A WOMAN'S GUIDE TO
DOCTORAL STUDIES

A WOMAN'S GUIDE TO DOCTORAL STUDIES

Diana Leonard

OPEN UNIVERSITY PRESS
Buckingham • Philadelphia

Open University Press
Celtic Court
22 Ballmoor
Buckingham
MK18 1XW

email: enquiries@openup.co.uk
world wide web: www.openup.co.uk

and
325 Chestnut Street
Philadelphia, PA 19106, USA

First Published 2001

A catalogue record of this book is available from the British Library

ISBN   0 335 20252 7 (pbk)   0 335 20253 5 (hb)

Library of Congress Cataloging-in-Publication Data
Leonard, Diana.
   A woman's guide to doctoral studies / Diana Leonard.
      p. cm.
Includes bibliographical references and index.
   ISBN 0-335-20253-5 – ISBN 0-335-20252-7 (pbk.)
   1. Doctor of philosophy degree. 2. Women–Education (Graduate) I.
Title.
   LB2386 .L46 2001
   378.2–dc21   2001021401

Typeset by Graphicraft Limited, Hong Kong
Printed in Great Britain by Biddles Limited, Guildford and King's Lynn

CONTENTS

viii   Contents

ACKNOWLEDGEMENTS

Except when quoting from published work, I have kept quotations anonymous to preserve the confidentiality of the more politically sensitive comments. I should therefore like to thank the following for general support and sharing, including in some cases letting me borrow their words and experiences:

Sandra Acker, Sue Adler, Suki Ali, Ulrike Baechle, Polly Barker, Tom Barker, Nicola Blaxill, Jeffrey Bost, Andrew Brown, I-Ru Chen, Amanda Claremont, Valerie Clifford, Kelly Coate, Bob Cowen, Angela Creese, Harry Daniels, Miriam David, Rosemary Deem, Sara Delamont, Debbie Epstein, Judith Glazer-Raymo, June Gleeson, Anne Gold, Norman Graves, Valerie Hey, Alessandra Iantaffi, Barbara Kamler, Jane Kenway, Diana Langmead, Ingrid Lunt, Jackie MacDonald, Julie McLeod, Melanie Mauthner, Louise Morley, Funiwe Njobe, Katrina O'Loughlin, Anita Pridmore, Phil Salmon, Eve Setch, the late Steve Sharples, Jasbir Singh, David Telford, Mike Trinder, Elaine Unterhalter, Kate White, Geoff Whitty and Flora Wilson. You have made the last few years fun, and I refer you to pp. 259–60! Thanks.

I should particularly like to thank Hannah Barker, Shereen Benjamin, Kuang-Hsu (Iris) Chiang, Martin Eyre, Akiko Nishio and Rachel Torr for reading an earlier draft of the manuscript. Also Judith Abrahami-Einat, Irene Bruegel and Richard Kuper, Bob Connell, Amy Elman (especially), Jeanne Favret-Saada, Irini Fragou, Chryssi Inglessi, Maresi Nerad, Carol Stack, Gaby Weiner and Grazyna Zajdow, to whose houses I have escaped to make time to write in the hectic world of the new higher education.

This publication uses data supplied by the Society for Research into Higher Education, by agreement with the Higher Education Statistics Agency. Thanks to Emma Sangster.

INTRODUCTION:
USING THIS BOOK

One of the things I've noticed about women students is that many have much less understanding of what is expected of a research student to 'get ahead'. I'm not referring to the actual work required, but rather that women tend to see that as perhaps the only thing needed. So they are much less likely to speak up, they seem less likely to choose a 'territory' and then defend it, they are much less likely to see themselves as being 'judged' on matters peripheral to the work at hand. And so they are 'failed' while unaware they are being tested at all.

(former vice-chancellor)

As an undergraduate I studied natural science at an elite university and certainly had no idea of what was needed to get ahead. Later I did a PhD in anthropology in Wales while not much the wiser, and I then moved into sociology partly because I was impressed by the liberatory work of C. Wright Mills. His famous book *The Sociological Imagination* starts with the phrase: 'Nowadays men often feel that their . . . lives are a series of traps'; and he goes on to argue the need to understand our personal difficulties in the context of social structures and public issues (Wright Mills 1970: 12 and 14). This guided me when I finally wrote up my own doctoral work on courtship, weddings and setting up home in South Wales (Leonard 1980) and in my subsequent involvement in the women's movement, in my research on gender and education and in teaching women's studies. But it was only recently that the profound changes in higher education in Britain led me to apply it to my own and my students' location within universities to understand how best to react. In higher education, understanding 'what feel like a series of traps' now seems essential.

At the same time, two colleagues asked me to write a chapter on gender for a collection on *Working for a Doctorate* which they were editing (Graves and Verma 1997). When I started to look at the literature, I realized just how little recognition there is of the differences between the experiences of men and women students in mainstream research and policy on higher education in the UK. It is also absent from most of the textbooks addressed to research students – despite all the work that has been done on gender and the labour market and on the differences between girls and boys in schools. Moreover, even less attention has been given to differences *among* women and men postgraduate students: between those who study full and those who study part-time, between those in different disciplines, between those who do their doctorates immediately after their first degree and 'mature women returners', between those who have lived all their lives in Britain and those whose 'domicile' is abroad or whose first language is not English, between lesbians and heterosexuals, who are single or in couples, with and without children, with and without disabilities, and so on.

I had by then worked with twenty of my own students who have successfully completed their PhDs and was starting to teach on a professional doctorate, which led me to interesting questions about the nature of the PhD itself. I knew there had been research on gender and higher education in the USA since the late 1960s and in Australia and New Zealand since the 1970s, and so I sought out the work specifically on doctoral students and added it to what I already knew from work on pedagogy, curriculum and assessment in schools, on women staff in universities, and from teaching women's studies, for example on violence against women and the sociology of the family. This produced a reasonably rich, if speculative, article which I was later asked to develop in relation to students from abroad (Leonard 1998). However, both these articles are largely about doctorates in the social sciences and (like the studies on which they were based) from the perspectives of faculty and policy makers rather than of students. They are also full of references so as to try in a typically academic way to convince people about the importance of gender. They are therefore not particularly easy reading.

I hope in this book to speak more directly to any woman who is going to undertake a doctorate and to giver fuller information on the 'series of traps' you are likely to encounter with either a traditional PhD or a new, 'professional' ('vocational', 'taught') doctorate. The book gives research-based information on how women are positioned inequitably within the supposedly liberal, cerebral world of postgraduate studies, and suggests how best to push back or move around problems and come out in front – without selling out. It is not a basic beginner's text on 'how to get a PhD' because these already exist and also because I presume doctoral students can cope with complexities. You need to consider the full picture to understand your own gendered situation and to work out your own answers – which are not easy ones. Also while the book is aimed mainly at women, it has a lot in it of interest to men since many problems are common to both sexes, though with a gender dimension. It should therefore be of interest to anyone sympathetic to feminism, especially men who try to be reflexive about their own masculinity and their position as men.

  The book starts with a chapter which gives an overview of the recent changes in higher education, and in doctoral studies in particular, in the UK (and in various forms, in most other advanced industrial countries). This is important in helping you to make sense of your location and to understand the mysterious events and acronyms: the 'RAE', 'Subject Review', 'massification', 'HEFCE', 'ILT' and others which haunt your supervisor. If you want to plunge straight into discussions more directly related to your own experience, skip this chapter and start with Chapter 2, which discusses making the decision to do a doctorate, and Chapters 3 and 4 on choosing where to study (or later chapters if you are further on in your course). But do return to Chapter 1 later on and keep it to hand for reference. You can't understand the 'traps' fully without it; and one of the well-documented differences between men and women students is precisely that women are less likely to recognize 'the rules of the game', as the opening quotation suggests.

The University of California at Berkeley graduate school has done some excellent work on gender and graduate studies. One study of undergraduates found that even women who intended to carry on to higher degree work had no clear knowledge of how graduate school worked and what they should study. 'Men, however, knew precisely what their emphases in graduate school would be and could name concrete steps by which they hoped to succeed'. A subsequent study of doctoral students revealed a similar striking pattern among students who were well advanced in their studies. The majority of women interviewed

> felt alienated and isolated in their departments. They did not know the informal rules and conventions of the dominant culture in their department. They interpreted their negative departmental experiences as personal failures, not as a reflection of a 'cool' departmental climate. They attributed any success to luck, rather than to personal competencies. They found solace only in the graduate student peer culture. In contrast, men described the factors contributing to their progress in terms of well planned strategies and personal achievements. They explained their negative experiences in terms of insufficient guidance, faculty aloofness and departmental factions. In addition, those men who felt alienated and who saw themselves as peripheral to the department . . . attributed this to their family conditions or their minority status. They were divorced and had to take care of a child, or married with children, or they were Black or Hispanic students.
>
> (Nerad and Stewart 1991: 15–17)

This finding, that women often lack confidence and are too inclined to attribute success to luck or hard work, and our negative experiences to our own shortcomings (rather than to institutional failings), has been well documented elsewhere too. Women are known also to be slow to put our personal development to the fore and while most men are flattered when someone suggests they should think about doing a research degree, not only are fewer women invited to do so, but those who *are*, seem almost to brush off the recognition.

I hope this book will encourage you to take the possibility of doing a doctorate seriously, to negotiate your way through the process of doing one, and to be successful in your own and other people's terms. It may be that some who read it decide that now is not the right time for them to do a research degree, though they would like to do one later. Promising women may decide realistically that they have other priorities – that they want a more rounded life or that they are not prepared to give up other activities, especially aspects of their relationship with partners and/or children, for this particular exercise. (Men, of course, may also decide not to do a doctorate. But in my own and other people's experience, men explain their decision mainly in relation to employment pressures, and they decide against it much less often. Large numbers of men in fact get kudos for doing part-time doctorates, especially in business or other vocational studies, while a large group of supportive wives bring up children virtually as single parents.)

If you do want to go ahead, however, it really is important to understand fully what is involved and to face up to the informal rules and homosocial cultures of universities. Otherwise you will be implicitly positioned and disadvantaged by them. Women need to make careful and clever career choices, whether or not you are willing to be associated with or involved in the competitive, self-promotional behaviour traditionally associated with dominant masculinities. If you don't know what you are doing, and especially if you come from a relatively under-privileged background, you may well have an unhappy time along the way, and end up in a low status institution and a low status position, as either a teaching or contract research foot soldier, on a short-term contract and possibly part-time, shortly thereafter ending up outside academia altogether. Moreoever, if you are coming to study in Britain from abroad, you need also to find out about and keep in mind the same sorts of informal rules for the situation to which you will be returning.

Facing up to informal structures and recognizing what actually counts in academic life (understanding its micropolitics) and when and how gender is salient, and how women and femininity are devalued, can however be a painful process.

Coming to have a feminist consciousness is the experience of coming to see things about oneself and one's society that were heretofore hidden. This experience, the acquiring of a 'raised' consciousness [has its] disturbing aspects [but it] is an immeasurable advance over that false consciousness which it replaces. The scales fall from our eyes . . . We begin to understand why we have such depreciated images of ourselves . . . Understanding, even beginning to understand this, makes it possible to change. Coming to see things differently, we are able to make out possibilities for liberating collective action and for unprecedented personal growth . . . Moreover that feeling of alienation from established society which is so prominent a feature of feminist experience may be counterbalanced by a new identification with women of all conditions and a growing sense of solidarity with other feminists. It is a fitting commentary on our society that the growth of feminist consciousness, in spite of its ambiguities, confusions and trials, is apprehended by those in whom it develops as an experience of liberation.

(Bartky 1990: 21)

Gender is certainly not given adequate attention in any of the guidebooks for students which have popped up as the numbers of graduate students have increased. In most texts there is in fact *no* mention of gender – or other – differences among students. At best there is a short section on women *and* one on overseas *and* one on part-time students. Gender is added on, not threaded all the way through and the *interaction* of systematic social differences is missed. This is also likely to be true of the courses run for research students by your university and of documents issued to you. They will cover some of the basic information/'cues' you need as a research student, but they are unlikely to cover any of the gender specific angles which fill this book. This is despite the fact that, as I have stressed, everything has a gender dimension; and women need (have a right to) more intellectual and personal support until the system which disadvantages us is changed. At present we are likely to be overtly or subtly 'othered' and alienated by the culture of the department or laboratory where we work; and have less or different access to financial support. All of which applies more strongly and in specific ways to working class, minority ethnic, lesbian, disabled and older women.

These biases and limitations in textbooks, induction and mainstream courses, and welfare offices are largely due to deficiencies in their own sources of information. The big names in UK higher education research are, and have long been, quite unaware of (and indifferent to) gender issues, so there is not the material for textbook writers and others to draw upon. A vicious circle exists whereby the obvious keeps not being seen, despite attention having been drawn to gender in higher education (HE) by feminists for thirty years and despite Equal Opportunities (EO) issues having been put (back) on to the universities agenda in the 1980s. However, the major changes associated with the 'massification' and 'marketization' of HE in the late 1980s and 1990s knocked such work for six, and it has only recently begun to return (though focused on class rather than on gender, and with a simplistic analysis).

What this book provides is not a self-help/improvement account. I shall not be suggesting that *the* problem is women's 'low self-esteem' and that what we need are specialist training courses for women in assertion, self-presentation (clothes and body language), communication and leadership skills so that we can acquire something we lack. Nor is it in the women's magazine mould of saying you can get ahead (get a doctorate quickly, and then a better job) while improving your marriage/partnership/sex life – and all without losing your femininity: your lipstick, orgasms, pleasure in shopping and other enriching 'differences' from men. I shall not (principally) be discussing what to wear and what body language to wheedle in. Nor does this book support the idea that men and women are different, and that this difference can be problematic (because it can cause misunderstandings) but it can also be enriching if both sexes practise mutual tolerance and adjustment; *however*, in science (or professional life, or academia, or management) 'masculine' 'rational' values *must* hold sway because of the nature of the field, and therefore, here at least, women must and can emulate men.

Rather, this book has a critical, inequality approach, seeing existing social structures as giving men advantages, and masculinity as actively reconstructing these structures, with women having to interact with men from less powerful positions in both public and private institutions. It responds to the self-help, *Cosmo* and *Men are from Mars, Women are from Venus* approaches (sometimes self-described as 'postfeminist') by asking critically 'what sort of difference?' and '*is* it enriching?' and 'in what ways is a field "masculine" and should it continue to be so?' That is to say, I seek to politicize gender, not to 'other' or pathologize or to glorify women; and I look to collective awareness and action for change. (Though I am happy to include assertion and leadership training, careful use of clothes and body language, and arguments for less masculine cultures and mutual enrichment, as useful tools. They are just not enough and at times can be problematic.)

I am certainly not going to suggest there are easy answers, because the power involved in gender relations is more complicated than 1960s and 1970s analyses of male dominance suggested – important though the early sense of outrage in the Women's Liberation Movement was in bearing witness to oppression in all aspects of women's lives. Feminism has moved on to develop new conceptualizations of the relations of men and women, and of what it means to talk of 'men' and 'women' in the first place. This book is therefore not written from a perspective of just uncovering instances of direct discrimination against women and deep-seated conflicts of interest between the sexes. Nor does it see gender as something laid down in our psychology in childhood: a fixed attribute at the core of every person's sense of self. Rather it sees gender as fluid and constantly reproduced (or challenged) through social practices. Gender is the effect of participating in particular social practices, rather than the other way around; and change and instability are always present. But so is inequality. It is not a question of socially constructed/performed differences giving rise to inequality, so much as inequalities in a binarily divided society giving rise to constructed and reconstructed 'differences'.

Moreover academia itself is not an institution which just reflects (or exacerbates) pre-given gender identities which people bring into it. Rather it is a place (yet another place) that actively *constitutes* gender: a site within which individuals construct and reconstruct themselves as gendered subjects by engaging in masculine and feminine ways of thinking and talking, and sexual and other social interactions. Its own social structures and discourses constrain, but do not dictate, individuals' possibilities. To take a concrete example, I shall argue that the very concept of 'being an academic' (or a 'professional', or a 'research student') is gendered and classed: they are built around a number of divisions of labour and attributes associated with middle class masculinity, which construct femininity and working classness as 'other', but which actually require and use the labour of women and the lower classes. Such ways of thinking constitute a fundamental challenge to customary ways of thinking. But they do explain better why it is so difficult to change.

There are also no easy answers because gender is not the only power relation in play. There are also issues of class and race and physical and mental capacities and age, and while we may disentangle these heuristically, in practice they are overlapping and interconstructed with gender. I shall try to keep the nuances. For instance, the going is tougher and there are fewer women in certain subjects and in more prestigious universities. There are also rather different problems for minority ethnic and working class women and lesbians than for white Anglo-Saxon Protestant heterosexual women from middle class backgrounds. While there are sometimes major problems (such as violence or harassment or discrimination) for women in universities, more often what we experience is an invisibility or 'trivial' put-downs, which we cope with, though they can accumulate so that at times and places they really get us down. As they do in the rest of life. (Some of the 1970s work does acknowledge this, but I think underplays it.) Also women fight back individually and collectively and enjoy the warmth of women's support and the joys and excitement of feminist research; and sometimes, of course, women use femininity to get ahead and/or personally contribute to their own or other women's subordination. More of such 'queen bees' later.

Whether you follow me through the more theoretical arguments or not, I hope the book fulfils its purpose of providing women (and men) with essential information and creative insights about gender and about change in higher education, on the basis of which you can draw your own conclusions and plot your own paths. I hope it is supportive and hopeful without being Pollyanna-like. It would be nice if the book also made people in higher education generally more aware that women matter. There are certainly problems for women (indeed for everyone) in higher education today, but pointing them out is not the same as saying women are simply victims, or that the whole enterprise is (now) intrinsically fraught and flawed. Rather it stems from a belief in the importance of reflecting on the issues so that newcomers can maximise the intellectual pleasures to be gained. Like Sara Delamont and colleagues' (1997) guide for supervisors, my basic philosophy is that good, useful, pleasurable doctoral studies are based on self-consciousness, not on intuition or flying by the seat of one's pants. Also that women's support for other women, formally and informally, is essential, and that women and sympathetic men must actively contribute and rejuvenate organizations, not just take what they need from them while looking backwards to the now faded legacy of the 1930s or 1950s or 1970s.

The advice provided is, as it is fashionable to say nowadays, 'research based', with references so that you can follow up particular points, and picky readers can contest them. There is a short list of suggested further reading at the end of each chapter.

Nadya Aisenberg and Mona Harrington (1988: 58–9) suggest the following 'rules of the game':

- Find out what's going on. You need an inside line.
- Gain practice in political skills, like how to run meetings and how to present proposals.
- Assume some opposition. You can't please everyone all the time.
- Be persistent. Keep pushing and people will often end up agreeing.
- Learn to say no and keep your eye on what is in it for you as well as others.
- Don't spend all your time servicing other people.
- Use contacts. The old boy network really works, so use the 'old girls'.
- Choose your fights – those that are really important.

1 | UNDERSTANDING THE RULES OF THE GAME

Since the late 1960s, higher education in many countries has become increasingly 'market-driven' in several interrelated senses. Concern has become narrowly focused on how well the national system is producing what the economy is thought to need. The efficiency and effectiveness with which education is being 'delivered' has become a central concern for politicians, for the quasi-governmental bodies which manage the public funds allotted to higher education, and for the individual universities and colleges themselves; and they have all looked to commercial sector management systems as the force for improvement. Moreover education is now 'marketed' – created, promoted and distributed as a 'product' for tangible returns – with different countries and universities in competition with each other for students and research funding. All this has produced dramatic changes worldwide. Britain (and Australia and New Zealand) are perhaps extreme cases in the speed with which their educational systems have been re-formed, but similar trends can be seen in most other OECD countries. They are certainly part of the agenda of international agencies such as the World Bank.

The higher education system I teach in today therefore feels very different from the one I joined in 1976. It is certainly different from the one I had hoped we would achieve in the 1970s and early 1980s (see p. 31). The power of professors and faculty generally is much diminished; we talk of 'management' rather than 'administration'; and government imposed 'regimes of surveillance', rather than academics' professional responsibility to students and the wider community, are supposed to be the means to ensure quality, excellence and increased productivity. Universities and departments and individual academics compete against each other, and the hours most academics work have increased considerably. In addition, our terms and conditions of employment are worse. Salary increases lag far behind the rate of inflation and more staff are on short-term contracts. The ratio of students to staff has greatly increased, so there is less time for each individual student, and teaching and catching up on administration spread into the evening, weekends and the vacations, which used to be used for individual reading and writing. Staff and students are mostly housed in dilapidated modern offices rather than quadrangles; while the facilities available increasingly depend upon the status of each university, each subject area, and each individual's own bargaining power.

For individual academics the decade from 1980 to 1990 in the UK saw a 25 per cent rise in student load, a 37 per cent decline in pay and 22 per cent less spent on libraries (Wilson 1991).

Women professors now work an average of close to 65 hours per week and men professors 59 hours (AUT 1994).

These changes have, not surprisingly, also impacted on doctoral studies – on what the degree is supposed to be about, the required backgrounds and future possibilities of students, the numbers of research students that universities want to recruit, the facilities available to them (libraries, laboratories, offices, computing facilities and halls of residence), and supervisors' and departmental relationships with students. They are therefore obviously going to affect your experience if you decide to study for any sort of doctorate, and if you are thinking of a career in higher education. Moreover, emerging contradictions within these marketization processes are repositioning the now much more diverse student body, and teachers and researchers, in a whole series of unexpected ways.

This chapter aims to give you an outline of these ongoing changes as they affect graduate studies because you may know relatively little about them even if you have recently graduated from a British university. The debates covered in the popular press are mainly around education in primary and secondary schools, and the only two topics in higher education which do get mentioned regularly are fees for undergraduate 'home' students, and who among such students has 'access' to which universities. The second half of this chapter, and the rest of the book, go on to explore how the changes have impacted somewhat differently, and generally harder, on women students and staff than on men; and on certain groups of women more than on others. Whereas issues of gender and 'race' in schools have been reasonably well recognized and explored in Britain, and there is considerable concern about the somewhat simplistic assertion that 'girls are now doing better than boys', the many times and places in which women and non-white, non-

British faculty and students do less well in the UK's higher education system, generally get overlooked. Most HE policy makers and researchers think gender and 'race' issues have been resolved among university students; this forms a vicious circle with the surprising lack of empirical research on student culture and experience at either undergraduate or postgraduate level in the UK, and the lack of HE research on gender. The main equity issue is now (again) the proportion of undergraduate students from poorer backgrounds who are getting into the 'elite' universities, with some belated attention to higher education and disability.

Changes in British higher education

Producing what the economy is thought to need, quickly and cheaply

Since the 1970s, the whole British education system, both universities and schools, has been redefined as *primarily* about skilling more and more young workers and providing professional and inservice courses in lifelong (re)learning for adults, rather than as being about expanding the minds and developing the capacities of citizens. Similarly, universities' research has been increasingly reoriented from substantially 'blue skies' pursuit of knowledge for its own sake, to an increased volume of short-term, commercially or policy relevant work, ideally supportive rather than critical of the government's position. There has been some, but relatively little, resistance by academics. We seem to have been overwhelmed by the speed of change, and many have been silenced by the insecurity of their jobs.

We have thus moved rapidly from an elite to a mass higher education system in the course of just thirty years: from 10 per cent of under 21 years olds in the early 1960s to now nearly 40 per cent having access to a much expanded, substantially (though decreasingly) publicly funded, system. Much of the increase in 'university' student numbers has been due to former polytechnics becoming universities in 1992, and to older students who had missed out on higher education earlier in their lives returning to learning as mature students: 50 per cent of first year undergraduates were aged 21 or over in 1997–8. Within this increasing population of university students, the proportion of women among 'home' undergraduates has increased dramatically: from one-third to more than half since 1986 (with women first outnumbering men in 1996–7).

However, spending on universities has not kept pace with the increase in size of the sector, and the unit cost per full-time equivalent student in England fell consistently throughout the 1990s. In addition, the government in England (though not in Scotland) phased out maintenance grants for home undergraduates and introduced a requirement to pay a contribution to the fee. This whole area of funding and how much universities can charge and, somewhat in contradiction, how to increase the numbers of under-graduate students from low income backgrounds, continues to be a hot arena of debate.

As a consequence of the reduction in unit costs, while the numbers of academic staff have increased, the increase has not kept pace with the increase in numbers of students. Also, because cuts meant there were years when there was little recruitment of staff, the average age of full-time teach-ing faculty members is now in the late forties, with many younger people as insecure contract researchers and part-time, temporary teachers (see pp. 138–41). Similarly, the increase in provision of books in libraries and space in laboratories has been well below the rate of increase in numbers of students (see pp. 100–1) and we all have to cope with working in crowded and under-maintained buildings.

Universities have therefore been under pressure to raise money from other sources to supplement the reduction in government funding: to recruit more students and to get funding for projects from the private and public sector as well as from the research councils and charities like the Wellcome Foun-dation and Nuffield. Since the numbers of 'conventional' (home, under-graduate) students in popular fields have been 'capped' by the government, universities have developed and diversified their postgraduate offerings, including welcoming more doctoral students (or having doctoral students for the first time in some post-1992 universities), and increasing their recruitment of international students at all levels.[1]

Postgraduate numbers have therefore 'skyrocketed' in Britain (as in most other OECD countries), and postgraduates now comprise around one-fifth of the total higher education student population and two-fifths of part-time students.

By 1997, 'the UK [had] more postgraduate students (about 300,000) than there were undergraduates in the early 1960s (about 270,000)'.

(Coffield and Vignoles 1997: 3)

In 1961–2 there were   26,700 postgraduates in the UK

    1979   100,900 postgraduates, 13% of total student population

    1994–5   315,400 postgraduates, 21% of total and

    1998–9   403,300 postgraduates, 22% of total.

Of the 1998–9 postgraduates, 101,000 were research students, 5.5% of total student population.

(Harris Report 1996; HESA 2000: Tables A and B: 6–7)

Most of these postgraduates, especially women, are taking taught courses which provide initial vocational training and inservice professional development, rather than primarily academic degrees, and most are studying education or business and administrative studies, followed by social, economic and political studies, and engineering and technology. Of those who do take academic degrees (masters and doctorates) most are part-time and pay their own fees.

> More than 10,000 new students started doctoral degrees in 1999, compared to just over 3000 in 1992.
>
> (Gillon 1999)

Universities have also sought to increase their recruitment of students from abroad and in particular from outside the European Union, since such 'overseas' students have paid 'full-cost' (three times as high) fees since 1979. The numbers of non-British students studying in the UK has thus risen from around 10,000 in 1963 to 150,000 in 1998 (including 70,000 from the European Union), of whom 89,000 are postgraduates. There are 33,000 international students, mainly from Asia and Europe, doing research degrees (HESA 2000: Tables 1c and 1g).[2]

International student recruitment (and provision of scholarships) has always, in every country, involved a mixture of motives, being tied in (more or less overtly) with national foreign policy objectives and overseas aid. That is to say, higher education has long been an important element in winning 'hearts and minds' and securing a country's trade and international security (which can be alternatively read as: in perpetuating colonialism and the education providers' economic, political and cultural supremacy). However, there has also always been a concomitant humanitarian motive: a concern to assist the progress and development of 'third world' countries (for the UK this means particularly low to medium income Commonwealth countries) and to promote international peace and understanding. Either way, there has generally been little concern to preserve 'other' cultures within the formal and informal curriculum provided for international students in Britain (or elsewhere in the world). It has been assumed that if 'they' come 'here', they want what 'we' provide.

More recently (early 1980s onwards) international recruitment has moved from being seen as a drain on resources to an income generator. British universities' earnings from selling education abroad are now substantial, and increasingly recognized as important. So much so that in June 1999 the Prime Minister, Tony Blair, announced that the numbers of overseas students in HE should be increased by a further 50,000, and that visa and employment conditions would be changed to facilitate this.

A study for the Committee of Vice-Chancellors and Principals (CVCP, now Universities UK, UUK) in 1997, the first on the impact of UK universities and colleges on the UK economy, confirmed that universities were vital players. Higher education had a £1.3 billion balance of trade surplus in 1995–6. It employed 715,000 full-time equivalent people directly and indirectly (only 43.3 per cent of whom were teaching and research professionals), that is more than 3 per cent of the UK workforce (McNicoll *et al.* 1997).

Britain's universities, colleges and private schools are being 'rebranded' to capture a larger slice of the lucrative international education market. A £5 million campaign was launched in eight countries over three years in 2000 (by advertising agency McCann-Erickson for the British Council). It was aimed to capture a quarter share of the world market for English-speaking university students by 2003, changing the image of an elitist system which is seen as honest and giving qualifications which have a high credibility for employers, but too set in its ways.

The international movement of students, not only from low to medium income countries to the major urban centres of Northern countries but also *between* high income countries, and of university staff for short and longer periods, is now increasingly an element in the general development of global labour markets for professional and skilled workers. It is motivated by the claimed benefits of a more global outlook, the promotion of intercultural skills, and the possibility of making useful future (business) contacts for an internationalizing economy. This is supported by international agencies. For example the World Bank, UNESCO and the North American Free Trade Agreement (NAFTA) foster international research teams and encourage the revision of national curricula to give a (supposedly) more 'international' focus. Internationalization has also given birth to a growing body of professionals who support international students in further and higher education (FHE).

The British Council is the UK's principal agency for cultural relations with other countries and its Educational Counselling Service is the central overseas educational recruitment agency. It has offices in most countries, and staff who will help students searching for a place to study. The Council's local information centres house the brochures sent out by each higher education institution (HEI), though the Council itself does not evaluate or vouch for the information provided. It is generally impartial as regards the various universities, though it will also do special representation for a fee (unlike other education brokers who make introductions in exchange for a proportion of the fees paid by the students who do enrol).

UKCOSA, the Council for International Education (formerly the United Kingdom Council for Overseas Students' Affairs), is a UK-based agency which supports the work of voluntary sector organizations, study abroad administrators, recruiters, student union sabbatical officers and staff, housing administrators and registry staff who work with international students. It runs a phone advice service and a range of training courses, conferences and seminars to update them on regulations and developments in immigration and employment law, financial aid, and regulations on fees and awards. It also tries to disseminate research findings and to facilitate the exchange of good practice.

Within the European Union, inter-European educational exchange has been promoted since 1987 as a cultural as well as an economic phenomenon, through a series of grant-supported programmes. ERASMUS (the European Action Scheme for the Mobility of University Students) aimed at assisting 10 per cent of all (first degree) higher education students – not just the wealthy few – in all member states to spend at least three months in the HE system of another member state. It has also funded staff exchange and visits and lasting inter-institutional cooperation networks. Its concern has been not so much the development of the sending country as the internal development and integration of the European Union itself. This has been further developed with LINGUA (programme to promote foreign language competence), TEMPUS, LEONARDO DA VINCI (action programme on vocational training) and SOCRATES (the successor to ERASMUS) programmes, which also encourage the 'Europeanization' of school and university curricula, foreign languages learning, and the development of joint teaching and research programmes. We are also now into the fifth in a series of Research and Development Frameworks which fund major projects especially in science and technology involving several member states. This can include funding for postdoctoral fellowships and general encouragement for the 'mobility of researchers' (see also pp. 134–5).

In addition, cheaper travel and new communications media are opening up huge new possibilities for 'open learning', and some universities have started schemes to exploit opportunities in 'offshore education markets'. More and more HEIs are looking to enter what they see as the lucrative market for distance learning previously dominated by The Open University, and/or to establish campuses abroad where students can begin courses before transferring to the UK to complete the second or third year of their (first or higher) degrees. On the other hand, The Open University has itself been seeking to enter new fields, such as teacher training and medicine. Despite (or because of?) the competition involved, there are worries about the quality and ethics of some of these new arrangements (see p. 86).

The concern with 'quality'

The rapid development of higher education has led to renewed debates about the link between employment, training and postgraduate education, the purpose of vocational degrees, doctoral training and research, and the impact of postgraduate work on future careers. These have included a number of stock-taking reports, notably the *Review of Postgraduate Education* (hereafter called the Harris Report 1996) and the more general *National Committee of Inquiry in Higher Education* (the Dearing Report 1997). Both were concerned with the appropriate balance between undergraduate and postgraduate degrees in different universities, and both reflected preeminent concerns with labour market issues ('the needs of employers') and with ways of assuring the quality of educational provision while not increasing the cost to the public purse. There have also been two White Papers on Science, Engineering and Technology (SET), one from the Conservative government in 1993 and another from Labour in 2000, and a Parliamentary Select Committee on Higher Education reported in 2001 (Office of Science and Technology 1993; Department of Trade and Industry 2000).

These all assume that an improvement in standards will be best achieved by the second aspect of market drivenness mentioned above: by universities (in common with schools and many other public services) being run increasingly in ways which approximate to (a particular form of) business management. The aim is to 'through-put' students under strict financial limits and quality control, with 'transparent' procedures and clearly stated 'learning outcomes' and 'assessment criteria'. Accountability to 'stakeholders' is to be achieved by tying government funding to how well an institution performs on a number of outcomes-based indicators (sometimes *reductio ad absurdum*) of research productivity, teaching quality, dropout rates, and employability of graduates. The assessments are conducted by outside agencies and the results are made public and published in national league tables. (On using these see pp. 99–100.) The audits of particular importance to research students are the Research Assessment Exercise (RAE) and the Subject Review (SR, formerly the Teaching Quality Assessment, TQA).

> The most boring practices, Michel Foucault has argued, can play an unacknowledged but fundamental role in society. So it is with the practice of audit . . . [This] has become an important means of regulating all of the professions, and it has had the effect of undermining the traditional virtues associated with professionalism . . . Of the distortions induced by the audit explosion . . . [p]erhaps the most interesting is the auditing of academic research. The research assessment exercise offers incentives for academics to teach less and write more . . . and there has become a visible

transfer market for prolific researchers . . . it encourages all universities to seek to become Harvard or Yale . . . Nor is the RAE neutral in terms of what academic research is done. For [it has produced a change] in favour of publication in prestigious journals rather than books . . . There are now, apparently, half a million scholarly journals in existence – to whose benefit, one wonders. At the same time, 'a whole menu of activities for which performance measures have not been devised have ceased to have official value. Editing books, [writing textbooks], organising conferences and, paradoxically, reviewing and facilitating the publication efforts of others fall out of account'.

(Bogdanor 1997: 22)

The Research Assessment Exercise gives a measure of the productivity of (the amount and quality of the publications produced by) the members of each discipline (for example chemistry or sociology) in each university, on a scale from 1 (low) to 5 (high). A star indicates a high proportion of staff are included ('are research active'), that is they have produced four good publications in the previous three years. The evaluation also involves consideration of the numbers of research students and completion rates. How much money each university receives from the Higher Education Funding Councils' coffers is a function of the 'mark' awarded.

There are separate Higher Education Funding Councils (HEFCs) for each region of the UK, with slightly different practices and substantially different budgets. The Higher Education Funding Council for England (HEFCE, under the Department for Education and Employment, DfEE) is much the largest with a budget of £831 million per annum in 2000. The Scottish Higher Education Funding Council (accountable to the Scottish Executive) had £114 million; the Higher Education Funding Council for Wales (responsible mainly to the Welsh Assembly), £42 million; and the Department of Education for Northern Ireland, which funds its two universities on advice from the NIHEFC, £24 million.

Assessment of each universities' performance is carried out by specialist panels of academics appointed by the funding councils. The quasi-competitive market so produced is affected by the politics of who gets appointed to the panels, and the relationships between them (influenced by past reputations) – more so than is usually admitted. In the 2001 RAE, women were poorly represented both as chairs and committee members: fewer than one in four panel members and only one in seven of the panel chairs were women. Moreover, the panels that women chaired were responsible for allocating less than 10 per cent of RAE funding (*Times Higher Education Supplement* (*THES*) 3 March 2000: 8). This doubtless contributes to our lack of success in getting proper recognition for women senior staff, and for feminist research (see p. 184). Pressure to produce a constant stream of publications has also not allowed for different pressures at different times in women's and men's lives.

Helen Mercer and the Equal Opportunities Commission (EOC) won a sex discrimination case against the London School of Economics (LSE) at an Industrial Tribunal in 2000. Dr Mercer was not given a permanent job after she had a miscarriage while on a three-year contract, and her suitability was questioned. The LSE chose a less well qualified younger man instead, who was thought to be better able to contribute to the next RAE. It was also found that LSE's appointments procedure discriminated against women indirectly in setting research output targets that might be incompatible with maternity leave (*Guardian* 14 April 2000: 13).[3]

As far as research students are concerned, the RAE has meant academics moving more of their time into research projects and writing, and out of teaching. (Of course a substantial number of those registered for research degrees already have academic jobs and so are affected in both ways.) The effects on supervision-as-teaching are perhaps more ambivalent than the effects on undergraduate teaching, since having research students is itself an indicator of research 'quality'. But there *is* a major problem of highly published supervisors who get headhunted and so move from one university to another, leaving their students with the Hobson's choice of either following them or starting over with someone new. There have also been lots of games of buying in visiting professors from external think-tanks so that their publications can 'count', but such individuals are simply not a presence at all as far as students are concerned. On the other hand, some would argue that the stress on publications has provided a more objective criterion when appointing new staff than the obscure 'potential' that older men used to stress in order to advance their acolytes, and that this has helped women. While it is perhaps a problem that there are now lots more journals to be skimmed, there are also lots more to publish in!

The format of the RAE is likely to change (again) after the Exercise in 2001, but something similar is pretty certain to continue. There will be skirmishes between the HEFCs and government, with each side asserting how well it has or hasn't worked, and the government making noises about wanting to promote more commercial scientific research and the universities trying to guard their autonomy and peer reviewing of research council grants. ('If the government wants more applied research it should fund it directly.')

Most British 'blue skies' research is funded through projects submitted to one (of effectively seven) research councils. Most are managed by the Office of Science and Technology (OST): Biotechnology and Biological Sciences (BBSRC), Engineering and Physical Sciences (EPSRC), Particle Physics and Astronomy (PPARC), Medical (MRC), Natural Environment (NERC) and Economic and Social (ESRC); with a Research Board for the Arts and Humanities (AHRB) which may become a full research council in due course. All have good websites; see for example www.bbsrc.ac.uk

The Subject Review is even more problematic and also subject to constant change to stop HEIs getting skilled at 'working to the test'. The Further and Higher Education Act 1992 made it a statutory requirement for the HEFCs to 'secure the assessment of the quality of education' within the university sector, and it does this through a Quality Assurance Agency (QAA) which is funded by top-slicing university grants. A Subject Review involves a team of inspectors for each subject area appointed by the QAA visiting each university (supposedly) every third year and assessing areas relating to the teaching of that subject and awarding grades. Currently these are numerical and published as league tables.[4]

Arguably inspections of teaching are not best done by snapshots, by outsiders, re transmission of skills and knowledge against declared 'learning outcomes'. The fundamental problem of trying to assess teaching lies in the assumption that it is one kind of activity, and excellence is one kind of excellence. But teaching involves at least two parties, teachers and the taught. The quality of teaching is not a quality of a teacher but of a relationship, aspects of which are defined by the character, talents and motivations of the lecturers. Teaching is not an action but a transaction, not an outcome but a process, not a performance but an emotional and intellectual connection between teacher and learner. Therefore it cannot be assessed as an attribute or skill of a teacher or a department, independent of the learners who have their own characteristics which affect whether and how much they learn (about what) from a particular teacher, and, indeed, how much the teacher learns from them . . . In fact the quality of teaching, which surely means an assessment of its effects on students, can hardly be assessed at all – in the short term. What can be assessed is not 'teaching' but the absence of teaching . . . We can and should pay attention to how much people actually do, both formally and informally, whether they actually get to their meetings with students sober and on time, read and respond to their written work, and the like . . . We can demand of university lecturers professional

> responsibility towards their jobs and a humane non-exploitative rela-
> tionship with their students. But, beyond that, we must depend on our
> appointment procedures [and staff development] to ensure teachers know
> their subjects and are competent to transmit knowledge, or broaden
> perspectives, or stimulate curiosity, or raise ambitions, or prepare stu-
> dents to learn throughout their lifetimes.
>
> (Trow 1994: 14)

Most of the things looked at during Subject Review visits are not teaching
as such, but rather the available facilities (the quality of the libraries and
classrooms) and the Quality Assurance mechanisms in place (such as whether
each course issues information to students on its aims and expected learning
outcomes; whether it keeps full records of feedback on essays; whether it
regularly reflects on its practice; whether it has regular systematic student
evaluations which are fed back into planning). Moreover, the assessment is
not against an absolute, common standard of performance across the universities, but rather against each institution's evaluation of how well it is
doing. (So if a department says it is achieving only a lowish level it can be
evaluated as doing very well against this.) So far the QAA has audited
only undergraduate and postgraduate diplomas and Masters courses, not
research degrees. Whatever the intent, SR comes across as oppositional
rather than supportive, and most universities say the best they get out of
such an 'inspection' is the fostering of team spirit before and during the
visit, and some extra forced reflection on their teaching, record keeping
and facilities.

> Asked about institutions that might refuse to volunteer for QAA audits, its
> chief executive said:
>
> > Volunteer is not the right word. The Funding Councils have a statutory
> > responsibility to assess the quality of the provision that they pay for and
> > they contract with us to carry out that assessment on their behalf. The
> > system is only voluntary for institutions in so far as they do not have to
> > receive public funds.
> >
> > (*THES* 7 January 2000: 1)

There are in any case real problems in trying to treat education like a
product you buy whose quality can be guaranteed by a kitemark. It is not a
question of 'do universities deliver to customers the course they expect to
get', except where promised courses are cancelled or very poorly delivered
or where there are very specific agreed skills and knowledges involved. Much

of what you gain as a student is not what you expect when you start, and some important learning is difficult and painful, especially initially. Teachers may be seeking, quite properly, *not* to fulfil students' (or employers' or local community) expectations, but rather to modify these and to enhance students' minds, characters and sensibilities. In addition, students are not easily equated with 'consumers' of a service. You have 'rights' as 'purchasers', but of an opportunity to learn, not of a guaranteed qualification with recourse to litigation if you don't get the certificate. We have, however, almost got to the point where any failure is seen not as a failure on the part of the student, but rather on the part of the 'producer' / the university teacher, with students' end-of-course evaluations influencing the assessment of faculty's capabilities; and vice-chancellors wanting more first class degrees to be awarded because parents and students choose universities with 'good' results. (Softer markers get better evaluations and litigious students cost the university a lot in legal fees, so efforts may be made to cool them down. Hence standards sag, and some of the effects of SR and league tables are the opposite of what is intended.)

Moreover, the focus on producing 'user oriented' services by encouraging innovation through competition, with a strong preference for practical pre-scription rather than reflection and analysis, assumes the main 'consumers' of education are employers. But this an oversimplification for short-term political ends. There *are* other issues and other groups who are stakeholders in the education system – including students and a generalized 'national public good'.

What is certain is that both the RAE and SR audits are hugely time con-suming and costly and have greatly increased the demands upon academics. They have also increased the competition between and within universities, and led some 'third division' HEIs to deliberate 'mis-selling' of courses.

Research by the Association of University Teachers (AUT) in 1994 suggested that the money spent by institutions (in addition to the cost to the funding councils themselves) on the (then equivalent to the) RAE was an annual £4.5 million, and the cost to the 'old' universities of the former TQA was £2.8 million. The AUT claimed that for the cost of these initiatives in quality assurance, each department assessed in the RAE could have afforded to employ an extra lecturer at the bottom of scale A; and each department visited for TQA could have afforded to employ another lecturer on the bot-tom of scale B.

A report for HEFCE in 2000 found red tape and bureaucracy cost univer-sities £250 million a year. A single Subject Review visit cost £75,000 (*THES* 4 August 2000: 1).

To try to improve efficiency, there has also been structural reorganization and greater Taylorization within universities: more separation of management (into something called the equivalent of 'the directorate') from the actual doing of research and teaching, with an emphasis on marketing and business generation, and (supposedly) rationalized and computerized administrative structures. Commercially based activities (for example costed consultancy instead of the free exchange of ideas with worthy organizations) now occupy more of staff's time, and universities' research output is exploited through patents and attached science parks or new linkages to the corporate sector.

Changes in doctoral studies

Serious concern with efficiency and effectiveness and management systems started to be applied to doctoral studies in Britain from the early 1980s. The issue of the very long time it was taking many students to complete their PhD theses and the high proportion who never submitted a thesis at all was raised by a House of Commons Committee of Public Accounts in 1979 and then by a government working party and the research councils (particularly the Economic and Social Research Council). While there were (and are) big differences between doctorates in different disciplines (see pp. 61–5), and the problem of dropout and time to completion has never been so marked in the sciences and engineering, research students in the social sciences and humanities were taking up to ten or more years before they were ready to present their theses, and as many as two-thirds used not to finish at all in some departments and some subjects. Even the Science and Engineering Council found 'failure' rates of at least 30 per cent.

Some 'wastage' in higher education is inevitable and students may gain a lot from their studies and produce publications even if they do not present a thesis. But the dissipation of funders' money and faculty time and effort (that is universities' efficiency) at doctoral level was deemed unacceptable, especially because of the hostility of the government of the time to the social sciences. The British tradition had been to have restrictive entry to undergraduate courses combined with an expectation (and support to ensure) that the great majority of those who did embark on such studies eventually passed successfully. Doctoral studies were out of line with such expectations and so a process of tightening up was begun. (While there was some concern with the waste of *student* energy, hope and money, this was low down on the list of priorities.)

The focus was initially upon getting the doctorate down to something that can be completed in four years (or six years part-time), with the thesis seen not as the *magnum opus* it had become in the social sciences and humanities in the 1960s and 1970s, but rather as an apprenticeship piece of work to be completed promptly. In those fields where the PhD consists of a lengthy independent project under the guidance of a single member of staff, the main concern was to improve the quality of teaching. The Economic and Social Research Council (and then some other research councils) applied pressure by refusing to give grants to students to study in universities which did not get acceptable completion rates, starting at 25 per cent in 1987 and rising over the years to 60 per cent completion within four years (with a longer term target of 70 per cent). Both the then Social Science Research Council and the Natural and Environmental Research Councils also introduced a requirement for universities to provide a substantial set of approved taught methodology and methods courses. Other sciences got involved in discussions of a Masters degree in research (MRes) to go between the undergraduate degree and a doctorate. This presumes that research students get state support to do a PhD, not for their own development and pleasure in learning, or to contribute a particular piece of knowledge, but in order to become professional researchers. All the policy statements of the 1980s and 1990s, and most of the funded research on the doctorate in the social sciences done at this time, were from the putative employers' and the universities' perspective, rather than those of students. Almost none looked at possible differences among students.

Institutions have consequently sought to improve the 'through-put' of their increased numbers of research student ('late completion' is now defined as 'after more than four years of full-time study') by introducing staff development courses in research supervision and bureaucratizing student progress (establishing statements of staff and student responsibilities; encouraging some form of memorandum after each supervision; requiring annual reports on each student; establishing departmental research committees to monitor all research students; and having better management information systems to track student progress). They have also made such improvements to student facilities as they can afford, tried to overcome the isolation of graduate students, and centralized these changes in 'graduate schools'.

Graduate schools (or divisions or offices or departments or colleges) have long been a feature of US universities with very large student bodies and excellence in research. They help protect the research capacity of the institution by demarcating undergraduate teaching from postgraduate and research work. The graduate school is headed by a senior academic (a dean or director) and membership is restricted: only certain teaching staff are accepted as members and only they can teach graduate students. It may provide a home for various non-departmental research centres, and collaborate with other universities in the locality. The graduate school covers all the bureacracy for graduate students, dealing with admissions, keeping student records, approving taught courses, appointing examiners, and hearing student appeals. It can be just an office, or it can be an important policy making unit which also monitors graduate work (hence the good information available on doctoral studies from the USA), and reviews departments and promotes improvements. It may also have budgets to pump prime projects and to provide some post-doctoral fellowships. It can provide an alternative home for students away from their departments.

At the start of the 1990s, only two UK institutions had graduate schools, but by mid-decade 33 had introduced one and a further 23 were thinking about it. This was mainly (as elsewhere in Europe) to develop the quality of graduate education, especially to protect the growing numbers of postgraduates from the overwhelming growth in numbers of undergraduates. For instance, a graduate school can support postgraduates in the competition for resources (for example in determining what the library buys, in the use of teaching rooms, in deciding what sort of residential accommodation is provided for how many months each year, ditto as regards the social life, student union, and staff time). It helps to provide a home for graduates who can get squashed between undergraduates and staff in departments. In places where there are not many postgraduates, it can gather together a reasonable size group to form a community, promote interdisciplinarity, and sort out the institution's responses to new Funding Council requirements. (Hogan 1994)

A United Kingdom Council for Graduate Education (UKCGE) was established in 1994 (comparable to the US Council of Graduate Schools) with an annual conference and occasional research and publications. It was initially based in CEDAR (Centre for Educational Development, Appraisal and Research) at the University of Warwick.

By the mid-1990s the policy focus on postgraduate studies in Britain had largely moved on to other discussions: of, for instance,

- The standard of information available in universities' brochures to enable funders to be able to judge what is covered in courses and the 'benchmark level' of a degree.
- Whether all universities, or only those of approved quality and with a 'critical mass' (see pp. 102–3) of researchers and research students, should offer PhDs.
- How formally to assess attainment in the compulsory research methodology courses, and whether to add additional required courses to firm up other 'transferable skills' acquired when doing a PhD (for example project

management, lateral and creative thinking, adaptability, oral and written presentation of findings, and so on) (see pp. 58–9).

- The employability of those with PhDs and whether all doctoral study should be broader, more practically focused and industrially relevant.
- The introduction of vocational or professional doctorates incorporating more 'skills for industry' (teamwork, professional and management development, up-to-date information technology (IT), commercial ways of thinking, presentation skills, and experience of research outside universities, see pp. 26, 71–3).
- Studentships in Industrial Research Organizations and the encouragement of new links to the private sector, such as developing more corporate universities like British Aerospace and Motorola universities (where staff do PhDs at nearby universities on topics useful to their firms as a form of staff development).
- New modes of delivery, for example distance or web-based courses and supervision.

The same old worries about completion rates and research training continue, however. For example, the Particle Physics and Astronomy Research Council was again planning to penalize physics departments where students took longer than average to complete in 1999 (*THES* 28 May 1999: 4); while the Arts and Humanities Research Board looks set also to require research training for the students it funds.

Other countries' concerns with doctoral studies

The market leader in academic and vocational doctorate production is the USA, with its different university system and very different mode of gaining a doctorate from Britain (see pp. 74–5). The USA has had mass higher education, including mass production of postgraduates (a million and a half students) and of doctorates (nearly 40,000 awarded per annum) for years. Moreover, it is (and has long been) also the leader in recruiting overseas students – who are still not seen as major money earners, and are often well catered for in 'international houses' on US campuses, though with little concern to modify US curricula and pedagogies to their needs. Rather the worry is that they will want to stay on in the USA after they finish their studies. Instead, the radical concern from the 1970s was to recognize and cater for the ethnic diversity among American *home* students, and for feminist demands – both of which have led to major innovations and an organized backlash in the 1990s.

In striking contrast to Britain, there is little overarching federal government responsibility for higher education in the USA: no national Higher Education

Council and certainly no equivalent of the QAA. Institutions do go through accreditations processes but the controlling bodies are mainly local – sometimes at state level (for public universities) or at the individual institutional (or grouping) level in the large private sector, with professional associations playing an important role. Both individual institutions and these associations give teaching and mentorship awards, and the professional organizations can tell you of departments which they have placed under censure for poor performance.

Most US doctorates are awarded by the 'research universities' (though there is a taxonomy of research degrees that differentiates between research I, doctoral I and doctoral II universities, depending on the number of doctorates awarded) and unlike the UK, vocational doctorates, notably the EdD, are ranked lower than the PhD. Like the UK, the USA has long been concerned about time to degree and dropout rates around doctorates. But they have also been even more concerned about the 'overproduction' of both PhDs and professional doctorates – of there being too many expensively trained scientists and engineers who are unable to find appropriate employment, and students with doctorates especially in English who end up with huge debts and no chance of academic jobs. There is also now concern about there being 'too many' women because they are now more than 50 per cent of undergraduates. It is argued that if men move away from higher education, the status of institutions will decline. On the other hand, there are certainly 'too few' African American men in higher education generally, and certainly at doctoral level.

On the opposite side of the world, Australia is rising fast in the English language higher education market (see p. 73) with a system based on the British one. It is now extensively and well marketed overseas, especially in South Asia (Indonesia, South Korea, Thailand, Malaysia, Vietnam, and the Philippines). Education (at all levels) was an important element in former Prime Minister John Keating's 'Australia in the Pacific' policy, and since 1984 (when two key reports were produced) it has been seen as both a way of spreading Australian influence abroad and a big money earner. There has been general 'export facilitation' by the Australian government and its agencies, and also specific support from, first, IDP Education Australia (a company owned and operated by the universities, with 35 offices in 19 countries) and, since 1995, the Australian International Education Foundation (a joint enterprise between the universities and the government). The 14,860 international students in the Australian tertiary sector in 1986 were increased to 47,165 in 1995; with 84,000 taking courses with Australian universities in 1999 (including 26,600 enrolled offshore). They comprise up to 14 per cent of students on some campuses, and up to 40 per cent in the most popular disciplines (economics and commerce) (*THES* 21 July 1999: 10).

Education is Australia's fifth highest source of foreign exchange earnings (estimated at £950 million in 1995 and A$2 billion in 2000 – 2 per cent of GDP). It provides 25 per cent of the operating revenue of the top enrolling universities. The 37 universities' brochures have helped to transform its image from a slightly dreary colonial outpost to a dazzling, middle class, beach society with the Anglo-Asian flavour of California. They use Asian born alumni to promote Australia as a safe, clean, English-speaking country, close to and in the same time zone as South Asia. More directly, universities use overseas agents in these countries who are paid A$1000–2500 commission on each student enrolled and there have been bribes accepted for students to go to particular institutions (Langmead 1999).

Australian university senior management tends to favour recruitment heavily biased towards full-fee-paying programmes in expensive fields, like law and business, and towards government-to-government aid in education, rather than selecting individuals purely on merit. Some of the most popular courses both commodify knowledge and assume cultural and political neutrality. Under such dispensations it is argued that health, welfare and language provision for students, and especially childcare provision, is not 'economic' and that those who need such support 'can't cut it' in uni-business. It also tends to produce newspaper headlines which suggest that, for example, the devaluation of the yen is a problem for Australian vice-chancellors (rather than for Japan and Japanese students). The problems of the effects on tertiary educational growth in third world countries of the establishment of satellite campuses by first world universities, and of the increased flow of students (and money) from third to first world countries, get downplayed.

On the other hand, some faculty, including the very large number of international student support staff in Australia, have both raised these issues and done innovative work on 'internationalizing' their education, seeking to develop culturally inclusive revisions of curricula and pedagogy and to promote intercultural understanding and acceptance. They stress social mixing as part of cultural, economic and interpersonal relations, and the need to give full consideration to those from a non-English-speaking background (NESB). But more than this, they have pioneered 'multiliteracy': encouraging symbiotic intercultural relationships, with those from formerly colonized counties and NESB communities in Australia actively participating in constructing new literacies to challenge neo-colonial legacies ('writing back'). They also have innovative patterns of undergraduate and vocational course delivery, including first year teaching 'offshore' (that is in the home country), encouragement of staff and student exchanges *to* the countries from which most of their international students come, and the development of cross-national research projects with a more global outlook with these countries.

Graduate unions

Student unions and branches are hard to maintain because the collective memory gets erased every few years. Even when a full-time organizer is hired, they usually move on after a few years, and leaders and members move on relentlessly to other lives. However, when they are strong, such unions involve graduate students in governance and alter the power relations on campus, including initiating general campus wide conversations about the purpose and future of higher education. They also offer individuals leadership training and an experience of taking control of their own lives, including working models of multiethnic and multiracial collaborations and feminist activism (Nelson and Watt 1999: 153–6).

The USA

While the possibility of 'putting yourself through graduate school', aided by individual colleges' scholarships and small grants for specific expenses (see pp. 129–45), is often spoken of in relation to the USA, most research students there support themselves substantially by working as research assistants or teaching assistants (RAs or TAs) often on very low wages. This has led to various forms of unionization. Starting in 1969 at the University of Wisconsin, US graduate students as employees have established campus unions which have functioned successfully not only at negotiating for salaries and benefits but also at handling other grievances. In other places students have affiliated with the American Federation of Teachers, the United Auto Workers, or the Communication Workers of America, for example. This became a growing national movement in the 1990s, as graduate employee wages failed to keep up with inflation. In several cases they had to go to court to confirm their right to organize with a major fight at Yale and finally success with a National Labor Relations Board ruling at New York University in 2000.

Australia

Australian graduate students are also strongly organized, but on a less economic and a more national and stable basis. The Council of Australian Postgraduate Associations (CAPA) split away from the (now undergraduate) National Tertiary Union, but they still work together and are based in the same building. CAPA has considerable clout and credibility with politicians, since it is good at getting media representation and most of the students it represents are fee paying 'customers'. It is funded by the postgraduate association of each university (out of the general service fee) at the rate of £300 per year per student. The union has a president on a student stipend equivalent, two admin staff and a researcher. A national executive is voted on each year, with 'a blood bath' at the annual conference around issues of representation. From 1990 to 1993 it set up its own Codes of Practice and forced universities to get staff to undergo training.

The UK National Union of Students (NUS) is a disaster area by contrast. It has long been party politicized and split, with 'Labour' in control and sections of the hard Left making bids for power. As I was told, 'Its bickering makes the House of Commons look sophisticated'. It doesn't have a permanent postgraduate students' officer, but one of the twelve members of the National Executive Committee takes on this responsibility. In the past it has neglected postgraduates, but this may be changing because in 2000 it published a booklet on *Increasing the Involvement of Postgraduate Students in Student Unions* and a similar one on overseas students. Its welfare department does, however, produce good, regular information sheets on finance, visas and so on, which are distributed to student unions and also on the NUS website.

In response to NUS neglect, a National Postgraduate Committee (NPC) was set up independently in the mid-1980s. This initially produced a *Journal of Graduate Education* (from 1995, but in abeyance) and a series of pamphlets on accommodation, sexual harassment and the terms and conditions of postgraduate research and teaching assistants, to assist in disputes with universities about provision (NPC 1992, 1993, 1995a, 1995b, 1998). It continues to hold annual conferences, to produce responses to government White Papers and to make representations to HEFCs and QAA. Its procedures are rather heavily bureaucratic and male science research student dominated (for example meetings are always at the weekend 'because science research students can't get away during the week', despite pleas about childcare) and it is not nearly as well funded as the NUS. It doesn't have a commercial wing like the NUS travel and insurance and is supported entirely by subscriptions from affiliated student unions and a handful of individual members. Nonetheless, its one (sabbatical) officer manages to do good work arguing, for example, for graduate students to have access to loans on the same conditions as undergraduates; and on the appeals procedures for 'failed' Masters and PhDs (see pp. 254–6). Moreover, unlike the NUS, the NPC has credibility with educational journalists.

It is also possible for UK research students to join the AUT or the National Association of Teachers in Further and Higher Education (NATFHE) (see p. 34).

Finally, it is worth mentioning that not all nation states are reacting to major events of the twentieth century by economizing their education. Some (Iran, Brazil) are rediscovering their pasts, others (Russia, Poland) are over enthusiastically embracing their pasts (Cowen 1996). Some continue to stress a demonstration of erudition – being encyclopedic and perfect – which is very unlike the past and continuing the UK requirement to demonstrate analytical skill.

This variety in what a doctorate involves and is for will become increasingly clear and contentious as countries seek harmonization and standardization, especially within free-trade groupings. To date our own superstate, the EU, has been mainly concerned with the admission criteria for first year courses, credit transfer systems, and comparability of levels of undergraduate degrees. But Masters and doctorates will not be far behind.

Some effects of the recent changes in the UK

What is being left out

In the new British version of Social Darwinism, many important issues in education are definitely on the back-burner: namely, education as a means to create and recreate a common (national) culture and to contribute to knowledge for its own sake; education as a welfare right of citizens for personal development; and education as a means to engineer a reduction in social inequalities. These all still get referred to, but in practice receive short shrift compared to 'wealth creation'. That is to say, most of the concerns of educationalists for centuries – the moral and cultural purposes of education of Socrates and Rousseau, John Stuart Mill and Tawney, Arnold and Dewey, not to mention Mary Wollstonecraft, Paulo Freire and Virginia Woolf get largely ignored. Where are love of learning for its own sake and the development of the human spirit; as central to a civilized society and an element in active citizenship; and as a contributor to the continuity and stability in society? What of the university as both critic and conscience of society and as a means of social engineering? What also of the concerns of the new social movements of the 1960s and 1970s which hoped to open up the university and make it responsible to, and useful for, the less privileged sections of society (see Table 1.1)?

This of course applies at doctoral level too. The current debates on postgraduate studies are but the latest phase of a concern with long history: whether higher education is for 'education' or 'training', with the pendulum currently well towards the (economistic) training end. PhDs are seen by government as a mixture of training for generic researchers and a form of national 'R&D'; and professional doctorates have been introduced to 'upskill' professionals for managerial level employment. Neither form of doctorate is now seen officially as pre-eminently a means to a more personally rewarding and satisfying life, nor as about making a significant contribution to communal knowledge.

Table 1.1   Three modes of university organization

	Donnish dominion as in the 1950s and 1960s (see Halsey 1992)	Emanicipatory sought by the new social movements of the 1970s	Managerialist promoted in the late 1980s and 1990s
Central concerns	Social responsibility, scholarship, equal access across social classes, tapping the pool of ability	Democratization, community relevance, sex and race equity	Competitiveness, universities as enterprises, profitability, quality and effectiveness
Type of leadership	Professorial power, senate democracy, hands-off administrators	Minimal distinction between manager and managed, dialogic, nurturant, collegial, often in opposition to the Establishment	Rational/technicist leaders to drag reluctant academics forward, line management, entrepreneurial
View of students	Apprentices, paternalistic, pastoral care	Active participants in policy and curriculum construction equality and mutual responsibility	Clients/customers to be serviced, marketing targets
Relationship to the state	Central civil service and universities should be above sectional interests, social representativeness, detached and objective, academic freedom	Concerned with connection to grassroots and new social movements	Forced pace of change, policy making a separate and distinct phase from implementation, more relationships with commercial funding sources
Accountability	Competitive entry, peer review, trusted professionals, ethics and integrity, absentee and incompetent lecturers tolerated for general freedom and good	To the community (asking 'whose side are we on?'), evaluated subjectively by the people it affects in different social situations	Market forces AND central state regulation, external evaluation of research and teaching, budgets tied to performance, short-term contracts for staff

Despite a rhetoric of lifelong learning supported by everyone from the OECD and the World Bank through UNESCO to New Labour, the perspectives of students, graduates and undergraduates alike, and their *pleasure* in knowledge, and *personal development*, are being largely ignored in both research and policy making in higher education. Students are seldom seen as 'stakeholders' in education, despite talk of 'consumers' in the 'global market'. Also despite what marketing elsewhere says sells products to consumers, personal 'happiness' and 'interest' and 'quality of life' are rarely mentioned. Instead students, including research students, are talked about as if 'they' were a drain on national resources. Yet such students make an important contribution to scholarship, they work long hours and tolerate low incomes (see Chapter 4). Further, in the concern to mass produce research students, 'they' are constructed as a homogeneous group, rather than diversity and different 'needs' and potential contributions being recognized.

> [A]n argument [for the role of research] based directly on economic benefit is clearly not enough. Arguments about indirect benefits in the economic context always sound very limp and unconvincing. It is only when you take them out of the economic context and call them direct benefits of an un-economic kind that they begin to sound convincing. The real justification [for government funding] is that research and research training are formative – not only of researchers and their attributes and identities, but also of social relations or social life. In that context, research is transformative . . . higher education makes a different kind of society possible . . . Now that may sound a bit general and abstract for a public position in favour of public spending on research training. I hope it isn't. It's a simple point really . . . education and research . . . are formative, they're productive; and because they (especially research) embody a reflective aspect as well, they are also socially transformative. Much of the future of . . . late-modern societies is tied up in their education and research systems.
>
> (Marginson 1998: 17–18)

Equity issues

As a consequence, despite 30 years of feminist, Black and minority ethnic and socialist activists arguing that higher education is part of the process of reproduction of the disadvantages of various groups in society, the issues these social movements have highlighted are largely absent from current national policy discussions and mainstream research. Gender is seen as something brought into the university, not created within it. The theme is, at best, giving everyone equal treatment and a fair chance (liberal, merit), not ensuring disadvantaged groups get equal shares and a fair outcome (radical, redressive, reconstruction). Gender is still separated from race and class, rather than their being seen integrally. More to the point, the enormous contributions these social movements have made to higher education's curriculum development, pedagogy, epistemology and empirical research are all ignored and confined to the specific areas of women's and race/ethnic studies (see pp. 175–91). With the result that what is in place in 'Equal Opportunities' is a 'short agenda' (Cockburn 1991), with little or crude analysis, and little effect.

EO work was at its height in British schools and technical colleges during the 1980s, with initiatives in higher education starting well behind. Even when they did, the 'old' (pre-1992) universities responded only cautiously and ambiguously and in confined and limited arenas to the politicized concepts of 'race', gender and disability when they arrived on their agenda. The 'new' universities (then polytechnics) were rather more concerned with EO because they were run by inequality-conscious local education authorities (LEAs) which insisted on, for example, targets for staff and student recruitment. But even in the polytechnics, what existed was often ad hoc, disparate and uncoordinated and inadequately underpinned by wider institutional policy. The few initiatives that *were* put in place were mainly concerned with staff, not with students, and they were inadequately monitored.

According to Sarah Neal (1998), although all four universities she studied between 1992 and 1993 had EO policy documents and various structures to generate and implement them, in their everyday, internal worlds, equality initiatives were the preserve of the management (not 'owned' by the general staff and student body) and marginalized and fragmented. Even at management level and among those who were closely involved, 'there was an absence of consensus [on] what equal opportunities actually meant and what the aims of . . . policies actually were'. She argues that although universities and academic trade unions are generally seen as sympathetic to issues of social justice and equal opportunities, higher education is also traditionalist and hierarchical, and *local* branches of the AUT and NATFHE are conservative and defensive, whatever the position of their national head offices (see p. 34). At grassroots level, both management and unions responded 'inactively' to EO programmes. They were 'apathetic', 'hostile and suspicious', or simply excluded EO from their remit, especially around issues of 'race'.

Neal agrees with earlier work by Maureen Farish and colleagues (1995), that genuine equality of opportunity is seen as unimaginable, unattainable and she adds *undesirable* within higher education, and so EO discourses and policies are depoliticized. Organizations try to maximize consent and minimize dissent by converting the issues into questions of 'fairness' and the removal of barriers, proposing technicist and rationalist approaches. They seek practicable solutions, like having policy documents, committees and specialist posts, and addressing issues of access, monitoring, fair interviewing, childcare, maternity provision, and wheelchair access. But they do not seek to raise awareness of historical patterns of disadvantage (especially those to do with race), nor do they question continuing power relations. They do not even properly publicize the limited EO strategies they do have 'in place'. She found many EO post-holders were isolated and stigmatized, and departmental 'consultants' were ineffective, untrained, and even unwilling. 'Race' and women's units were sometimes separate from, and mutually antagonistic to one another; or else homogeneous solutions were proposed for all inequality issues.

By the late 1990s, even this little had fallen further down the agenda of both national policy and individual institutional management. Official reports still incorporate a litany of 'women, ethnic minority and mature students', but gender and race issues are deemed to have been resolved among students because women and non-whites are now proportionately represented at undergraduate level. Most parts of the Dearing Report (1997) and supporting documents do not even give gender breakdowns in their statistical tables and never by gender *and* race or age or class background.

Admittedly, the Commission on University Careers Opportunities (CUCO) of the CVCP/UUK and the University and Colleges Staff Development Agency (UCoSDA) have been making new efforts in the 1990s. A new joint Equality Challenge Unit was launched in 2001 in association with various professional associations, to increase the numbers of women *staff*, especially at higher levels and in SET (continuing the concern of initiatives in the 1970s and 1980s). But this is very little and very late, and it is still at the level of doing surveys, setting up registers and databases, issuing guidelines, 'launching' fixed, short-term, lowly funded initiatives with other agencies, holding one-off seminars, running training programmes, and doing yet more evaluations – when the case is already made. The initiatives are too few and too modest to achieve much success, and are based largely on persuasion. Moreover, to repeat, they are all for staff (Bagilhole 2000).

The central offices of the academic trade unions, AUT and NATFHE, have been involved in EO issues since the late 1970s and have annual women's meetings, national women's committees and women's newsletters. They also run gender training workshops as well as funding and publishing research and policies on a wide range of EO issues. These include many of interest to students (some jointly and in association with the NUS) such as on age discrimination, gender neutral language, sexual harassment, and consensual relations between staff and students. Both unions now also have active lesbian, gay, bi and transsexual committees, as well as longstanding antiracist activities.

These equity discourses are liberal rather than feminist (see p. 178) and barely scratch the surface of the relentless reproduction of class, gender and race privilege in HE. It is still very difficult to get gender differences defined as *oppressive and unfair*. Indeed there is some evidence of a growing resistance to initiatives for women:

- A series of gender-equity-is-a-luxury discourses exists (maternity leave is unfair to employers in the current context; the issue is to increase output and relevance to secure the position of the universities, not social justice; equal pay would be fine if we could afford it but there are greater priorities like labs and libraries – or even a lift for disabled people).
- A masculinity in crisis discourse is growing (men are victims of masculinity too with its effects on their health, family breakdown and so on; they equally need a 'men's officer' on campus; men have been unfairly disadvantaged by EO programmes and policies).
- Various attempts are made to set generations of women against each other ('1970s feminists had it easy: there were more jobs and better social security and grants then' versus 'the young women are letting down what the older women worked for').
- We are all said to be postfeminist now: we have grown beyond the need for EO.

Most of these are appropriate and recycle EO discourses individualistically: equality is equated with equal treatment for each person and an issue of individual rights not of group disadvantage. In addition there have been some very negative responses, even violence, against women complainants who have sought to use the formal equity processes in the USA, Canada and Australia. These serve distinctly 'to discourage the others' (see pp. 215–17).

In between the focus on boys' underachievement at school and women's underachievement as professors and vice-chancellors, issues of women's and men's differential performance at first degree and especially at doctoral level tend to go unremarked. But even if we were to accept Dearing's (1997) simplistic assumption that issues of gender are resolved at undergraduate level with the 50:50 balance in (home student) numbers, this is certainly not the case at doctoral level. Only 40 per cent of those doing doctorates are women and there is a much more substantial deficit of women among international students in the UK at postgraduate than at undergraduate level (see pp. 35, 53, 69).

However, the original research councils' enquiries in relation to the PhD in the 1980s did not include either social justice issues or the needs of foreign students as part of their remit. So, not surprising, either they did not notice differences among students, or they did not consider them important. As Sara Delamont pithily commented, 'an all-male committee . . . consulted male experts to produce a report focused on male graduate students' (1989: 52).

Consequently the changes introduced were assumed to be for (and so they best fit) full-time, home, young, geographically mobile, trainee 'scientists' (whatever their discipline). Hence they can present difficulties for all who do not fit this profile because of their domestic commitments, residence, career profile or discipline. Part-time, international, older and non-mobile students remain, as they always were, 'different' or 'non-normal'. It is they who have (or rather are) a problem: who are deemed to need (and at best will get help) to adjust to the existing system. In other words, past lack of concern with gender (and other) differences among students means that even if women and international students do not encounter direct discrimination, we still have to work in a system which positions us against the grain. Far from the specific difficulties of working class, overseas, mature, part-time and disabled women research students having been sorted out by (the limited) EO initiatives of the 1980s, they were rather continued and reconstructed under a new dispensation. The research councils have not required universities to monitor doctoral applications and completions by sex and race, nor to address the chilly climate which exists for all women and Black students (see pp. 201–14). Despite the current focus on audit and indicators, these by and large miss (ignore) structural differences (inequalities).

However, even in the absence of top-down attention to their particular needs, and with few role models, women are moving themselves into higher education en masse, from the bottom up; and, as Heidi Mirza (1995) points out, this is doubly true of Black women in Britain. They have exercised 'instrumental achievement strategies' in a world of limited opportunities. Despite a popular press which presumes Black underachievement, many minority ethnic groups are in fact over-represented as students in higher education relative to their population size (though very under-represented as staff).

Equal opportunities and antiracism has been traditionally presented as playing an important role in explaining the presence of black women in institutions of Further and Higher Education. It is my position that their presence is in spite of [such] practice not because of it. The motivation to 'go on' comes from the women themselves, an issue long ignored in the many studies that focus on 'race', equal opportunities and access ... The black female presence cannot simply be explained in terms of institutional access and changing white attitudes. This is a partial and liberal explanation. We should be clear, equal opportunities, antiracist and access programmes have not been about developing a political strategy for black people in the workplace or in universities.

They can even be a distraction and the identity politics they foster can be regressive, divisive and harmful (Mirza 1995: 150–2).

The one arena of government and non-governmental organization (NGO) policy and practice which has picked up gender and HE as an issue is overseas aid. The first (and so far only) study to look at women students from the poorer countries of the world studying in the UK was carried out for the World University Service in 1983 (Goldsmith and Shawcross 1985). It found that the poorest countries still have the fewest women relative to men studying in the UK (even though the students are often on UK government development aid funding), and that the numbers of women were and are also low from OPEC countries where there used to be obvious restrictions on women's education and where there are still limitations on their geographical mobility. Even ten years later, women comprised less than 30 per cent of all students from parts of south east Asia and Africa and under 15 per cent of those from Pakistan, Libya, Saudi Arabia and Iran (Wright 1997). Those few women from these countries who do come to the UK are also often from a narrower range of social backgrounds that their men compatriots.

Elaine Unterhalter and Kees Maxey followed up South African students who had studied in London during the Apartheid regime. They found that while all were upper or middle class, women came from even higher socio-economic backgrounds than the men. The women were much more controlled both financially and in terms of where they put their allegiance by their families and also by the liberation movement (the African National Congress, the ANC). Fewer women finished their PhDs (Unterhalter and Maxey 1995).

The Department for International Development (DfID, the former Overseas Development Agency, ODA), the British Council, and Commonwealth funding bodies have all accepted feminist concerns for women's welfare, together with arguments about the important role played by women in developing countries, and they have produced some major changes, despite various problems (see pp. 135–6). Staff in these agencies having been monitoring the gender of award recipients by subject, level of study and country of origin from 1985–6 onwards, and are described as fully sympathetic to increasing the proportion of women. The result is that the proportion of women among new arrivals in the UK on, for example, the principal government development-oriented scheme, the Technical Cooperation Training awards, increased by nearly 50 per cent (from 14.5 per cent to 20.25 per cent) in the 1980s, even if only a small minority of women are doing as advanced level courses as doctorates (Threfall and Langley 1992: 26–30).

The European Union is an even more heavyweight potential force for women's rights, and though its response is liberal and slow, it too is moving on women and research. A first Women and Science conference was held in 1998, which asked for and got political commitment from the Commission to promote women in science. (In EU-speak, 'science' includes social science.) There is now a Women in Science Sector; greater representation of women on decision-making bodies (advisory groups, evaluation and monitoring panels); and a policy report on gender aspects of science policy in the EU. *Promoting Excellence through Mainstreaming Gender Equality* was compiled by twelve women experts and includes harmonized data on gender and science across the member states. It was presented to Research Commissioner Philippe Buisquin in December 1999 and discussed in The Hague in spring 2000. There was special stress on the shortcomings of peer review system for the majority of grants. The Commissioner wants to encourage exchange of best practice and a coherent approach to promoting research by, for and on women in Framework programmes (*Cordis focus* 24 April 2000).

EU students on ERASMUS and other educational exchange schemes have been monitored by gender for some time, given the EU commitment to equal employment, vocational training and educational opportunities. However, the monitoring, which has been done by a team at the University of Kassel, has found next to no gender difference. This is, however, probably an unfortunate instance of evaluators not finding things, not because they are not there, but because they use quantitative methods and do not ask the right questions (Teichler and Maiworm 1997).

One of my students, Akiko Nishio, has been studying Japanese postgraduates at the University of London. She initially drew on the questions asked by the ERASMUS evaluators, but *on these questions* she found almost no differences between men and women. However, other questions and her own participant observation experience showed the women were usually young and single and funded by their parents, or they had accompanied their husbands and were using their time in London to study, while nearly half the men had been sent by their companies and brought their wives with them. Almost all the men said they had decided to study abroad in order to advance their careers, but women's reasons were much more varied. They included wanting to experience living abroad, to escape social pressures at home, and to accompany their husbands. Only a few mentioned improving employment opportunities. Nishio's work shows the importance of considering international students culture by culture, since the circumstances of, and replies from, say, American or Kenyan students in London might be expected to be rather different (Nishio 2001).

Improvements for research students

The situation is not all gloom. While not concerned specifically with improving the situation of 'marginal' groups of students, the UK's post-1987 focus on providing taught courses for doctoral students, whether doing a PhD or a professional doctorate, has been welcomed by some women and international students. It provides both more systematic presentation of methodologies and also support by bringing students together in a cohort. Improvements in the quality of supervision and the aim to complete the thesis promptly have also actually suited such students rather well. Certainly the competition to enrol students has meant that any good student, man or woman, is likely nowadays to be accepted to do a PhD; and some of those accepted will be working in the post-1992 universities which have extensive experience in catering for older and minority ethnic students. On the other hand, the student buyer needs to beware, because as noted there are some cowboy institutions and supervisors about, and there is increased pressures on even the best intentioned to take your money regardless (see pp. 86–9).

Your progress is certainly now better monitored and recorded (and, it is hoped, any possibility of your dropping out forestalled), though there is also more chasing up of fees and no longer a leisurely period after you have completed three years' registration when you can use the library or labs and get supervision for free. Arguably teaching now risks becoming over-bureaucratized, with the relationship between you and your supervisor over-controlled (with specifications of timings, sequences and uniform skills which *must* be covered, and required pieces of assessed coursework) and too much like relations of contract rather than those of personal and professional responsibility. There is certainly greater clarity in student handbooks as to what you can expect, and what is expected of you; and somewhat better provision of support services, for example help with English or in finding accommodation (though the provision of childcare is still very poor). Supposedly 'customer care' has reached the universities. In addition, because some students feel they have entitlements and are being increasingly litigious, universities are reviewing their complaints and appeals procedures, with encouragement from the QAA (see pp. 255–6). It is hoped that you won't be needing this, though it is helpful to have it in place!

In addition, a combination of the possibilities afforded by information and communication technology (ICT) and the pressures for cost-effective teaching of more students, is leading to the introduction of distance learning elements in some courses. Some of you may benefit from the new modes of course delivery and location, though others may prefer the older style of personal contact. In any event, ICT should augment rather than replace face-to-face teaching and interaction with other students. But it is useful to be able increasingly to access library and World Wide Web resources and to get email tutorial support at a distance, and it is also helpful to those with home responsibilities to have some of the more stringent residence requirements relaxed (allowing you not to have to leave home for long periods).

As cheaper travel is routinely producing greater flows of people, knowledge and culture across national borders, classrooms are increasingly international, with diasporic sets of academics and students generating exciting new curricula and pedagogies. Whole new postcolonial perspectives within disciplines are being opened up, involving issues of space and place and differences in ways of learning and arguing. Traditions are being reworked and hybridity flourishes.

Problems for research students

More dismal aspects of the recent changes for research students' experiences are fairly obvious, for example poorer facilities and the fact that while you may have an increased chance of getting a postgraduate teaching assistantship (to help with the mass of undergraduates), this is likely to be a casual, often minimally supervised post, and that there are poorer future job opportunities (see pp. 54–8, 261). University teachers and researchers also now have less time to be collegial and for time-consuming individual relationships with students, even if a sense of professional identity has made them try to minimize the passing on of these effects to their students. Everyone has necessarily become more instrumental and rational, looking to build a career and giving the hierarchy at least minimally what it wants, whether that is getting more research grants, or working 9 a.m. to 5 p.m. in offices, or becoming a 'line manager'. Some have embraced this new entrepreneurial professionalism whole-heartedly, even if most women academics (and many men) feel it is not what they wanted from a job they had hoped would compensate for low pay by allowing them to focus on the life of the mind and the welfare of students. There is also a worry that we could now be moving towards the same mass/over-production of doctorates (credential inflation) as has concerned Americans.

A couple of less obvious and more general issues are also worth mentioning. One is that despite the ending of the binary divide between polytechnics and university, there is now *more* rather than less differentiation among HE institutions because of the encouragement of competition. As in the USA and Japan, the UK now has a marked, gradated hierarchy of universities (though without the private/state split). At the top there are universities with ancient endowments and/or which score highly on audits of research activity, attract major research grants and successfully commercially exploit their staff's intellectual discoveries. At the base there are institutions which carry the bulk of first degree and pre-degree level teaching, with a low income per student. That is to say, the wealthy Oxford and Cambridge and some of the colleges in the University of London are followed by the 'Russell Group' (named after the hotel in London where their vice-chancellors started meeting), with various 'old' universities and the post-1992 universities midway in the '94 Group' and the 'Coalition of Modern Universities' jockeying for position and trying to work to preserve their advantages, with poorer places below them. (For more details on the importance of where you study, see pp. 98–111.)

A second general issue is that what the research councils have set in place for the PhD has now veered sharply towards a presentation of research degrees as *training*. They are supposedly about the acquiring of competencies, not to write a particular thesis, but to become a generic researcher; and about trying out of these skills in a short apprenticeship project – even though there has been no research to say if those who attend such training regularly complete more quickly, do better theses, or are more (or less) satisfied with their doctoral experience than those who do not. (Some research students simply skip going to the classes.) Moreover only *some* skills are now stressed: there is no longer time, for instance, to learn another language (see pp. 80–1), and arguably the time taken up by the taught element combined with the pressure to complete 'on time' is undermining the contribution made by PhD research to the creation of new knowledge.

This is most marked in the social sciences, where most of the first year (60 per cent of the 44 weeks) must be taken up with courses and where there was the first big push for, and a continuing stress on, completion within four years. Here the past focus on independent assessment of the nature and significance of a research question, and the quality of the process and product of answering it, is being replaced by a stress on developing a pre-specified (less ambitious, more limited) problem. That is to say, intentionally or not, the ESRC's pressures are acting as 'a powerful mechanism for research steerage' (Ozga 1998). The PhD thesis used to be a major piece of work on which authors could draw for their first monograph and several important articles. Increasingly, however, even in the humanities (where the AHRB has still not made a requirement for taught courses) all doctorates are becoming 'Kentucky fast research'. That is to say, they 'should' *all* now be pitched at a 'manageable level', with the capacity to succeed under pressure, and time management, of paramount importance – rather than a PhD at least tackling an issue of importance to the discipline and the individual student, however long it takes. In the natural sciences, more original work has always waited till postdoctoral level, but research here has been steered towards 'more boring but patentable paths' (Power 1997: 100).

This is evidenced in the increasing number of texts for students which recommend modest, safe efforts, for example replication of existing work in a different context, rather than research for pleasure, significance and originality. This is not necessarily what students want, especially not what self-funding, part-time, older students in humanities and social sciences want. Many (especially women?) want to undertake a voyage of guided intellectual exploration of a specific problem. These students are not odd, in the sense of being either occasional or idiosyncratic. They are probably the majority in many fields.

Nor is this narrowing down of the PhD in the long-term national research interest. The research councils have sought the high ground of presenting a PhD as largely a matter of the proper application of appropriate methods, analytic procedures and existing evidence to bite-sized problems, soluble in four years. This makes research seem like an issue of technical rationality. It risks losing sight of the more important elements of intellectual creativity. It keeps the councils away from both the messy, confusing, political issues of human concern faced by professional researchers, whose problems and practice go beyond the application of given skills to manageable problems, and the intriguing issue of how genuinely *new* knowledge is constructed. It also avoids the issue of just how much time it may take for such work to be produced.

Most researchers in the long tradition of studies of socialization into the professions talk about people needing to acquire not only technical knowledge but also 'shared tacit knowledge' by 'situational learning' in order to do their work. Schön, for example, in his widely read book *Educating the Reflective Practitioner*, talks of the issues facing a civil engineer building a bridge and points out that 'the most important areas of professional practice . . . lie beyond the conventional boundaries of professional competence' (Schön 1987: 7). They involve political, social and aesthetic elements. These are not usually formally taught so much as 'caught'. They include a feel, a knack, a gift for working in the laboratory or field, or with informants, or for finding sources, which comes from 'doing' and experience. Professional research practice also includes a powerful disciplinary *habitus* concerning aesthetic criteria – what constitutes 'elegance' and 'excellence' in a piece of work (Bourdieu 1988). It is such distinctions and discriminations, the artistry of handling indeterminate zones of practice: of framing problems, of implementation, of improvisation, and of writing an argument, which furnish the framework for knowledge production. And these are learnt by coaching.

> What is required is the 'freedom to learn by doing in a setting relatively low in risk, with access to coaches who initiate students into the "traditions of the calling": who help them, by "the right kind of telling", to see on their own behalf and in their own way what they most need to see' (Schön 1987: 17).

The vital element in doctoral research is learning to exercise disciplinary judgement, that is to say, acquiring the academic equivalent of 'good taste': knowing when an experiment has 'worked', how best to gain access to a research site, how to evaluate sources, how best to choose theories and critical cases, what there is to be seen in the data, when a reading is plausible and an analysis correct, how to construct an argument, and how to write and present a good paper. Newcomers need neither to be left to reinvent the wheel nor to have didactic teaching. Rather they need a practicum, with supervisors who can demonstrate, advise, observe performance, detect errors of application and point out correct responses. This is the induction which students find exciting and the reason why they submit to many years of (often unpaid) work. It is also why it is essential for academics to combine teaching and research – not to acquire a knowledge base, but to have a feel for the process of *construction* of disciplinary knowledge.

If the social sciences and humanities PhD is to be crammed into only two or three years of work on the dissertation itself, this creative element will simply be displaced to be learned either in a period as a postdoctoral student, as in the sciences, or in an initial period of employment before 'tenure' is granted, as in the American system; *or* it will result in a decline in British research standards, which is the reverse of the research councils' intention. (Paradoxically it is probably now only while doing a PhD that researchers can actually undertake scrupulous data collection, and give the analysis and interaction between data and theory something approaching the full attention and time that is required for high quality original work.)

A new form of academic masculinity

A final general issue worth exploring is a thread which runs through the new managerialism in higher education, the attempts to homogenize students ('they can be any age, culture or gender so long as they resemble a young British man'), and attempts to rationalize the doctoral degree as 'training'. This commonality is that academic professionality, in both its old, professorial and new, managerial forms, and the entire Enlightenment project of Science, is gendered. They have embedded within them an antagonism, a project of masculinity, of (super) rationality, of scientism, of independence which attempts to keep safe and secure and strong by keeping or driving out or denying elements associated with femininity (emotions, bodies, acceptance of the diversity of humanity, personal interconnections). These 'mind-forged manacles' makes such projects lopsided and finally counterproductive and destructive.

Celia Davies has traced the history of the concepts of professionalism and bureaucracy and noted that

> women's struggles to enter the professions in the late nineteenth century and early twentieth century . . . were not just a matter of doors and minds being closed to women, but of the values that were embedded in the notion of the practice of a profession reflecting a masculine project and repressing or denying those qualities culturally assigned to femininity.

When the professions developed in western countries they based their right to prestige and control and remuneration upon possessing a monopolistic knowledge and mystique, which they argued had to be gained by lengthy and heroic individual effort. This knowledge was possessed by individuals and exercised by them in a visible and active way. But the very notion of what it was to act and be competent as a professional derives from a masculinist vision that does not recognize its partial and dependent character. A profession requires, and cannot exist without, a complimentary 'other', feminine part. That is to say, professionality creates a dependence within, and disables, those who come to the professional in the capacity of client. This distance and subordination is maintained by allowing only fleeting and distanced/detached encounters between the professional and the client. However, such 'consultations' are (have to be) sustained by a great deal of preparatory and follow-up work done by others, who cope with the emotions and the embodied and particular characteristics of the clients. The persona of the professional does not acknowledge, or trivializes, this work as 'details' or 'support', although 'he' relies upon it. (Not to mention other aspects of the bodily and emotional 'needs' of professionals, which are also largely provided by women domestic supporters.) Those who do such support work may be praised in speeches and acknowledgements, but their work, and they themselves, are actually regarded as low level (Davies 1996: 669).

In the nineteenth and early twentieth century, women were excluded entirely from the profession of university teaching and research. But by the 1950s and 1960s we had been allowed in to do particular, limited, aspects of the work, in subordinate positions (Smith 1978). Today most routine teaching, student pastoral care and empirical research in universities depends upon junior teaching staff, 'academic related' ancillary and administrative workers, and contract researchers (all mainly women) who deal with the whole student and the whole research process, so that senior men can deal with just students' minds, make rational strategic policy decisions, and/or create theoretical breakthroughs. These subordinates are the ones who take the 'can do' their 'new manager' bosses have to declare to the state (and which they convert into 'must dos' for their staff), and actually operationalize it and perform the 'making do' characteristic of the grassroots of organizations. They are the women personal assistants who field the phone calls and make people happy with the decisions the senior men make (Clarke and Newman 1997).

The government's devolution responsibility to quasi-governmental organizations and institutional senior management teams to operationalize underfunded central policies by 'hard nosed' accounting ('managing demand') requires attempts to Ford-ize teaching by treating all students as the same (and as 'heads' not 'leaky bodies'). It also leads to attempts to rationalize the PhD as the application of agreed skills to defined problems, bracketed off from issues of individual, social and public purpose and with disciplinary knowledge treated as a dangerous residue rather than an intrinsic feature of knowledge production. These have in common that they give secure feelings of being in control: of purpose and direction and rectitude. But this is not because of their fitness for purpose, let alone their proven efficacy. It is because of their association with (a form of) masculinity.

There is no going back to the old 'donnish dominion' in the universities of the 1950s, nor would I want to since that was also, though differently, masculinized, and also but differently problematic. I would like to have tried more of the emancipatory model of the second column of Table 1.1 on p. 31. But many of the changes of the managerialist university do have much to be said for them, not the least being that research students are much less often left to sink or swim. The problems are, rather, first, that the new reconstruction of the relationship between the public and state around the figure of the individualized market consumer, which Britain has experienced during the 1980s and 1990s in all our erstwhile public services, is quite inappropriate *for education* in many respects. Second, that we are being forced along by a new masculinism which, like the old, over-values rationality, individual autonomy, objectivity and scientism, and now also political passionlessness and economism (Leonard 2000). Third, that the researcher we are seeking to produce through the new rationalized supervisory system of bureaucratized 'care' and monitored progress, is still 'the man of reason', the autonomous 'independent scholar' who transcends his (or now her) body and seeks after truth (in the PhD process, though less in professional doctorates) sharply separated from practical everyday affairs (Johnson *et al.* 2000).

Further reading

Among many recent books seeking to understand what is happening to universities globally and nationally, collections are useful in showing the general areas of concern.

Burgess, R. G. (ed.) (1997) *Beyond the First Degree: Graduate Education, Lifelong Learning and Careers.* Buckingham: SRHE and Open University Press. This includes articles on what is happening in the USA, Australia and Europe, postgraduate qualifications and employment, and 'lifelong learning'.

Jary, D. and Parker, M. (eds) (1998) *The New Higher Education: Issues and Directions for the Post-Dearing University*. Stoke-on-Trent: Staffordshire University Press. Articles here cast a critical gaze at the effects of mass higher education, diversity and stratification among universities, marketization and managerialism, funding for students and research, and changes in professional education.

Scott, P. (ed.) (1998) *The Globalization of Higher Education*. Buckingham: SRHE and Open University Press. Considers the internationalizing of British, European, Commonwealth and South African higher education and its effects on staff, students and policy making.

Useful analytical accounts of what is happening across the public sector in the UK

Clarke, J. and Newman, J. (1997) *The Managerial State*. London: Sage. An exposition of how public services have been 'depoliticized' by government saying it is just deciding on the maximum size of money that can be given to the police, medicine and higher education, and leaving it up to the sectors and institutions themselves to work out how to cut back and squeeze to work within inadequate budgets.

Power, M. (1997) *The Audit Society: Rituals of Verification*. Oxford: Oxford University Press. A discussion of the explosion of political demand for accountability and control, the attractions of managerialism, and the unintended and dysfunctional consequences for the audited institutions and their staff members (but not students). Chapter 5 looks at the RAE and the QAA.

Changes in higher education

To keep abreast of changes in higher education, it is worth reading *The Times Higher Education Supplement* weekly. For more in-depth reviews you might join the Society for Research into Higher Education (SRHE) Postgraduate Issues Network. This was established in 1995 and is 'primarily for academic staff such as supervisors and senior managers, although it is open to anyone interested in postgraduate education [and] some of its most active members are students with a management or research interest in the area.' It meets one afternoon a term and has produced booklets on various aspects of supervision and overseas postgraduate students (Cryer 1997a; Okorocha 1997; Denicolo 2000; Smith and Gilby 2000).

Specific research on doctoral studies

Becher, T., Henkel, M. and Kogan, M. (1994) *Graduate Education in Britain*. London: Jessica Kingsley. See pp. 61–2.

Burgess, R. (ed.) (1994) *Postgraduate Education and Training in the Social Sciences*. London: Jessica Kingsley. This contains the first findings from the ESRC Programme on 'Research into Training' which funded nine projects from 1988 to

1991 (following the concern about times to and rates of completion of social science PhDs, see pp. 22–3).

Delamont, S., Atkinson, P. and Parry, O. (2000) *The Doctoral Experience: Success and Failure in Graduate School.* London: Falmer. See p. 70.

Gender and higher education

Glazer, J. S., Bensimon, E. M. and Townsend, B. K. (eds) (1993) *Women in Higher Education: A Feminist Perspective.* Needham Heights, MA: Ginn Press. Provides 40 key US articles including Patricia Hill Collins, Sandra Harding, Frances Maher, Adrienne Rich and Bernice Sandler.

Morley, L. (1999) *Organising Feminisms: The Micropolitics of the Academy.* London: Macmillan. Based on the doctoral study of a leading writer and activist, this uses interviews with academics and postgraduates (including research students) in Britain, Greece and Sweden, to trace the interconnection of power and knowledge, showing how power is exercised rather than simply possessed. It is quite densely written but covers a lot of ground, including the difference in the trajectories of feminism and Equal Opportunities initiatives.

Wisker, G. (1996) *Empowering Women in Higher Education.* London: Kogan Page. An introductory account which discusses undergraduate students, including mature women returners, issues of women staff's recruitment, promotion, leadership, and balancing home and work, and three chapters on the changes that women's studies have made to courses and teaching.

Woodward, D. and Ross, K. (2000) *Managing Equal Opportunities in Higher Education.* Buckingham: SRHE and Open University Press. A more optimistic view of EO as a tool in the hands of sympathetic senior managers. The authors suggest changing tack and arguing for EO as part of 'customer care' for students and of human resources development for staff. It contains chapters on disability and sexual orientation which discuss the history of concern with these areas and give good lists of contacts.

International students

McNamara, D. and Harris, R. (eds) (1997) *Overseas Students in Higher Education: Issues in Teaching and Learning.* London: Routledge. Chapters cover the history of changing attitudes to overseas students, student experiences and orientation programmes, learning and language needs, cross-cultural counselling, learning support and evaluation, intercultural learning, gender, and studying in Europe. There is particular attention to student from Hong Kong and South East Asia.

Ryan, Y. and Zuber-Skerritt, O. (eds) (1999) *Supervising Postgraduates from Non-English-Speaking Backgrounds.* Buckingham: SRHE and Open University Press. Aimed at supervisors and international student advisers, and primarily Australian focused, but specifically on research students and certainly worth reading if you come from migrant background or a NES country and don't speak fluent English as a second language. It includes some personal accounts and case studies of African, Iranian and Chinese students and a case of a mismatched student and supervisor.

Notes

1 The extent to which UK universities depend on public funding has been declining, and varies a lot from one institution to another. The wealthier universities have substantial income from endowments and interest on capital, while all universities try also to earn money from conferences and other business ventures, donations, overseas students' fees, and from projects from the EU and industry. For example, only 9 per cent of the London Business School's and 23 per cent of the London School of Economics' income came from the funding councils in 1997, though they also get public money for research projects through the research councils (*THES* 3 March 2000: 1).

2 Differential fees for overseas students began in 1967. EU students are funded by the UK Treasury and distinguished from UK domiciled, 'home' students in the statistics collected by the Higher Education Statistics Agency. Non-EU students are officially described as 'overseas' students. I shall refer to 'other EU' and 'overseas' students collectively as 'international' students.

3 The regulations have since been changed to allow an HEI to indicate the situation of staff who have taken maternity leave, or career breaks, who hold part-time contracts, who are disabled or who have been absent for long periods with illness. The trade unions would like the fact that this is possible to be made clearer to those who may be left out or penalized.

4 Subject Review is one of several quality reviews conducted by QAAHE. In SR, six topics are currently assessed and given a mark out of 4 (a maximum score of 24) for each subject area. The CVCP/UUK have fought to get rid of numerical scores, so as to avoid fine rankings. In January 2000 it was agreed that in future there will be just three aspects of provision: teaching and learning, student progression, and effective use of teaching resources. Each will be marked as failing, approved or commendable, with a subcategory of the last 'exemplary', alongside a detailed narrative report. A 'concise' summary 'for external audiences' will also be issued.

2 | DECIDING TO DO
        A DOCTORATE

Figure 2.1 London's Transport Museum postcard from a poster by Chas Pears (1930)

The 'dreaming spires' of the ancient university, the lure of just the name 'Oxford', or the image of the scholar in 'his' library, all represent group fantasies or social utopias for the aspiring academic, just as the imagined, longed for, community of scholars continues to be a reference point which academics frequently invoke as representing the 'real university' of 'the past'. These fantasies are productive and sustaining of the desire to be a certain figure, the independent scholar. The body of the scholar that frequents these spaces often is the tweed-coated figure conjured up by [a] library full of leather-bound tomes . . . Of course, it is a masculine figure, even though women have managed throughout the history of the PhD to imagine themselves into these spaces, and hence to submit themselves [to] the pedagogical practices that both rely on and sustain these fantasies.

(Johnson *et al.* 2000: 139)

Do I enjoy being an academic? That means, do I like working in this tower office on the floor? No furniture, boxes piled in the corners, wet carpet from leaks in the roof, listening to the thunder building up out-side, keeping notes of what I have to do to follow up today's work tonight, keeping an eye on the clock not to miss a late afternoon doc-tor's appointment and remembering to pick up a child from child care on the other side of the city. Is this [the] blissful devotion to the uninter-rupted pursuit of knowledge which Doctoral study offers? I'm really not impressed. I have one more hour. Do I keep editing this chapter, inserting some notes from my 'working chapter file' or dash over to the library to follow up on some muddled references from an earlier chapter? (which I probably won't be able to find on first effort). Everyone always tells you to be careful about references. You know you have to be absolutely pedantic about references. So why is there always a page number miss-ing? Why don't graduate students have secretaries? Why don't mothers have wives? It's pouring. Keep editing; it's relatively dry in here.

(Fleet *et al.* 1999: 686)

Why do a doctorate?

If you are considering the major commitment of studying for a doctoral degree (whether a PhD, MD, EdD or other, see pp. 71–3) you probably have a number of good reasons – and by 'good' I mean here 'reasons which are likely to end up with you getting your degree'.

Vocational improvement

- You may want to enhance your career opportunities and future earning capacity if you already have a job, or want to get a job, in higher or further education; or in order to do your current job better. This includes nowadays those of you in academic related jobs (such as librarians, administrators, student support staff); those in the former polytechnics and in fields like art and design and accountancy that used not to require their staff to have doctorates; and those outside the academic sector, in industry, government departments and other public sector agencies.

- As a further credential to help you because you are from a marginal group (a woman or Black, for example) within a tight professional job market.
- Or to gain skills in a western country which are needed for future jobs in your home country.

Personal development

- You may want to develop your ability to think independently, creatively, deeply and investigatively, especially if you have had past experience in an education system focused on rote learning or if your present job doesn't stretch you intellectually.
- As a way to go abroad, or to use time constructively if your partner is located in another country for a few years.
- To show you are not 'an 11+ failure', or simply to prove you can do it and to feel a better, more clever person.
- Or as a diversion after a divorce; to find your own pathway; or because you feel burnt out and need recharging intellectually.

Contributing to knowledge

- You may want to do a particular piece of research, or to do some research in general.
- To solve a particular problem or because you have an exciting idea or have thought of a new way of approaching a field.
- For intellectual excitement, intrinsic interest, and because of a deep interest in a particular discipline and wanting to make a significant contribution.

Helping your community or benefiting society

- This is especially common among non-western students and among politically committed people (including feminists).

You may also be motivated by some less common reasons, which are less hopeful in terms of your ultimately successful completion. They may suggest you should do some rethinking. These include:

Problematic reasons

- Drift: not being sure what else to do. If this applies to you, consider a shorter MSc course by tuition and research.
- Because you enjoyed being a student and want to continue as one. In which case a doctorate, especially a PhD, will come as a shock, because it is a very different experience.
- Because you can't get a job and you are offered a grant, generally in the sciences. But will starting a PhD, living on little or no money for several years, and then dropping out actually help?
- Just because further study happens to be a convenient thing to do – to stay in a particular place or because of life changes.
- Because 'everybody' expects you to do a doctorate.
- Specific to women, so as not to continue to be Miss or Mrs or Ms. In which case, consider studying medicine and becoming 'a proper doctor'. Most medical practitioners haven't taken a PhD or an MD, but are qualified on the basis of two bachelor's degrees.

There is some pattern to these choices. Various types of doctorates are undertaken for rather different reasons and at different points in life in different disciplines. They are done more for vocational reasons and by younger and full-time students in the sciences, and more for personal development and part-time by those who return to study after a period of employment, and in the social sciences and humanities. But you need always to do a doctorate with real commitment and pleasure, and as an apprenticeship to doing many more research projects in the future. Any doctorate is an intellectual challenge: a move from a past higher education experience of testing out and using received knowledge to the very different experience of producing new knowledge. A professional doctorate is about using theoretical insights to improve your professional practice. They are not simply convenient settings in which you can get support for a sustained piece of writing. A thesis has to fit a particular mould, so you will almost certainly have to do a lot of rewriting if you subsequently want to publish it, or parts of it. It is therefore not the best thing for you to do if you are mainly interested in activism, or in journalism and getting ideas across to the general public (where research is swift and secondary), or in writing a novel, or a textbook which clearly explains other people's ideas. But your research *can* produce work which is both innovative and influential and which is completed within a reasonable period of time and which attracts commercial or media attention and reaches a wide audience.

In any event, if you do decide to do a doctorate for whatever your individual reasons, you will not be alone. The numbers of research students are increasing and more than 100,000 individuals are currently registered for a 'research based higher degree' in the UK, including over 10,000 from other parts of the EU and 23,000 from the rest of the world (see Figure 2.2 and pp. 12–13).

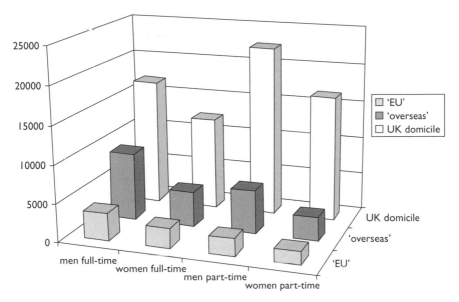

Figure 2.2 Students studying for a research degree in the UK, by sex and domicile, 1998–9
Source: HESA 2000: Tables 1c and 1g

Does a doctorate deliver on these expectations?

To a considerable and possibly an increasing extent, yes.

Vocational improvement

There have been some gloomy prognostications about the poor financial returns to doing a PhD and about the unemployment of those with doctorates (especially among scientists and those in English departments in the United States). For instance, Ernest Rudd found some years ago (see Rudd and Hatch 1968) that a comparison of successful British PhDs with their contemporaries after a few years in employment (ten years after graduation) showed that those with PhDs had a different pattern of employment. They tended to be in jobs that, for graduates, were relatively poorly paid, and the average pay of those with doctorates was less than that of a matching group of graduates without one. He suggested this is partly because they are more likely to be in employed in education, which is a poorly paid sector. But even if each field of employment was looked at separately, those with PhDs seldom had any advantage.

However, recent work which differentiates by gender suggests this picture needs repainting. Investment in higher education gives higher financial returns to women than to men. In the UK, women get a very high earnings-benefit from a first degree and an increasing rate of return with increasingly higher degrees. That is to say, doing a doctorate is probably a good 'investment' if you are a woman, but a more questionable one for a man.

> Using data from the National Child Development Survey of all individuals born in one week in March 1958, and looking at their earnings when they were 33 years old (i.e. in 1991), taking just those who had got the 18+ examination (A levels), and controlling for other characteristics which could also affect labour market outcomes, Richard Blundell and colleagues found that
>
> > The impact of higher education on women's wages was. . . . considerably larger than its impact on men's wages. Women with non-degree higher education qualifications (NVQs level 4, HNC/HND, professional or nursing qualifications) had hourly wages on average 26 per cent higher than those with just A levels; women with first degrees had hourly wages on average 39 per cent higher and women with higher degrees had, on average, **43 per cent higher wages** than this base group.
>
> Men showed a different pattern, with improvements of 15, 21 **and only 16 per cent for a higher degree.** (Blundell *et al.* 1997: iii)

The actual interconnections between achieving a doctorate and differences between men's and women's career development are hard to track in the UK because the statistics collected are not sufficiently 'robust' to support an analysis. While HESA (2000) and the Institute of Employment Studies (for the Association of Graduate Recruiters) collect information annually on the employment of first degree graduates, and there have been occasional follow-up studies of where graduates are working a few years later, little information is routinely collected for those getting postgraduate qualifications. Moreover the figures often don't distinguish within this group between those getting doctorates and those getting other postgraduate qualifications (let alone cross-tabulating by gender and domicile). They also don't record what happens to those who go abroad. Plus of course employment studies are complicated by the indeterminate length of the doctorate and by quite a number of students already having, and continuing, employment while studying, or getting jobs while they are finishing their doctorates. If you do a doctorate you may experience a number of early moves: going first into temporary research or teaching contracts and then into permanent jobs; or first into higher education and then into commercial jobs. In addition, the importance of having a doctorate varies with the discipline. Only a minority of employers value a PhD in information technology and engineering, while a PhD is virtually a prerequisite for careers in biotechnology and biology. It is a requirement for most lectureships in sociology, but less important for a lectureship in law. It is also rather too soon to say, and certainly too soon to comment in detail, on how professional doctorates are going to be valued by employers.

We need a proper study of all those who got doctorates in a particular period (and not just occasional follow-ups of the rather select group whose doctorates have been funded by the research councils). HEFCE was told by the DfEE to develop its own performance indicators for employment rates by 2000, so the 'employability' of those with doctorates seems set to become increasingly important, even if hard to measure. But until this information is available we have to rely on occasional commissioned studies of particular groups (which inevitably means looking at the state of the market in 1990 or earlier).

The Institute of Manpower Studies at University of Sussex has carried out a number of studies on the employment of those who got doctorates in the late 1980s to early 1990s in the sciences and social sciences – but from a 'needs of the labour market' rather than a student perspective. Although they don't, unfortunately, tell us very much about either gender differences or international students, they do say that they found neither scientists nor social scientists in general had much difficulty finding employment related to their studies, though for many a PhD was not a prerequisite for the job they got.

The unemployment rate of newly qualified scientists with PhDs is considerably lower than for first degree scientists. Of the three-quarters of those with doctorates who entered employment in the UK from 1985 to 1988, about one-third stayed in higher education, though this varies with the discipline. Among the largest group, biologists, more go into education. Within universities, most are researchers (this includes the postdocs, who are classified as 'FE and training' but are in fact research assistants), with only 10 per cent becoming lecturers immediately. Another third go on to do research in private industry and commerce, especially chemists who go into the oil and chemicals sectors, and physicists and mathematicians who go into R&D in financial and business services. Around 10 per cent enter the public sector (though this is probably an under-estimate because it excludes the Ministry of Defence, which would not give details for the survey); and the remaining small percentage go largely into teacher training.

Of those with PhDs in social sciences, most go into jobs in higher education, though it varies a lot by subject area: 70 per cent of those getting psychology, sociology and economics PhDs in this period became university lecturers or researchers, against just over a third of those who studied business studies or geography. The latter are more likely to go into market analysis and town planning. Social science doctorates are also well represented in independent research institutes and public sector organizations (the civil service and central government departments: the Home Office, Department of Health, local health and education authorities and voluntary bodies/charities, including development agencies). The less than 10 per cent who go into industry and commerce are likely to join either very small organizations (for example management consultant agencies, advertising or specialist legal firms) or very large ones (such as in television or banks, where they tend to get used in research functions, rather than in administration, marketing, legal or personnel). Employers outside academia don't seek out social scientists with doctorates – they don't advertise for them specifically – but rather recruit them in the same pool as other graduates (first degree and especially Masters students). So the possibilities for employment are tied in with the market for these less qualified applicants. On the other hand, this market is growing rather than declining, and alongside efforts to improve 'professionalism or overall staff quality', employers may welcome those with a doctorate because clients are impressed by this qualification and increasingly expect staff to have such a degree. International organizations and posts overseas especially like staff to have doctorates.

(Pearson *et al.* 1991; Connor 1994; Connor *et al.* 1994)

Such studies tend to assume a particular career path, which is not necessarily the one travelled by many women. Men are twice as likely to go on to study for a higher research degree directly after they graduate – 18 per cent against 10 per cent of women in 1996–7.

There has been a longstanding assumption

that the pattern prevalent among male disciplines and male academics was 'normal', i.e. the academic career was linear. Successful scientists went to university to do their undergraduate degree, then their doctorate, followed by a postdoctoral position, then they moved to a tenure track position. This may still be the norm for some, and it is noticeable that women scientists conform to this picture more so than their sisters in the humanities and social sciences or the health sciences. [But the] entry point to an academic career and the preparation for an academic career vary between disciplines and institution types [research institutions in industry, government departments and other public sector organisations, teaching and research universities, and teaching-only institutions]. Plus there is generally now recognition that an interruption to an academic career, or a slow-down, is not indicative of ability or commitment. But this is harder to maintain in the natural sciences than in the social sciences as knowledge and skills seem to date faster.

(Moses 1995: 7)

We have no more than impressionistic information on what sorts of jobs men and women have been doing if they start their doctorates later. Nor how many people doing doctorates already have a job in academia. Nor what happens to people's careers as a result of getting a research degree. Do those who continue part-time in their jobs while they study, or who go back to the same job as they had before, get promotion? Might they use doctoral studies as a mechanism to change their lives, and not want to go back? Does this differ or is it the same for men and women? What happens to the many women in science who leave it once they have a PhD (see pp. 206–7)?

Certainly a doctorate in no way guarantees an academic job nowadays, and some groups do find it harder to get university jobs. For instance, although universities are keen to enrol mature students (see pp. 12–13), they have often discriminated against mature candidates who applied for positions in their departments in the past, not even considering those who were over 45 if they were applying for a first position (and not warning individuals about this at the point of entry to their PhD). This may be changing as a result of new national and EU legislation. However, should you be an older would-be research student, it is probably more worth doing a PhD for 'education' rather than for 'vocational training'; though this is not to say that no older people ever get jobs. Also, to date universities have not been major employers of non-white staff, though it is hoped this is a generational phenomenon. Currently, however, only 6–7 per cent of academic staff in the UK are non-white (against 15 per cent of students) and just over half of these Black staff are not British nationals (and more are men than women). Only 1.6 per cent of academic staff are non-white British women (Carter *et al.* 1999). Black staff are also somewhat more likely to experience poor terms and conditions than whites: of those on fixed-term contracts, 34 per cent are white British against 48 per cent non-white British.

On the other hand, a doctorate increasingly gives you a portmanteau qualification for research-based employment. Previous gloomy arguments used to say that doing a PhD would be of little use in future jobs outside academia because what doctorates produced were specialists in very narrow fields who were not wanted by employers because they were 'too qualified'. Nowadays, however, with an increased proportion of young people getting first degrees and Masters (see pp. 12–13), and increased numbers of graduate students looking for and finding employment *outside* academia in industries based on the production of knowledge rather than goods, there is an increasing demand for skilled and certified researchers in expanding, new, quasi-professional fields. Many institutions, government and private research establishments, corporate labs, NGOs and think-tanks, can and want to use the 'transferable skills' and 'competencies' acquired while getting a PhD, even if not always your detailed field-specific knowledge. This has been obvious in science for some time, but it is also occurring in the social sciences and humanities. Consultancies and independent schools recruit staff with PhDs for kudos, while historical and literary 'research and development' is arguably now done as much in museums and record offices, for newspapers, magazines, broadcast media and film, in advertising, consultancies and quangos, as in universities, and in association with cultural tourism and the general heritage industries.

However, these jobs often require rather different modes of working from the isolated scholarship associated with some PhDs: they use 'more transient and heterogeneous sets of practitioners, collaborating on a problem defined in a specific and localised context' to produce 'transdisciplinary' knowledge (Gibbons *et al.* 1994). Employers are therefore inclined to see those with doctorates as having lost useful years of work experience – of team working, negotiating and presentational skills, training in computing, project managing and teaching. So it is helpful to include some proxies for these during your time as a research student (and professional doctorates may specifically include them) and to recognize that even the archetypal humanities PhD provides more 'relevant' experience than is sometimes realized.

Pat Cryer, who is the originator and convenor of the Postgraduate Issues Network of the SRHE (see p. 46), argues that 'Surprisingly few doctoral students are aware of their employability.' They can't see beyond their contribution to their field of study and look only for jobs in their specialist area. But in fact they acquire important skills which give a competitive edge.

All PhD students will, by the time they finish, have spent three or more years on their research, with all its various highs and lows. This feat should develop the transferable skill of being able to see any prolonged task or project through to completion. It should include, to varying extents which depend on the discipline and the research topic, the abilities to plan, to allocate time and money and to trouble-shoot.

In addition, the PhD researcher needs to keep up with the subject, to be flexible and able to change direction . . . to think laterally and creatively and to develop alternative approaches . . . Adaptability is highly valued by employers who need people able to anticipate and lead change in a fast-moving world, yet resist it where it is only for its own sake. All PhD students should have learned to set their work in a wider field of knowledge. The process . . . should develop the transferable skills of being able to sift through large quantities of information, to take on board other points of view, challenge premises, question procedures and interpret meaning.

All PhD students have to be able to present their work through seminars, progress reports and their thesis. Seminars should develop confident presentation, and group discussion skills. Dealing with criticism and presenting cases ought to be second nature. Report and thesis-writing should develop the skills needed for composing reports, manuals and press releases and for summarizing bulky documents.

The doctoral road can be lonely, particularly in the humanities and social sciences. Yet the skills of coping with isolation are transferable and can be valued highly by employers. They include: self-direction; self-discipline; self-motivation; resilience; tenacity and the abilities to prioritise and juggle a number of tasks at once. Students working on group projects should be able to claim advanced team-working skills.

Further examples of transferable skills are many and depend on the interests of the student and the nature of the research. Think about advanced computer literacy, facility with the Internet, and the ability to teach effectively. Negotiating skills in accessing resources can be highly sought after. And doctoral students are used to networking with others, using project management techniques, and finding . . . their way around specialist libraries or archives.

(Cryer 1997b: 1)

Women who read this book should also be able to argue they have additional political awareness, understanding of micropolitics, strategic thinking, networking and language skills in relation to women's issues, which *should* be a selling point in jobs outside academia.

Personal development

Surveys suggest students' personal expectations are more likely to be fulfilled by doing a doctorate than career aspects. Few regret doing a doctorate, or what it has cost them. Of course, the most disgruntled may get left out of samples; there are certainly horror stories of bad supervision, wasted time, too heavy teaching requirements on low pay, and exploitation in labs (see pp. 89–92, 139–41); and initial hopes may have been changed and modified along the way. Nonetheless, 'a self forged through tackling the difficulties of research, especially when stress from other sources is high, is a new self. So is the self that overcomes the doubts about ability to do the work' (Francis 1997: 18).

Within Zen there is the *koan* system. A *koan* is a puzzle the 'master' sets his students on the road to self-discovery. The student ponders on the meaning of the riddle until its elements become clear and enlightenment occurs. The path, we are told, is poorly lit, difficult to navigate, with few meaningful directions. The art of solving the *koan* comes not by presenting the correct answer but by asking the right questions. Such a scenario bears more than a passing resemblance to the PhD process.

(Gorry 1997: 15)

So was this whole undertaking worthwhile? For a long time, my successfully completed thesis came to symbolise nothing but pain and resentment . . . But now, at a greater distance, I know that the PhD allowed
me to make a journey of which I was immensely proud . . . The pay-off
now comes through how I can express the impact of so much personal
and professional learning in my life.

(Salmon 1992: 62)

As overseas students the cost of a PhD can be high both financially
. . . and psychologically. In consequence, we carry the fear of failure like
an unconscious second skin. This makes standard difficulties appear
larger than they really are . . . But this account of my experience reads
worse than it was. There are always rewards, and many: the pleasure of
being able to carry out research; of mastering each step; of satisfying our
curiosity; of learning about new worlds; the letters and encouragement
from home; the sympathy, solidarity and companionship of fellow students; the daily support and protection of the group of friends we create
. . . And on our return home, once everything is past and done with, we
will be ready to explain that doing a PhD is sort of being in heaven and
there will only be old letters to remind you of the difficulties, the fears
and insecurities. Because returning home, my friends, is another story.

(Arregui 1991: 41–2)

Contributing to knowledge and benefiting society

Work done for PhDs is also a very important element in national knowledge
production. Whether each thesis builds a small step onto an established paradigm (as in the sciences) or each student establishes their own topic where
there are competing paradigms (as in the humanities and social sciences), some
very important research is done by research students and some theses have
opened up whole new fields. (The pressures to complete within a fixed number
of years, filling of time with required courses, and the need to earn supplement-
ary income during the final year(s), may mean the numbers able to produce
a genuinely novel research project will dwindle however: see pp. 42–5.)

An analysis of publications arising from PhD theses in four fields of social
science and their impact in the late 1980s concludes that 'work published as a
result of theses work in the UK makes an appreciable impact in the wider
literature of the disciplines'. In two of the areas investigated, 'the mean cita-
tion frequency was much the same for postgraduate students as for established members of staff.' The Australian Academy of Science noted that

senior academics estimated that 95 per cent of all research done in chemistry departments in the 1970s was carried out by postgraduate students; while a more recent Dutch government report argues that PhD students are carrying out 'the major part of university research'. American science policy debates talk of PhD students as the 'dynamos' of research, and federal concerns about increasing or cutting back postgraduate provision is partly to do with guaranteeing the national research capacity. (All cited in Advisory Board for the Research Councils (ABRC) 1993: 10–11. See also pp. 189–90.)

In the 1980s I got funding from the ESRC to do an overview of ongoing research on gender (with Margaret Littlewood),[1] and every single one of the projects on sexuality was then being done for a PhD or unfunded for individual interest. By 1994, the British Sociological Association national conference was on sexuality and it attracted the greatest number of papers ever for an annual conference (Allen and Leonard 1996).

However, doing the work and producing a thesis is not sufficient. You don't write a doctorate (or a Masters degree dissertation or a workplace-based study) to be read by just your supervisor and examiners and your mother. Publishing and generally disseminating your ideas is equally important and an essential element in registering your ideas, especially in science. It does not hurt to start considering this from the very beginning in all fields. Build it in to your progress by choosing a 'sexy' topic and approach, and by giving papers as you go along. Think of your audience as a support group. Think also about getting the attention of policy makers and community activist groups by more popular writing, lecturing, and using websites and so on (see pp. 244–5, 256–8).

Differences among doctoral students

Disciplinary differences

Tony Becher undertook a long and very influential ethnographic study in Britain and the USA of 'the culture of disciplines', *Academic Tribes and Territories* (1989). He then worked with colleagues on the British arm of a five nation research study on the history and contemporary funding of research and graduate education (Clark 1993), which covered three 'archetypal' disciplines: history, economics and physics. They later extended this to cover modern languages, sociology and biochemistry, and published their account in *Graduate Education in Britain* (Becher *et al.* 1994). This stresses both how research education is shaped by the epistemological and cultural norms of individual disciplines and the forms of organization which are deemed to be required to produce know-ledge in that discipline; and also the differences between elite, middle and lower rank universities. They conclude that there is a major difference between the experience of doing a PhD in the sciences and doing one in the humanities and the social sciences.

> Broadly, science research students are closely involved in the production of new knowledge by teams of established researchers; [while] students in other subjects are for the most part inducted into the individualistic tradition. Science students may make indispensable contributions to disciplinary research but [they] may not be expected to achieve the same degree of individual conceptualisation or integration as their peers in the social sciences and humanities.
>
> (Becher *et al.* 1994: 185)

Becher and colleagues stress however that there are also differences *between* different arts and science subjects (that is between history and languages, and between physics and biochemistry), and differences *within disciplines*: 'physicists may be theorists or experimentalists, concerned with fundamental, strategic, enabling or applied research. Sociologists may draw on scientific, literary, historical and[/or] philosophical traditions' (Becher *et al.* 1994: 185).

The differences between sciences and humanities and social sciences affect the whole doctoral process and are threads running throughout this book.

If you are a scientist, you usually choose a field of specialism and then join a specialist research group in that area. This group will have funding and can support and use students, but it is designed primarily to optimize the production of new knowledge rather than to educate students. Individual research students have to fit into this structure; and your work has to be geared to the instrumentation and consumables which are available in the labs to which you are attached. If you decide you need new equipment, getting authorization for funding and waiting for it to be delivered can cause serious delays. If you are a student in the arts and humanities or social sciences, on the other hand, you are much less likely to be funded to do research, but will nearly always develop your own topic, which will be distinct from that of established members of the departmental 'community', even if it relates to the interests of the one person who is your supervisor, and even if you choose your place of study for its library or other facilities.

If you work in science, you will usually be assigned a supervisor from the team and often work alongside him (and it is usually a him) every day, and in the company of postdoctoral researchers, lab assistants and technicians. You may, however, in practice not get that much opportunity to talk to your supervisor outside the lab, unless you are 'male, drink alcohol . . . and are sports loving or clubbable' (Delamont *et al.* 2000: 156). Even then you could have difficulty in tying your supervisor down to talking about your own piece of work. You may be given a specific problem or technique to work on, and, if you are lucky, get help with practical problems from postdocs and technicians. But since everyone is working in a related field, competition can be fierce. Although labs look like collective environments, they can effectively consist of a number of research students all working alone – fearful of others discovering the same thing before them. This can make students feel very isolated. Women and international students especially can be both ultra-visible and lonely (see pp. 201–9).

If you work in the humanities and social sciences, by contrast, you will spend a lot of time initially defining and refining your topic, deciding the appropriate methodology to use, finding sources and doing fieldwork on your own. You may feel even more isolated and unsupported, culture shocked and in limbo (though this is changing). Even your supervisor's interests may soon be substantially different from your own, despite it initially looking as if you have a lot in common. Little is organized for you outside the taught courses in the first year. There is no timetable, no set reading, and little feedback unless you seek it. Academic interaction in seminars and conferences can be competitive and down-putting, especially if you lack middle class heterosexual confidence (see pp. 202–8). A competent supervisor will indicate to you areas you should follow up, but in the end it is your responsibility to check what other work exists in the field, to filter through possible theories, to decide on the research design, to defend the interpretations, to be 'original enough'. On the other hand, there is much less likelihood of someone else publishing 'your' findings when you are too far advanced to change track. The issue is rather finding anyone else with similar interests.

Science, social sciences and humanities students are all likely to feel under-supervised and to estimate that they see staff less than staff think they do. However, given the help from postdocs and others who are around in the lab, and who are specialists in the techniques of the lab, poor supervision is a somewhat less central problem in the sciences, although experiments or computer programmes that don't work can be really panic making, and postdocs and technicians may be chauvinistic. In either case, you may lack physical (and maybe symbolic) space in the department: to work, to be seen as part of the community, or even to hang your coat.

All research students who complete have in common that they work longer hours and for much less money than those they graduated alongside. There are pressures on scientists to be present in the lab, sometimes for over 50 hours a week. Students in arts and social sciences tend to work more in bursts with breaks, and at home or in the library. All are now required to take some generic research training course in their field. Also for all, towards the end, the thesis occupies every hour of the day.

If you are a scientist, you can expect to finish a PhD in three years or less, but you probably can relatively easily (and will need to) continue as a salaried postdoc, when you are in a more leading role in a team, for another three or four years to make a more major contribution. Social scientists and those in the arts need a minimum of four years full-time to produce a PhD, and even those with grants won't have them for more than three years and so will have to get a job or a loan for the last year. But in these fields you should produce a major piece of research which you can publish as a mono-graph and draw upon for articles for several years – usually over your name alone. If you are a scientist, on the other hand, you are likely to be one of up to thirty authors of a large number of articles produced by your team by the time you write your thesis.

Although the rubrics vary somewhat from one university to another and as between PhDs and professional doctorates (see pp. 24–6, 71–3), all doctoral students have to produce 'unaided' work which is 'original' and 'makes a significant contribution to knowledge'. It is generally presented in the form of a thesis, though in some disciplines and some universities it can be presented as a portfolio of published material. Part of the attempt to reduce the degree from a *magnum opus* has been to say that it should com-prise 'the work that can reasonably be expected to be achieved by a hard worker within 3 years' (ABRC 1993). But many students remain worried about what is 'enough': enough experimentation, enough hours contribut-ing to the team's efforts, enough of a contribution to knowledge, and enough originality.

Estelle Phillips's own doctorate was on 'The PhD as a learning process' (1983) and she later conducted a project on quality in the PhD as part of an ESRC programme following the Winfield Report. Her best-selling text with Derek Pugh (three editions: 1987, 1994 and 2000) gives fifteen different ways in which a PhD can be original and make a significant contribution to knowl-edge. These include:

- Carrying out empirical work that hasn't been done before.
- Making a synthesis that hasn't been made before.
- Using already known material but with a new interpretation.
- Trying out something [in the UK] that has previously only been done in other countries.
- Taking a particular technique and applying it in a new area.
- Bringing new evidence to bear on an old issue.
- Looking at areas that people in the discipline haven't looked at before.
- Continuing a previously original piece of research.
- Carrying out original work designed by the supervisor.

- Providing a single original technique, observation or result in an otherwise unoriginal but competent piece of research.

(Phillips and Pugh 2000: 63–4)

Phillips says that her interviews show 'basic agreement concerning what examiners are looking for in a good candidate [in the social sciences] . . . conceptual understanding, critical ability and an explicit and well structured argument'. She argues for using various points along the way – regular monitoring of work in progress by the supervisor, having a formal upgrading from MPhil to PhD, getting preparation for the viva, including a (formative) viva – as ways to make sure a student stays on track and can work out what is required (Phillips 1994: 137).

Becher *et al.* stress, however, that 'standards' for PhDs vary between disciplines, between specialisms within the same discipline, and between universities of different status. There is always a viva voce exam at the end, with usually two examiners, where you as the candidate have to demonstrate your ability to initiate, argue and defend your ideas. But in sciences with relatively dominant paradigms, the examiners are likely to be selected with little reference to the student and you may not even know who they are going to be until close to the viva. In value-laden areas, with conflicting schools of thought, the tendency is for supervisor and student informally to discuss who would be appropriate and for the supervisor's recommendation to be treated more or less as a formality if the proposed examiners are senior scholars. Either way, you want high status examiners because their identity is part of people's later evaluation of the worth of your thesis (see pp. 247–8).

It is hard to give a comparable overview of what is expected of the still relatively small number of students doing the professional doctorates which have been established since 1990 (see pp. 71–3). These have often been set up swiftly, chiefly in clinical psychology, education and engineering, and each university is seeking a niche market and to attract a slightly different clientele from those they see as their competitors. The degrees may be taught and examined jointly by academics and senior members of the profession or industry; their approach to curriculum, pedagogy and assessment, and their professional ethos, tends to vary with the specific staff expertise and target group. However, such degrees typically involve more required taught elements than PhDs, and students put together a portfolio of work which includes evidence of their innovative and critical application of knowledge to their professional practice (research designs, evaluation reports, papers for professional rather than academic journals, conference presentations and videos, or working models) with a less extensive, and more workplace relevant, thesis. They may also include some team projects and evidence of managerial, leadership and budgetary skills.

Gender differences

Becher *et al.*'s (1994) work treats students as a relatively homogeneous group in each disciplinary area. However, there are obvious differences between the life chances and experiences of men and women; and of course there are also systematic differences *among* women and among men, and these social divisions all intersect and co-construct each other. So while disciplinary differences affect everything about doing a doctorate, including administrative procedures, ethics, health and safety, intellectual copyright, and research design, so too does gender. But it is never just a question of the discipline, and never just a question of gender.

Unfortunately, it is not always clear what the gender and other differences among students are in Britain, because the necessary research has not been done. One has to dig around and I have drawn on work in schools and on higher education in other countries, as well as on general sociological work on the labour market, interpersonal interactions, family relationships, and on harassment and violence, in writing this book (see pp. 2–7). Conversely, the many and important gender differences discussed here suggest the problematic nature of the assumptions underlying many current policies and much 'research-based' generalization on British higher education. For instance, men and women students' motivations for doing a research degree differ somewhat.

Ingrid Moses, on the basis of a national study of *Barriers to Women's Participation as Postgraduate Students* in Australia in the 1980s, found men and women were equally dedicated scholars, but women were slightly less likely to be vocationally oriented, less likely to have drifted into doing a PhD, and less likely to be centrally concerned with salary and promotion than men, though they aspired equally with men to high status, currently male-dominated, careers. Women often start to do a PhD after a period of employment (and most have had several jobs rather than a period out of the labour market caring for children) as part of a personal development progression, while most men undertake research directly after their first degree, as a 'closed loop' continuous, planned educational career. Women talked to Moses of undertaking a PhD because of 'a need for a change', to counter job burnout, or as 'taking charge of one's life' and prioritizing their own self-development (Moses 1990, 1992).

Equally, women research students are consistently less satisfied with graduate school than men (in the USA, UK and in Australia, see pp. 199–200) because of the structure of knowledge acquisition. This tends to be competitive and isolating and they find it alienating. Also they get less attention, less financial support and have less possibility of interacting with women faculty and of finding women mentors and sponsors. Women also experience a different conflict between study, work and family from men; and they may take somewhat longer to get their degrees.

While the discipline is a primary source of identity in postgraduate studies and provides the framework for the research, there are major differences in the experiences of women by discipline. Some subjects are more and some less woman/feminist friendly. This is tied in with the proportion of women and the absolute numbers of research students in a given department. Where there is a sizeable number of research students in a department and a high proportion of women it is much easier to establish academic peer groups and networks which can improve women's freedom of interaction and participation. But even when women are in the majority they still usually do less well (see also pp. 94–6, 161–6).

Kim Thomas's PhD (1983–7) was funded by a studentship provided by Aston University as a result of pressure from a group of women staff. Her work has parallels with Becher's work, but looks at *Gender and Subject in Higher Education* at undergraduate level. She shows how the gender-specific connotations of certain particularly 'masculine' and 'feminine' fields of study (physics and physical sciences, and English and communications) affect how individuals construct and reconstruct (or as some would now say, 'perform') their sense of themselves through their chosen subject; and how the possibilities differ for men and women (Thomas 1990; see also pp. 179–80).

Surprisingly, given the under-representation of women in science at undergraduate level, women are overall more evenly spread across the fields at doctoral level than men (see Figure 2.3). Roughly one-third of women doctoral students study SET and maths, another third humanities and social science, and the remainder medicine and related fields, business, law and architecture and planning. Half of all men study science and engineering.[2]

Other differences

Other important differences among research students come from their range of countries of origin and domicile, and first languages. But research on international students not only has not differentiated by gender, but also has nearly always lumped all foreign students together, not even differentiating between those from high and those from low to medium income countries. But self-evidently there are differences by economic circumstances and between national educational backgrounds, and within each national group by source of funding. Moreover each student also brings with them a personal history which by doctoral level is complex and established. This diversity

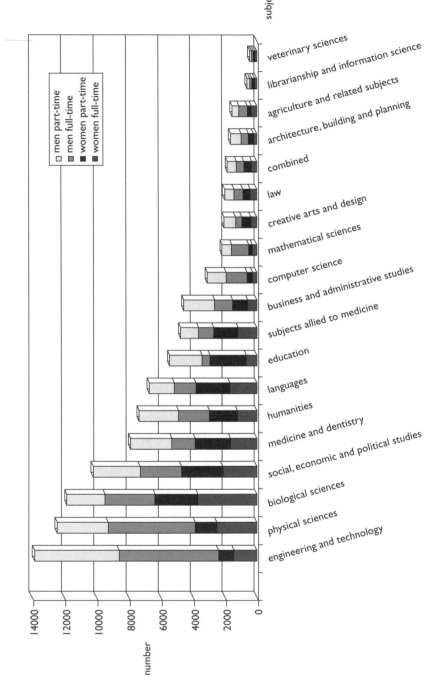

Figure 2.3 Students studying for a research degree in the UK, by sex and subject of study, 1998–9
Source: HESA 2000: Tables 1c and 1g

Table 2.1 Top twenty countries of domicile of international research students in the UK, 1996–7

	Women		*Men*
Greece	845	Greece	1210
USA	747	USA	1136
Germany	549	Germany	1115
Malaysia	466	China	1060
China	458	Malaysia	989
Italy	458	Iran	813
Canada	457	Turkey	611
Irish Republic	410	Irish Republic	596
France	373	South Korea	581
Japan	317	Taiwan	570
Taiwan	292	Canada	549
Spain	267	Saudi Arabia	537
Thailand	258	Italy	518
Brazil	233	France	479
Turkey	229	Pakistan	472
India	224	Japan	438
Portugal	217	India	415
Mexico	165	Japan	377
Australia	149	Brazil	372
South Korea	146	Mexico	342

Source: HESA data supplied to the author by the SRHE.
Note: Figures include full-time, part-time and 'other' registrations.

makes an important contribution to British universities' intellectual and social life (see Table 2.1).

What doing a research degree involves

Earlier sections of this chapter stressed the differences between the experiences of research students in different disciplines. You may think you realized this already because there were differences between undergraduates in sciences and arts, and between physicists, ecologists, historians and anthropologists in your previous time in higher education. However, these differences become more marked at doctoral level because the difference between academic fields is central to the PhD experience. Doing a PhD is essentially about full socialization into a discipline; about what the French sociologist Pierre Bourdieu calls acquiring the *habitus* of each discipline. This involves acquiring not only various competences but also an artistry to employ them in changing circumstances and sense of 'good taste' which enables you to recognize work with flair when you see it: which is ingenious, apt and performed with bravura (from a particular disciplinary perspective). Like other professional socialization, this requires not just applying ideas and techniques that are already known. It is not a case of repeating experiments or fieldwork or using sources that are known to work, which you did at undergraduate level. It is the exciting and mind-expanding experience of finding out how to produce and evaluate new ideas and data, which may or may not be appropriate and which may or may not 'work'. It is finding out what it means to *be* a physicist or a psychologist. This is 'caught' as much as 'taught' (see pp. 42–3); and especially in the early stages of what is necessarily a lengthy process, it can be a disorienting experience. People often can't put into words what it involves, even though they can point you towards examples of past good work and practice and offer suggestions on how to improve your own.

Paul Atkinson, Sara Delamont and Odette Parry studied the academic socialization of doctoral students as part of the ESRC programme of the late 1980s, extending an original concern with the social sciences to include a number of natural science fields. They have produced two very different books (as well as many articles) on the basis of this. One book is essentially practical, for supervisors (Delamont *et al.* 1997) and another is more theoretical, from a sociology of education and knowledge perspective (Delamont *et al.* 2000). Both are well worth reading, especially the sections on the fields closest to your own, because they help to articulate what the socialization process is aiming at, from laboratory research in biochemistry through computer-based modelling in artificial intelligence and physical geography to field research in town planning and social anthropology.

What the experience of doing a doctorate is going to be like for you will therefore be very different in anthropology from chemistry – and also hard to gauge until you start. Doing a British doctorate is as different from doing a British Masters degree as each of your previous phases of education has been from the one before. It is therefore well worth reading not only Becher (1989) and Delamont *et al.* (1997, 2000) but also some of the other textbooks on doing PhDs which look at particular fields, especially those with accounts by individual students (see pp. 83, 111–12), even if you are doing a professional doctorate. It is also worth reading accounts by practising researchers who try to demystify the research process in their field generally (see pp. 172–3).

Deciding to do a doctorate is obviously much more problematic than the decision to do a Masters because the degree takes so much more time, is much less directed, and is known to have a lower success rate. But it is also much more mind expanding; and although it is risky, it is less so than it used to be. Success depends on autonomous work and can involve huge expenditure of emotional energy and sometimes debilitating soul searching. You are also likely to have to work under terms and conditions very far from the Ivory Tower ideal, as the opening quotations on p. 50 suggest. There will certainly be times when you feel nobody cares, the whole thing is misconceived, your topic is trivial or what you have to say about it is trivial, or that someone else is going to come up with the same topic, completed, a year before you. It is then worth remembering that most people who start but fail to get a PhD do so *not* because they submit and are below standard, or because they are pipped at the post, but because they give up before completing. This happens sometimes because the reality is too different from what they expected or because they don't have the flair or dedication needed for research, but more often it is because they drifted into doing a PhD or allowed or devoted too little time to the research and were disorganized, and/or life events intervened (though cf. pp. 201–33). If you choose your supervisor or lab with care, have a manageable, worthwhile topic, keep a sense of where you are going, plan to complete within a set time, build in giving occasional papers to get constructive, critical support from other students and staff, and keep the pressure level on yourself high but controlled, you *will* be successful.

Although a doctorate is a somewhat scary and isolating experience, you can (should?) be sure of the support of your supervisor in the British system. They will be keen to see you through, not only because you have a personal relationship but also because an incomplete doctorate is a waste of time for supervisors too, and a reflection on their professional competence. You should also get support from within the lab or department, including regular departmental seminars and social meetings (often Friday night at the pub, which can be tricky if you don't like that sort of atmosphere). Your own supervisor may run student seminars; there will be other research students in the student union and societies, on field trips or retreats; contact with library and computing staff; membership of the professional association and its meetings and conferences; seminars you yourself organize; email or world-wide web contacts with people with a similar interests; and, towards the end, perhaps some teaching which supports your belief in your ability. You will also have the huge pleasures of concentrated reading, constructing arguments, serendipity, being recognized as expert, membership of a specialist network, and making events happen.

Differences between the various types of doctorates

The first doctoral degrees recorded were awarded in Paris in circa 1150, but the PhD was begun in what was later to become Germany in the early nineteenth century. Until the 1870s, German universities were the only ones in the world which geared themselves around the twin ideals of teaching *and* research and which stressed the freedom of students to learn, often primarily working on their own, and of teachers to pursue highly specialized research. Students were attached to a specialist seminar or institute, though they might move from one to another, and their career prospects were dependent on the sponsorship of their *Doktorvater* (literally their 'doctor father').

American and British students studied in Germany and the reputation of the German model, and the advance it gave German science and medicine, led both the USA (from the 1860s) and the UK (from the end of the First World War) to adopt modified versions of it.

The first US PhDs were awarded in 1861 by Yale University, and the first to a woman, Helen Magill, by Boston University in 1887.
The first UK PhD/DPhil[3] was awarded in 1918 by Oxford University, and the first to a woman, Evelyn Mary Simpson, also by Oxford, in 1922.
The first Australian PhD was awarded in 1948 by the University of Melbourne, to a woman, Erica Wolff (Noble 1994: 22).

Previously the doctorates of British universities, the highest degrees awarded, were named after particular (professional) faculties – law (LLD), theology (divinity, DD), medicine (MD) and more recently, 'letters' (arts, DLitt), science (DSc) and social sciences (DSocSc). These are supposedly substantially above the PhD in maturity and scientific accomplishment and relatively few are applied for and awarded. The UK PhD was originally an intermediate degree between the Masters and the DLitt or DSc. The latter was to remain essentially an acknowledgement of an established body of work from a mature scholar or an advanced thesis done while already in university employment – as is still the tradition in many European countries.

Various countries are also now introducing 'vocational' or 'professional' doctorates. The boundary between a PhD and these other doctorates is (still) somewhat blurred, but generally the PhD is centred on the traditional disciplines and prepares candidates for 'pure' research and a university teaching career, while professional doctorates focus on innovation in the *application* of knowledge, and may well involve group projects and research on workplace-based problems. In Britain and Australia the new degrees seek to remain on a par with the PhD, although in the USA, where professional doctorates have a much longer history and are often vocational training immediately after the Masters rather than for experienced and senior professionals, they are not as highly valued. In Britain professional doctorates now exist in clinical psychology, education, business studies, and engineering. But in the USA there are a large number (currently around 60), while in Australia, 62 programmes were developed in 17 different disciplinary areas in the 1990s, though the EdD is far and away the most popular. The discussions around professional doctorates have certainly renewed and reinvigorated national and international discussions about the role of the PhD (see pp. 24–5, 238–42).

The new four year EngD in Britain is aimed at the next generation of research managers in industry – people who do research but who also have business skills. Candidates work for three years on an individual project in a company, where they are treated as employees and given full resources. They also do a fourth year of coursework, based either in employment or in the university, with both an academic and an industrial mentor. The coursework broadens their horizons through learning about different aspects of the field and including requiring students to find out more about how the business in which they work operates.

This degree has proved very popular. While the large Engineering and Physical Science Research Council filled only 85 per cent of its PhD studentships in 1998, the demand for the EngD was such that the scheme was expanded from 75 to 100 places, doubling the number of university-based centres taking such students (*THES* 4 June 1999: 32).

Differences between doctorates in different countries

With the general internationalization of higher education, doing a doctorate can provide an opportunity to travel, and it is likely some readers of this book may want to give serious consideration to doing their doctorate in another country. This may well particularly interest women – for personal growth, to learn about another culture, or to get away from home pressures. Alternatively, you might want to use one of various schemes to spend part of your time – a term or a year – abroad. Despite British hesitations, it is possible to acquire a working knowledge of another language before you go. At the very least, spending five minutes imagining yourself participating in a seminar in another language will make you sympathetic to your foreign co-students if you stay in Britain. Moreover, knowing a bit about different doctoral education systems allows us to see better the strengths and weaknesses of our own. It stresses that what we have is but *a* system: a social construct. Things can be organized differently.

Much of the experience of doing a doctorate in the UK (except for the mandatory research training and the viva, see p. 241) is common also to Australia, New Zealand and South Africa. These follow the British system in having relatively short degree lengths: three years (first degree) plus one year (Masters) and three or four years (doctorate). Australia is also attractive because it is now particularly well geared to recruiting and supporting overseas students (see pp. 26–7). The North American system (including Canada) is different, and however; it is important to know about it because much of the research on women or gender and on 'race' and graduate studies (as well as on women and non-white faculty) has been done in the USA and is sometimes presumed to apply generally. However, work on race in particular does not translate easily to the UK context because of different patterns of class and ethnicity, and the existence of historically Black colleges in the USA. So overall research needs to be read carefully because simplistic comparisons can disguise as much as they illuminate.

The initial work for a PhD in the USA is not dissimilar to the US system of undergraduate credits, in which graduation is achieved by the accumulation of 'credit hours'. This is fundamentally a system for measuring time (class attendance), writing (of semester papers) and knowledge (courses will be planned to cover 'major' and 'minor' areas of expertise). For the Masters and PhD, it involves 'the accumulation of credit courses across an appropriate range of disciplinary fields, which are likely to be useful for work in that thesis area and that thesis topic'. It is expected that reasonable grades will be maintained in the courses attended, normally expressed in a faculty or graduate school requirement for a certain GPA (grade point average). Toward the end of this sequence of courses there will usually be a 'comprehensive examination', individually set but taken by all candidates to demonstrate that they have mastered sufficient of the associated knowledge to begin fully concentrating upon the doctoral 'dissertation'.

The writing of the thesis is guided by a dissertation committee of probably at least three people. The shape and lines of argument get hammered out in this committee, where a great deal of the quality control work is done. The candidate must convince the committee that the major methodological and methods choices (of the theories examined earlier) are clearly and correctly made and displayed, and that an appropriate range of intellectual perspectives has been brought to bear on the thesis. These processes are likely to be supplemented by a full public presentation of the doctoral dissertation proposal within a seminar open to the faculty.

Thus the American PhD can and should be seen as a highly structured experience, with a considerable sequence of controls over the timing and pacing over access to the start line for the dissertation. Rather charmingly there is even a phrase 'ABD' which means that a candidate has finished a doctorate – 'all but the dissertation'. In other words, in English terms, the candidate has not begun the main task – writing a thesis. Less charmingly, each of the quality control points means the possibility of an individual being 'cooled out' of the system in the first couple of years. However, the system also means progression through the system with a peer group, perhaps less loneliness because of class attendance, and often smaller 'theses' (written in a couple of years) than in Britain.

(Adapted from Cowen 1997: 192–3)

The American PhD system thus has two rather separate programmes. After they have gained their Masters and passed the comprehensive examination, candidates start a whole new part of their programme with the dissertation, and it is only the latter period that is covered by some of the guides available (see p. 83). Some elements – the exhaustive library review, construction of a researchable problem and related hypotheses, the conduct of experiments or fieldwork or location of primary sources in archives, the elaborate analysis of data, and the lengthy literary writing up and discussion of the results especially in the humanities and social sciences – are the same as for UK candidates. But the need to 'handle one's dissertation committee' and the form and predictability of the formal oral 'defence' of one's thesis, are not. The American PhD also needs to be seen as part of a ten-year selection process for university appointments, which goes up to and includes the work done as an assistant professor, before tenure is granted. (It thus has similarities with a UK science PhD which extends into a post-doctoral fellowship.)

However, the USA is both an obvious choice for native English language speakers, and appears to be ahead of the UK in a number of ways. It has a long history of mass higher education (which is what the UK has moved to); it has a structured taught element in the PhD (which is what the UK is said to have moved to, see pp. 22–5); and it is far and away the world's top producer of PhDs and the top 'receiver' of foreign students – one-third of the total and two-thirds of the English speaking. The US system gives a broad and thorough grounding in many literatures, and credit for this (positive feedback). Moreover, the private institutions, and especially the elite universities which dominate overseas recruitment, offer attractive financial aid. However, there is also great variation in quality between universities, high attrition rates, less one-to-one attention than is given to individuals in the UK, and even with scholarships, most students end up with very substantial debts. Plus 'the search for the demonstration of brilliance and creativity and ideas to change intellectual fields' occurs more in the postdoctoral or assistant professor phase of a career, and is judged by publication rather than the PhD thesis (Cowen 1997: 197).

Wherever you choose to study, you should obviously aim to be based in what is recognized as a good university, and a good department, for your subject area *in the country where you plan to live in the future* (see pp. 92, 106). In many countries, although there is formally reciprocity with reputable universities abroad, and a doctorate from one is accepted as okay for a job application in another, in fact many academics look down on foreign PhDs because of the different systems. So if you do study abroad, keep in contact with some academics in your home-base (see the section on mentoring on pp. 166–9) and try to publish a few articles in international journals before finishing your thesis. While the future is doubtless with the internationalization of postgraduate (and postdoctoral) training and individuals moving to study not only from poor to rich countries but also between high income countries (see pp. 13–15), such travel may not give you much of an advantage in employment terms at present – though as a trail-blazer you should benefit in the future.

Can you cope?

Before you undertake a doctorate you will obviously have done some serious cost analysis of whether you have not only the intellectual, practical and literary strengths, but also the emotional resilience. This will involve being prepared to do some marked reordering of your day-to-day life. The degree will have to be first or second on your priority list for several years if it is to get the time and attention it needs to be finished reasonably swiftly. This is probably not a time for other grand passions! There are, however, a number of 'myths' you can challenge.

Your intellectual abilities

One reason women often come late to their doctorates is tied to a phenomenon widely noted in the literature on gender and education in many countries (and noted in the Introduction): that girls and women are trained not only to be more self-effacing and diffident than boys and men, but also to think that *if* they were good enough, someone would have noticed and encouraged them to proceed. However, with doctorates, as with so much else in life, it is certainly not true that intelligence is identified and rewarded. Women are less likely to be seen to have PhD 'potential', either by themselves or by others, not because they could not do one successfully, but because what we do is 'read' differently, because the curriculum and pedagogy are not chosen with us in mind, and because we do not get the same opportunities to interact with women teachers and researchers as undergraduates and Masters students as men students do with men faculty (which is one reason why we are less likely to understand informal academic processes than men). Women are also therefore less likely to get first class degrees (the work women do is less likely to be perceived as exceptional and women are less willing to 'play the game' to the same extent). Not having first class degrees, women are less likely to get funding for a research degree. Women are also less likely to get same-sex supervisors or mentors as graduate students. Where faculty do recommend women to do postgraduate work, the women are likely to be under 30 (Moses 1994).

So, particularly if you are older and considering doing a doctorate, look to and believe the support and encouragement you get from family and friends; and at any age accept that you should be confident and prepared to put yourself forward. There is in any case no empirical evidence of a correlation between good marks in undergraduate examinations and success in research (Hudson 1960, 1977; Miller 1970, quoted in Phillips 1994). Recognize your tendency towards self-deprecation and don't torpedo yourself. Yes, you can cope, and yes, it will be worth it. Be encouraged by work on mature women undergraduates who have started with an overwhelming lack of confidence, but who have been surprised to find how low this is on their list of concerns a few months into term, once they have had some positive feedback (Merrill 1999). In the end, doing a doctorate itself should train you in more realistic self-assessment and increase your confidence.

Time demands

Even if you register only part-time, you should ideally put in some work on your research every day (to an equivalent of two days' solid work a week), if possible in a place where you can leave the work spread out in between times (see pp. 116–26). It really *cannot* be fitted in to odd half days at the weekend. This doesn't mean cutting off your social, domestic life and active life entirely. On the contrary, you need these for balance: to ensure you stay healthy and supported. But it does mean organizing everything around the doctorate (and not the other way about). You need 'time out' from the degree work, not displacement activities. This requires the development of a lot of practical and interpersonal management skills and a self-imposed schedule which accepts that there is a lot of hanging around and false starts, that some time inevitably gets wasted, and that there will be unforeseen events during the course of a long project, so slack has to be planned in. You don't want to emerge a workaholic, but nor do you want a dissertation or other crisis to take you unawares and stall your progress, or to throw you off completely so you waste all the time you have already invested.

> I was told a long time ago that I should treat my PhD as a job not a hobby. And I think that advice is very, very important. Personally I never treated my PhD as lightly as a hobby, but it took a long time to be fully aware of the PhD as my job.

Getting a doctorate is a long haul. It is difficult to give even rough figures of just how long, because in the past universities were quite casual. They were not always aware of the status of their students and long completion times included periods of part-time enrolment and a liberal approach to intermissions. Practice and record-keeping have now been tightened up; but information is still hard to come by because completion rates and times are now commercially sensitive information. However, although there used to be high rates of non-completion before 1990, more recently at least two-thirds and possibly three-quarters of those who have started doctorates have managed to complete.

What can be said is that it will take you at least three years full-time, and five part-time, probably more in the humanities and social sciences, especially if you suspend for a period or for any reason move supervisor or department. Women may take somewhat longer on average to complete than men, but we don't have a higher dropout rate. The average gender difference in time is probably due to there being more men in fields with shorter times to completion, rather than to women's 'domestic responsibilities'. According to US data, there is no significant difference by sex *within* the major fields. Indeed in some fields women, and certainly in most fields international students, finish more quickly than men and home students (see pp. 197–201).

The low income and status

Money is, however, and is likely to remain, a problem in doing a doctorate. It is expensive. Unless you can get a grant (preferably from the Wellcome Foundation, which pays a living wage) or have a job within the university, perhaps as a research assistant, or can get funded by your employer (see pp. 131–42), all of which have strings attached, you will have to meet your living costs and pay substantial fees, as well as needing money for equipment, books, fieldwork expenses, lab fees, and attending conferences. And think of the earnings forgone!

Living costs vary in different parts of Britain and postgraduate fees vary from one university to another and by discipline, and according to whether you are full-time or part-time, and a 'home' or 'overseas' student. But even for a part-time home, arts student, they are quite substantial – if you have to pay them yourself. Cost is probably not the top item in deciding your choice of where to study, but you should certainly shop around a little, comparing university websites and student handbooks, and if you are abroad, talking to people who have studied in the UK and consulting the British Council. (See also pp. 100, 106, 129–30.)

But as an investment in your own growth a doctorate may still be a worthwhile thing to do. Certainly before you dismiss the possibility, recall that as women we have a hard time thinking of anything like self-fulfilment as justification for going into debt. We will do it for our children, for a car, or to fix up the house, but not for ourselves.

However, the initial loss of status and money for middle-aged individuals with jobs who either give them up, or go part-time, is certainly stressful; and especially hard for women, who often lack other sources of prestige. It is also difficult for younger students to continue on to doctoral level, especially if you have debts remaining from your undergraduate course, when your contemporaries are earning three times as much. It is hard for anyone to occupy the subaltern position of student, especially if you are made to feel uneasy, or even intimidated, by those who seem cleverer than you feel you are yourself.

Your other responsibilities and social life

Because it takes so long and is so demanding, doing a doctorate is obviously difficult (though not impossible) to combine with other demands, be they young children, needy partners, elderly relatives, a new job, or whatever is culturally expected of women in your milieu. Doing the degree part-time may seem the solution for 'home' students, but if you can't put in the time mentioned above and allow yourself some time off at the weekends, think again. You can't simply 'find' all the necessary time by better time management. You will have to *make* time by putting some other stuff on the back-burner (see pp. 116–23). Then you will only have to deal with your guilt and other people's reactions to your absence, your preoccupation and your single-mindedness!

There are obvious ploys, like planning special times with your young children and partner (if you have them), and involving older children and/or your partner with campus activities. Some women have access to domestic help, others exchange babysitting with other students. You can schedule time to keep in touch with relatives at home, and maybe work some of the time 'at a distance' (back at home) now that UK residence requirements are no longer so strict and since information and communication technologies enable you to stay in touch with your tutor. But the problems won't go away; so seek comfort and don't become immobilized by guilt. Form informal support groups with others in a similar situation at college and eat a regular lunch together (see pp. 161–6). If you are single or in a same-sex partnership or from a minority culture, be sure to make time to maintain support from your domestic and social life, especially if you have to move to a new location such as a small town when you are used to the city, or vice versa. Many experience a lot of stress in the first year of doing a doctorate, especially if it involves moving home and culture, so be forewarned.

There is less you can do about the still continuing (though less strong) assumptions by *some* people in the university (as in other occupations – we just expect better from intellectuals) that your career *should* take second place to marriage, and that to be happy, women must be mothers and mothers should do most of the care for children. This is less directly or less frequently expressed to women today than it was in the 1950s to 1970s, and it is more accepted that families can be fitted around work, just as work can be around families. But these sentiments are still there, and materialize in the lack of childcare on British campuses, the greater demands on women to prove themselves serious students; in giving women teaching rather than research assistantships; and in the relative lack of faculty interest in finding employment for women students when they graduate.

Language skills

Doing a doctorate in the UK requires a fluent command of English. It helps to have this from the start because the pace of progress through the degree has been speeded up. If you are from a non-English-speaking background you will be asked for a certificate of English language competence (International English Language Testing System or Test of English as a Foreign Language) at a specified level. Your university will however probably also have academic literacy support available for you once you arrive, which covers not just questions of language, but also constructions of argument, including disciplinary differences in modes of writing (see pp. 234–47). Some home students also find this useful. However, there will be only a certain amount of such help available.

I was told: 'The reality seems to be that students get few chances and often extremely short time to have one-to-one sessions of language support free of charge. They find they have to pay almost as much again as an overseas fee for a Masters or PhD to attend enough courses on English for academic purposes and to have a private language tutor (costing £5–15 per hour), especially when they submit the final version of their coursework.'

However, the ability to read and speak foreign languages is, unfortunately, no longer a necessity for 'home' doctoral students, except for the specialist languages required for instance, for fieldwork in anthropology, or to do comparative studies or to read texts in history. Having such skills is, however, a tremendous asset – and one we might expect women would be more likely to have (given who mostly takes languages at GCSE and A level).

In other European countries, and a generation ago in the UK, language was not an option, but a necessary part of everyone's education. It made available sources that were not available in English. It provided access to the thinking, and subjectivity, of other peoples. Above all, it cast a light, of necessary distance and self-examination, upon the student's own language. Goethe said in the context of literature: 'The monoglot is deaf.' The same applies to the study of the social sciences. Ninety per cent of the World Wide Web may be in English: but 70 per cent of the world's books, and a higher percentage of its newspapers and other sources are not. This issue, addressed in [the Robbins Report on Higher Education of 1963], was not addressed by Dearing [in a similar report in 1997]. On its own it seriously disqualifies any claim that the social sciences in this country are facing the challenges of a changing world.

(Halladay 1998: 12)

Disabilities

Students with disabilities are somewhat more welcome in universities than in the past, and universities now have obligations towards them under Part III of the *Disability Discrimination Act (DDA) 1995* (relating to access to goods, facilities, services and premises). However, quite what these obligations are is not clear because of, currently, an 'education exemption'; and good intentions do not often equal, for example, £40,000 for a chair lift to access one part of the building. A far lower proportion of research students and professors are disabled than the presence of such workers within the UK workforce as a whole (2.3 per cent and 1.2 per cent against 11 per cent) (*THES* 14 July 2000: 20–1; HESA 2000: Table 11b).

Academia tries to preserve a Cartesian 'life of the mind', not acknowledging the materiality of its own production, and ignoring the bodies that support and increment its existence. The presence of disability, and even more gendered disability, is threatening . . . Disability is feared because it is seen as a hopeless situation of passivity, lack of control and of happiness . . . Since academics are seen as independent people, the negative image of disability as a state of dependency does not fit in with society's image of higher education . . . But academia can certainly prove to be a stimulating and challenging environment for disabled women, on condition that it stops asking itself what women cannot do and starts acting on how society can be changed to enable disabled people to participate fully within it. Research that is participatory and emancipatory, led by and conducted with disabled women, is, indeed, the first step toward a more articulate and public awareness and understanding of the group, whose members will also as a result become more powerful and influential.

(Adapted from Iantaffi 1996: 182–4)

If you have special needs, there should be a Welfare Office in each university whose staff can provide you with information about what is available (or the information may be on the university website). They should also provide help with getting you what you need if it is not provided when you arrive. The student union should give you back-up. Shortage of funding is not helping in this as in other areas (see pp. 144–6), but Equal Opportunities policies, combined with Quality Assurance pressures, including a code of practice on disabled students which came into force in 2000, are (finally) leading to training programmes being run for staff to inform them of their obligations under the DDA. Audits are also being undertaken to prioritize and cost recommended actions. The HEFCE has run initiatives to help universities adapt their campuses, while the Scottish Funding Council has financed the appointment of disability advisors in each HEI. In addition women students with specific disabilities have written accounts about how they managed to do higher degrees, which are helpful and encouraging; and Disability Rights publications give examples of good institutional practice (including from SKILL, the national bureau for students with disabilities). You (and the student union) can try putting these in front of the university's authorities. You might also consider studying with the Open University, which has good support for disabled students generally.

Further reading

There are a number of general advice books aimed at research students in the UK, and more in the USA, which are worth reading even if they barely mention gender issues. Those aimed at supervisors are also useful in giving you a sense of the relationship from their angle too. Books giving general advice on planning and managing research projects are covered in the further reading for Chapter 5; on the actual writing of theses and on academic and other careers following a doctorate in Chapter 8.

General texts for UK doctorate students

Brown, S., McDowell, L. and Race, P. (1995) *500 Tips for Research Students*. London: Kogan Page. One of a series of books on '500 tips for . . .' by these colleagues. To be dipped into, but from the ticks in my library's copy, certainly enjoyed by many. Helpful on time and self-management, starting teaching, study skills and giving a paper.

Cryer, P. (2000) *The Research Students' Guide to Success*, 2nd edn. Buckingham: Open University Press. Written in a conversational style with lively anecdotes, by a specialist in the field of student support. It is strong on finding and using available resources and on transferable skills.

Delamont, S., Atkinson, P. and Parry, O. (1997) *Supervising the PhD: A Guide to Success*. Buckingham: SRHE and Open University Press. Well worth reading to get the view from the supervisor's position (and ideas to feed to your supervisor if they are not doing things the way you'd like). See pp. 157–61.

Phillips, E. and Pugh, D. (2000) *How to get a PhD: A Handbook for Students and their Supervisors*, 3rd edn. Buckingham: Open University Press. Research based and useful, but it comes down heavily on the side of doing things in such a way as to get a PhD with certainty rather than pushing the limits or combining with a more radical agenda.

Salmon, P. (1992) *Achieving a PhD: Ten Students' Experiences*. Stoke-on-Trent: Trentham. A supervisor's humanistic account of some research students in education. It stresses the personal development aspects of doing a doctorate and provides an interesting contrast to Phillips and Pugh.

Specific fields

Allan, G. and Skinner, C. (eds) (1991) *Handbook for Research Students in the Social Sciences*. London: Falmer. Covers a lot rather swiftly, but it has four students' and two supervisors' personal views and a chapter which points out the importance of gender and race. It also covers study skills and the management of research and looks at various social science methods from the perspective of a research student considering using them.

Burnham, P. (ed.) (1997) *Surviving the Research Process in Politics*. London: Pinter. This has first-hand accounts of handling the doctoral student role and the realities of the research process in political science and international studies, by full-time students, teaching assistants, an academic who is completing a doctorate, and several overseas students.

Graves, N. and Verma, V. (eds) (1997) *Working for a Doctorate: A Guide for the Humanities and Social Sciences*. London: Routledge. An excellent collection which includes three students' perspectives, a chapter by Denis Lawton on how doing a doctorate differs from other phases of education, and good coverage of gender and intercultural issues.

Murrell, G., Huang, C. and Ellis, H. (1990) *Research in Medicine: A Guide to Writing a Thesis in the Medical Sciences*. Cambridge: Cambridge University Press. Directly largely at medical practitioners but relevant to all experimental sciences.

Texts for US doctoral students

Caplan, P. (1994) *Lifting a Ton of Feathers: A Woman's Guide to Surviving in the Academic World*. Toronto: University of Toronto Press. Widely quoted and covering the whole spectrum of women in the academy in North America (with sections on doctoral students). It can be depressing to read problem after problem and it is hard to follow up references, but it is comprehensive.

Kerlin, S. P. (1995) Surviving the doctoral years: critical perspectives, *Education Policy Analysis Archives* (electronic journal), 3(17), November. A student perspective, with a good bibliography.

Peters, R. L. (1997) *Getting What You Came For: The Smart Student's Guide to Earning a Master's or Ph.D.*, revised edn. New York: Noonday Press/Farrar,

Straus and Giroux. This provides good general information should you be thinking of applying to study in the USA.

Toth, E. (1997) *Ms. Mentor's Impeccable Advice for Women in Academia.* Philadelphia, PA: University of Pennsylvania Press. An amusing, sharp account written in question and answer mode 'for academics of all genders and sexual persuasions'. It has chapters on graduate studies ('the rite of passage'), job hunting, conferences, first year on the job, and so on.

Vartuli, S. (ed.) (1982) *The PhD Experience: A Woman's Point of View.* New York: Praeger. An important collection of very readable personal accounts covering stress, personal relationships, older women and much else; but out of print and quite difficult to get hold of.

Differences between doctorates in different countries

Cowen, R. (1997) Comparative perspectives on the British PhD, in N. Graves and V. Verma (eds) *Working for a Doctorate: A Guide for the Humanities and Social Sciences.* London: Routledge. Humorous, reflective and erudite.

European Journal of Education, 1998, 3(2), special issue on Postgraduate Education in Europe. This includes reports from members of an EU network that focused on policy and practice in ten European countries. It has an editorial by Robert Burgess and articles on seven member states: Austria, Belgium, Greece, Germany, Portugal, Spain and UK.

Professional doctorates

Maxwell, T. W. and Shanahan, P. J. (1997) Towards a reconceptualisation of the doctorate: issues relating to the EdD degree in Australia, *Studies in Higher Education*, 22(2): 133–50. There is little as yet on doing professional doctorates outside the USA, but this article has an interesting discussion of what the differences between PhDs and professional doctorates should be if the latter are to complement and be on a par with the former.

Notes

1 Project on gender/women (C/00/26/2058).
2 Aggregating the 1998–9 figures for biological sciences, physical sciences, engineering and technology, mathematical sciences and computer sciences; and the creative arts and design, humanities, social, economic and political studies, languages and education; shows 34 per cent of women research students are in the first cluster and 38 per cent in the second (with the 17 per cent in medicine and dentistry, subjects allied to medicine, and veterinary sciences), against 49 per cent, 27 per cent and 11 per cent of men (HESA 2000: Tables 1c and 1g).
3 Oxford and the universities of Buckingham, Sussex, Ulster and York call their PhD equivalents a DPhil.

3 | WHERE TO STUDY?
Finding the right supervisor
and the right university

Although it may not feel like this when you are trying to find a supervisor and get started, it is something of a buyer's market for potential doctoral students. Chapter 1 showed what student recruitment looks like from the universities' side and why they probably want *you*, especially if you are a good lab scientist or a capable, self-funding humanities student. Moreover individual academics are often keen to take on research students because, in addition to publishing and getting funded research projects, having research students helps to develop their professional identity and career. For those with already established reputations, research students can provide a way of doing surrogate research – of keeping on top of the field, researching an area of potential interest, getting specific intellectual stimulation and new insights, and establishing a new academic network and joint publications. Research students are also a way of getting assistants in the sciences. Overseas students may provide an occasion for future travel; and some students are taken on for fun (which can include sexual motives, see pp. 209–18, 224–7).

All this is to say that if you are a good student, man or woman, home or international, and even if you are older than 'normal', you can be selective. It is therefore worth taking time and shopping around. Women in particular may lack self-confidence and feel flattered by, and accept too readily, early offers. However, it is a really important decision because your degree will, de facto, be evaluated by where you did it and by your supervisor (and your examiners, see pp. 247–9). This is an especially important consideration if you want an academic job. It is also important to work in a relationship of mutual respect, in a university that can provide the resources you need. On the other hand, even though students often blame failure on their supervisor, a good student can succeed with little or poor supervision, and a hardworking, less able student can also get through. However, a disorganized student with a poor supervisor is a recipe for disaster.

In the current competitive climate, however, as a 'buyer' you should beware. There is some misrepresentation with individuals and institutions trying to hook you in (and obviously not only in the UK but also worldwide). In particular, some universities which are relatively new to doctoral supervision, will accept people even though they are really not good enough to be able to cope, especially if their English is poor. So if a couple of good universities advise you against doing a PhD, and suggest you do a Masters course or a language course first, do take their advice seriously. Don't think that the one (with a poor research rating) which does offer you a place is necessarily doing you a favour. They could be letting you waste time and money, and/or starting you on the long path to a not very good degree.

> If you are contemplating doing your research degree in a university [or with a supervisor] unfamiliar to you, it is well worth spending a few days on the new campus to make the necessary enquiries. This may seem an extravagance, but it is really a good investment. Do not forget the PhD will take . . . years of your life: you are risking a great deal. In comparison with the risk, a few days may be very well spent.
>
> (Lawton 1997: 5)

Being proactive about finding a university and a supervisor, doing some homework on potential supervisors, and making it a two-way negotiation may feel a bit strange, especially if you are used to respecting seniors and following wisdom. But one of the major elements of the British system is getting you to develop your powers of independent discovery while another's learning to be self-reliant and self-directed. This is just starting as you need to go on. Also, one of the good sides to marketization is that there is now a lot more formal help available – better brochures, websites, attempts at Quality Assurance, postgraduate unions, and from British Council offices abroad.

If this sounds daunting, it may be best not to skip doing a Masters course, even if this is allowed, so as to build up your confidence and insider knowledge, or to take a short refresher course. This will give you up-to-date knowledge and let you read potential supervisors' recent work. If it has good methodology element, it will also probably make it easier to get funding subsequently, and maybe exemptions from later methodology modules – so your doctorate will not take longer in the long run. Should you then decide *not* to go ahead with a PhD, you will have a degree at the end of a year's full-time study anyway.

Individual supervisors

I will start by discussing choosing a supervisor because in the British system they are chosen at the start and are integral to the registration process. Getting a good supervisor is also the element that has been most stressed in both the training *and* the educational perspectives on the PhD, and by students themselves in humanities and social sciences. But while the identity of one's supervisor is clearly important, how important she or he is varies with your discipline. One reason the supervisor is so significant to non-science students is partly the lack of other sorts of support in such departments. Chapter 1 (pp. 22–5, 41–5) also suggests that one reason why a training approach stress this element is because poor supervision is the cause of low completion rates which the university could tackle at least cost (by better monitoring of student progress and staff development programmes for supervisors), that is, without providing other potentially useful but more expensive sources of support. You would be well advised not to focus on your choice of supervisor to such an extent that you don't also look at the other good and bad features of a place (see next section) – even if, as in for example anthropology, the lineage is the central element of professional identity.

Supervisors also need to be kept in proportion because the structure of academe positions them as quasi-parents and there is a tendency to project all one's student woes on to them (see pp. 90–1, 200). This applies especially if your supervisor is a woman, because you can find yourself expecting her to be all-giving and all-powerful. But in the end it is your thesis. A supervisor is just a good guide for a beginner, who helps to make you think how you are tackling a problem, by probing and prodding with questions, and who gives support and reassurance that you are staying on the right track. Ultimately, the decisions that are made are up to you. There is a limit to what you can ask of tutors.

If you were to make a list of what you are looking for in a supervisor, you would probably say you want someone:

- who is very knowledgeable about the specific subject you are interested in
- who can get you the resources you need (especially important in the sciences)
- who is good at communicating ideas and committed to teaching
- who has an international reputation (for sponsorship)
- who wants the same sort of relationship as you do – which may mean someone who will become a personal friend or someone who stays 'strictly professional', but either way is sympathetic, encouraging, and treats you with respect and
- who can keep the concept of the PhD in perspective for you.

It may therefore help to know that what existing students actually stress is none of these, but rather availability.

Availability

What this means obviously varies with the individual student. Do you want someone who directs you, or who acts as a sounding board? Who knows what you are up to at all times, initiates meetings and chases you up, or who leaves you to organize your own time and follow your own paths and style? Who takes direct responsibility for the standard of the thesis and lets you know forcefully if they think your work is poor, or who leaves decisions to you and is uniformly encouraging and supportive? Since what you want may anyway change over time, it is perhaps hard to know what to look for at the start. But there are some specific problems you should bear in mind.

   First, is he or she likely to be there? Do they have study leave due? Or likely to do extensive fieldwork? Or facing a tenure decision? Or running a spin-off chemistry company? Or with very heavy administrative responsibilities (such as a dean or head of department)? Or planning to retire? You need consistency and continuity if possible. Academics with brilliant reputations may not be the best choice. They are too busy jetting off to conferences, so students can end up with supervisions at Heathrow airport as the great man passes through. (Not common, but I have known it to happen.)

> Universities make appointments to enhance their reputations and for political ties – like Kissinger at Columbia (in New York). Students enrol thinking they will get someone who is really big in his field – and you're right, that's where they are, 'in the field'. They are not teaching. They are hardly ever even seen on campus. A university may advertise in its brochure the numbers of its members who are Nobel laureates or have national medals of science, and who are members of national academies. But you are unlikely to meet them if you go there, let alone be taught by them.

   In the sciences, it is important that your supervisor's lab is well funded and will continue throughout the period of your research, and beyond, so that it gives you postdoctoral research possibilities and that it is wealthy enough to send you to conferences.

   Second, how routinely overburdened is your supervisor? The increased working hours of academics are now comparable to those of junior hospital doctors. An average lecturer works 55 hours a week during term time, and women more than men.

A survey by the AUT based on time diaries kept for 2 weeks by 1500 academic and professional staff in the 'old' universities, showed that one-third of the time they worked was outside 'office hours'. Research and research supervision was additional to lectures, seminars and tutorials, marking, assessing and administrative duties (AUT 1994).

Some good supervisors by mid-life have (too) many research students, in addition to these already increased workloads. So do consider a younger one, who will have had supervision and training for the role (though note that the longest hours are often worked by young academics under pressure to make their mark). Some supervisors have rationalized by having their own student group seminars to supplement or complement one-to-one tutorials.

Joel Marchand of HotDocs, a confederation of research student associations in France, suggests that while a professor in hard science subjects may supervise one or two research students, the most eminent specialists in arts subjects in France supervise dozens of theses at a time. He claimed to know of one very famous history professor who had 150 research students (*THES* 9 August 1996: 8). This may be an urban myth, but do ask a potential supervisor how many other research students they have. Ten is a reasonable maximum.

Feminist staff in particular feel stressed by their concern to support (women) students while faced with the open-endedness of student demands in an 'entitlement culture'. Conversely they find themselves too much locked into doing pastoral work and teaching to complete their own PhDs or to get promotion.

Maintaining the type of relationship with which you feel comfortable

Another element of 'availability' is just how open and honest you feel you can be with your supervisor: whether you can talk about your problems without feeling foolish, and what sort of relationships exist in their lab – where you will be spending at least 40 hours a week. Your supervisor has to be both a supporter and a devil's advocate, and sometimes critical even when you may feel more or less suicidal. But not destructively critical. There is a fine line to be trodden and it needs to be walked in the context of respect and interest – with feedback coming promptly, and pointing out the good as well as the bad.

A woman who wanted to study in Australia strategically chose a prestigious university and two supervisors, one a mainstream senior academic in her main field and the other a rising star in a new field. She hoped the combination would help her get a scholarship and also would cover the two disciplines which her topic crossed. When she arrived it emerged that the senior person was on study leave and the 'star' would do the first year's supervision. She accepted this, despite the fact that she had never been able to read beyond page 5 of his latest book, which she found incomprehensible. She spent much of the first term settling in socially, but was soon floundering badly academically. She was refused upgrading at the end of the first year. Fortunately the university took the matter seriously – overseas scholarship holders failing is a cause for concern! The dean said her main department should have appointed someone to cover for the individual who was on study leave, and she should consider changing to a less turbo-charged second supervisor who did not intellectually intimidate her.

You should discuss the *process* of supervision with your supervisor, if not at the very start then certainly early on (see pp. 157–61), and return to it again whenever you feel you need to. One of the good things in the new concern with mutual accountability, protocols for the relationship, monitoring and specification of the stages and elements in doing a doctorate, should be that features of the process, relationship and results can be put on the table – made visible, explicit, negotiated and, if necessary, contested. This is after all part of developing your problem defining and solving skills along the way to getting your degree.

The traditional mode of supervision is private, individualized, laissez faire, with an open time scale, assuming the autonomous young scholar will thrive on benign neglect – veering into outright neglect and magisterial disdain, emotionally distanced, disembodied and super rational.

Alternatively the supervisor may speak of exposing what is in the students themselves, when in fact what is in play is Rousseau's 'well-regulated liberty': a hidden curriculum of subjection while preserving the forms of freedom – of rationality and independence gained through practising restraint and submitting to pedagogic norms. Here supervisors favour indirect modes of intellectual direction and passive reinforcement rather than direct negative statements. This allows them to manipulate students to their preferences without directly appearing (to themselves at least) to be doing so. Students find this hard to read! So be aware that 'would it be a good idea to . . . ?' and 'is it really advisable?' may well mean 'go and do it' and 'stop doing it'!

A different fantasy is sought after in some feminist pedagogy, which seeks pleasure in the identification of teacher and student, with the supervisor 'infinitely patient, available, confident in her knowledge, an intellectual and sexual role model who uses her long office hours therapeutically to help students develop subjectivity and self esteem and to solve personal problems', ending up exhausted and burnt out herself. (These first three types are drawn from Johnson *et al.* 2000.)

Phil Salmon, by contrast, describes agreeing to a supervisory relationship as an agreement to work in long-term close collaboration: to embark on a journey together. She sees the supervisor as a critical friend who has a personal affinity with the student and the work itself, who supports the project even when the student loses belief. She favours the PhD cohort where the students give each other credence and help each other over the blocks which can occur when they would not want to see their supervisor because they have nothing to present (Salmon 1992).

Anna Yeatman favours making it a more contractual relationship to ensure accountability, guide timing, and minimize waste and pain. She says expectations on both sides and their situation in a wider frame of graduate programme management (departmental and university policy) should be made explicit, visible and contestable (Yeatman 1994, 1998).

There are also occasional attempts to provide amusing typologies of 'least wanted' supervisors, though the research base for these seem thin. They do however suggest some of the problems, and there *are* some emotionally and materially exploitative relationships to be avoided.

The 'young turk' has just got his doctorate and wants to put a distance between himself and his students, and does this by being 'tough' and marking them down.

The 'career doctorate' supervisor's own thesis took ten years and at some level she wants you to live through that too.

The sadistic professor uses power to ventilate personal and career rages on students via 'upholding standards' and so on.

The sexist supervisor converts supervision into flirtation or misogyny.

The Hamlet complex professor doubts every version of your thesis and often rejects his own earlier endorsements of it, and his own advice, and keeps wanting to go back to square one to consider other approaches.

The passive-aggressive supervisor presents as a friend who will do anything for you, but contradicts this by small and large acts of dissertation sabotage (not reading your chapters for ages, not supporting you in getting access to research locations, criticizing you in public) because she doesn't like students or supervising but feels guilty about such role aversion.

The envious professor perceives you as a threat and acts to head off the competition.

(Adapted from Sternberg 1981: 148–51)

More important is the taboo subject of exploitation of students by supervisors: where students' interests are sacrificed to those of their supervisor. This can involve simple pirating of student's ideas, demanding senior authorship in jointly published work based on the student's ideas, using cheap student labour for tasks (from interesting to menial) of benefit only to the supervisor, or demanding a particular form of thesis or unnecessary extra work simply to make it formally acceptable to maintain the supervisor's reputation, or taking on students for the kudos and then neglecting them. Even if sometimes students feel exchanges are not unfair because their supervisor also does deals in return – providing a thesis topic and funding by cutting off a bit from the work he wants done, getting joint articles published, going out of his way to find scholarships, teaching assistantships and jobs for his students, and/or writing gilded lily references.

Knowledgeable about the specific subject and with a reputation in the field

It seems obvious that a supervisor should know the field you intend to study. But they don't necessarily need to be expert in just the tiny area you are interested in. It is more important that they are really interested in your topic, are up to date with the wide general field and can make eclectic and illuminating suggestions, and are compatible with your politics and epistemology. Also that they know (or are willing to learn) about the culture/country/context you come from and/or intend to study, if it is not their own. One possibility is joint supervision, though note that US literature is full of accounts of the problems of handling a committee, with internal issues of seniority and sensitivities among supervisors.

One of the problems we have, in the social sciences in particular . . . is that topics are very difficult to supervise. New topics are continually arising to which no one staff member is really well-attuned in a supervisory capacity, either because methodologically there is no one doing what the student wants to do, or more often because no one can break open the general context of content in which that student wants to work. In such a situation, we need more, rather than fewer supervisors. Students need to be able to locate in one institution while receiving co-operative supervision (perhaps electronically) from people working elsewhere who are closer to their topic. Students shouldn't necessarily have to move. There may be good reasons to stay where they are . . . we should move to a more complicated way of handling supervision, and continue the trend in the last decade towards multiple supervisors, with all the protections and all the richness and additions which having more than one supervisor can provide for the whole process.

(Marginson 1998: 22)

It is essential that your supervisor is a good sponsor – able and willing to get you the resources and contacts you need and to network you to colleagues and other students working in the field. (You can use a mentor to do this as well: see pp. 166–9.) Your supervisor will automatically become your referee for jobs for some years after you get your doctorate, so they need to be someone held in good esteem in the discipline. If you don't use your supervisor for this, people will want to know why.

Good at communicating ideas and committed to teaching and to women

Supervising doctoral work is a genuinely complex teaching task and needs considerable commitment of time and energy – but staff have often been expected to do it as a sideline. The student used, according to Bob Connell, to be supposed to 'absorb the necessary know-how by a sort of intellectual osmosis between great minds' (Connell 1985), just as supervisors themselves had supposedly picked up the teaching skills by 'sitting next to Nelly'. Courses for supervisors have of course been run by staff development centres in some universities for 30 years or more, and more recently by the Open University, and there have also been informal in-house training sessions where old hands pass on good practice – though it is usually the same keen people who attended regularly, and the worst supervisors who probably think they don't need help. However, in future, higher education teachers are going to *have* to have formal teaching training and be accredited (a new variant of the central control discussed in Chapter 1). Initially this is being directed at undergraduate teaching, but doctoral teaching is likely to follow (see also Subject Review, pp. 19–21, 100).

The Institute for Learning and Teaching in Higher Education (ILT) was launched in 1999 'to be the professional body for HE staff involved in teaching and the support of learning.' It will eventually act as a gatekeeper, accrediting training courses run by individual colleges and universities and issuing individuals with certificates of competence to teach in higher education. Currently membership is voluntary (but everyone expects it to become compulsory) and it costs £25 to apply with a £75 annual fee.

It got off to a bumpy start. Some of the launch documents which were circulated were sexist (a 'good' application from a man and an unsuccessful one from a woman, and sex stereotyping comments from sample referees, and so on). It stands charged with being unaware of or indifferent to existing validation processes – by professional bodies, the QAA and the research councils – and it moved too quickly and then had to change its membership procedures three times in the first year. Initially it had neither a public EO statement nor did its practice recognize systematic differences among staff or students. So, while the unions gave it a cautious welcome, they came to have reservations about its potentially damaging and divisive effects.

When looking for a supervisor, the best way to find out is to ask other students who are or who have been supervised by them (including alumni in your home country) and to check (discreetly) with the departmental research tutor or the graduate school of the university in question on the supervisor's track record with students. How long have past students taken to complete? What has happened to those who have completed? Did they go on to postdoctoral research or to jobs? What contact is maintained? In the sciences, how does the supervisor behave in relation to joint publishing and are they good with women and overseas students?

What women students specifically need

The self-help literature talks a lot about handling one's supervisor (or in the USA, one's supervisory committee), but the significance of gender in these interrelations is very seldom mentioned. However in studies of Sydney and Melbourne universities and a national study of Australia, Ingrid Moses (1990) found that the informal nature of supervision seemed to deny women the support we particularly need. Most women said they were satisfied with their supervisor, though they were less satisfied than men (which is also the finding from other studies), but women, especially older women, did not get as much access to or help from their own supervisor(s) as men, and they also generally missed out on 'the beneficial aspects of regular and frequent interaction with other academic staff in the department'.

Two important ingredients of a successful graduate career mentioned in the American literature . . . are a close relationship with an academic sponsor and integration with a student reference group. These provide the essential professional socialization and foster the development of the

> appropriate self-image. However . . . the gender of the graduate student will affect the likelihood of their receiving sponsorship from academic staff, so that male students have a better chance of being sponsored than females. Gender will also be one of the factors influencing membership of student peer groups. Women may be less likely than men to be included in those informal learning situations that arise outside the research situation or the formal university seminar.
>
> (Taylorson 1984: 147–9)

Is it, then, generally helpful to women students to have a woman supervisor (recognizing this will not always be possible, since most supervisors are men)? Well, certainly not just any woman, since not all women have empathy with women students and some are downright hostile. Moreover men are particularly useful as sponsors (see pp. 167, 248). But in general women supervisors, or if not supervisors then other women staff, are certainly helpful to women students, for a number of reasons. For instance, men and women often do not understand each other's conversational styles, and men supervisors seem particularly to misunderstand women students' silences and their use of narratives and personal experience, and to see them as inappropriate to academic settings (see pp. 160, 205).

> I was thinking about the relationship between the supervisor and the PhD student, especially when the supervisor is male and the student isn't, and trying to combine the work I've done on when women keep silent. The intensity of the one-to-oneness seems to compound the tension for some women, and allows the men to see the silence, not just as resistance, but as defining the student as not good enough. Women's best response to learning and teaching is often in the small supportive group where there are spaces for silences and inarticulacy and risk-taking. The intensity of the supervision doesn't allow for spaces and silences. I'm thinking about the dread that several women faculty in my own institution feel at the imminence of their supervision interview; and they are women who have no difficulty giving papers and teaching vast classes of postgraduate students themselves.

Problems of gaining access to a busy supervisor and cultural confusions are both probably exacerbated for international women students who do not fully understand British mores and whose supervisors are certainly unlikely to be versed in foreign gender interrelations (given they don't recognize those of their own society). There are also issues of (hetero)sexualization of relationships and romantic attachment which get played out differently when supervisors are women (see pp. 224–7); again these get read differently when the two individuals are also from different backgrounds. Caroline

Wright (1997) notes that the British Council has begun to tackle this issue in its guidance to overseas students and visitors. She suggests it should develop this further, and that each university should inform students how interchange and proximity between the sexes is generally acceptable in Britain and does not indicate sexual interest. But they should also make clear their policies on, and the support available to deal with, sexist and racist harassment, and with romantic involvements, if and when they do occur.

This does not mean, however, that men who are not comfortable being taught by a woman should express such views and be assigned to a man supervisor. Liberals may argue the same rules should apply to both sexes, but radical analysis requires differential treatment for dominated and dominant groups. Patriarchal views should be engaged with and not tolerated, whether they come from men from 'home' or 'other' cultures, where such ideas may be said to be endemic. There are in fact continuing political differences, and major recent changes, on this issue in most parts of the world; and many men from 'other' cultures, as many men from the UK, hold (and others should be encouraged to hold) egalitarian values (see Gundara 1997).

If you want to do research on gender, or if the field you are interested in has a possible gender dimension, do try to get a gender specialist as a supervisor, or at least make sure you have access to one as a co-supervisor. If not, attend a good related course on women's studies in the university (see Chapter 6). Be warned that many men (and some women) academics have not read the literature on gender, despite 25 years of feminist scholarship. Even though they may express an interest, they will not be able to help you do the necessary overturning of sexist paradigms to ask important research questions. They will probably send you off 'to talk to a feminist they know', far too late in the day for it to be helpful to your research project! If you want to study another country, get a specialist on gender relations and feminist theory in that country, since obviously there are important cultural variations. Academics sometimes take on supervising a particular topic because they hope that through working with a student, they themselves will learn. But most have no notion of what has been achieved (theoretically, methodologically and empirically) by feminist researchers; so you could end up simply not know what you are missing until it is too late – and 'what you are missing' is both scholarly insight into your material and the intellectual excitement and sense of solidarity that exists in this rapidly growing field.

Women staff, especially senior women staff and professors, are also useful to women students because they are more likely to be skilled in supporting topics low in the pecking order of importance in the discipline, which includes many areas popular with women. Women are also used to handling issues of 'objectivity' versus 'commitment' in research, and arguing for the legitimacy of particular (feminist) theoretical frameworks and methodologies; and likely to believe your accounts if you need help because you are being harassed.

How to find this person

In many disciplines you can simply write to someone whose work you have admired or who you heard speak at conferences and ask if you could talk with them about the possibility of studying with them. I'm generally happy to talk with someone for an hour on an open basis – it is flattering, usually interesting, and I know the field and can suggest someone they might match up with if our areas of interest aren't appropriate. I wouldn't necessarily recommend myself because I have a lot of students already. So don't feel committed to the first person you talk to, nor slighted if people pass you on. Alternatively, attend a short course or seminar given by the person and make your interest known to them. Or go to conferences and attend their paper and speak to them afterwards. Go also to the postgraduate sessions at conferences and the women's caucus and ask around. Go back to someone who taught you at undergraduate or Masters level and ask for suggestions, and then write mentioning your previous teacher's name. If the person you approach wants you to start via the formal application route, they will tell you, and/or they will often ask to see an outline of a possible topic, or something you have written, as the basis for a discussion.

If you don't get a reply, this is probably bad news anyway. It could indicate inefficiency, overwork, or arrogance. But not necessarily. See what the gossip network has to say. There may be a good reason and you should persevere. It could be they are away or on study leave. There is not always good administrative cover in universities.

If you are keen on a specific institution, visit it and talk to the registry and the research student association or student union. Then speak to someone, better a few staff, in the potential department, and their existing or recent students. Some universities have student guidebooks on the web about how helpful individual staff are to students. Alternatively (though this needs to be handled carefully) choose the university and department and ask to work with someone initially. Then, when you get there, talk to other staff and attend a class or two. This is a professional relationship, not a marriage. Consider joint supervision if one person is empathetic but another one knows the field.

This is difficult of course if you are from overseas, though looking through websites will give you information on individual staff as well as institutions (though see pp. 104–5 for reservations) and their email addresses. When you are close to making a decision, have a long telephone call with your potential supervisor, at an agreed time. Even if this is expensive, it is a good investment – difficult though it may be to speak in a foreign language in the middle of the night.

Getting a feminist supervisor, and/or someone who knows about gender, race or sexuality, and the 'brands' of work in these areas, is not always easy.

Feminist academics are thin on the ground and Black feminists an endangered species. Moreover, even though women academics are often attracted to teaching and prepared to take on quite heavy loads, this makes it difficult for them to do research and publish – especially since extra pastoral work makes its way to their door anyway. Quite frequently they are under pressure and often unable to bridge the gap between available resources and legitimate student demands. So joint supervision is also worth considering as a possibility here – but don't use someone else as supervisor and expect 'free' input from the women in the department or assign them a different role from the men.

> Sometimes it's quite insulting. I remember one in particular, this one student who was sort of dry running a thesis proposal, and at one point I said 'You really shouldn't be talking to me. I'm just a [thesis] committee member [in the North American system]. You should really be talking to your supervisor about this.' And she said point blank: 'Well . . . I wanted to make sure it was good before I went to him'.
>
> (Acker and Feuerverger 1996: 413)

Differences between disciplines and departments

Since doing a PhD is about becoming a full member of an academic discipline, it is the discipline or disciplines or interdisciplinarity which provides both the framework for the research and your new primary source of identification. There are, in addition, variations within disciplines in the interests and the prestige of different departments. It helps your curriculum vitae (CV) to have attended an elite department because generally employers favour them, but such places can be very selective and pressure students to excel. They also usually regard not getting an academic job afterwards as a failure. This may not suit you: it may make you feel inadequate and discouraged – especially since a mark of prestige can be a chilly climate for women. Student satisfaction seems to be less in 5* departments. On the other hand, staff in lower status institutions are under equal if different pressures, have fewer resources or backing, and generally less research experience.

> It used to be UC Berkeley sociology department's boast, as a mark of its status, that it had never appointed a woman member of staff. The results can be read in the collected accounts of the experiences of the first women who gained their doctorates there (Orlans 1994).

To find out about the academic prestige of a particular department, you can look at its ranking on the RAE and the Subject Review (see pp. 16–21). Subject by subject scores are published annually in 'league tables' in newspapers, in the general guides for prospective students (such as those produced by the British Council and the *THES*: see p. 113), and they can also (and probably more conveniently) be accessed on the *THES* or the *Guardian* websites (www.educationunlimited.co.uk). Individual universities which score well usually include this information in their prospectuses.

While these 'performance indicators' do give some comparability across institutions and departments, based on evaluations by external 'independent' agencies, they were not designed for student use, and certainly not for prospective *research* student use – even if education ministers now speak of them as 'clear summative judgements for public consumption' (quoted *THES* 12 November 1999: 3). Rather, they are instruments for making universities implement government policy, without capital investment, in what has become an adversarial game (see pp. 18–21). Central government and its officials (through the HEFCs and the QAA), not student 'consumers', decide what is looked at and how quality is assessed; while the universities respond to constantly changing rules and increasingly frequent visitations with creative accounting, manipulation of data, and careful self-presentation. None the less do browse them, for they loom large in your supervisor's concerns!

There are other points to bear in mind when reading them, however. First, the focus of most newspapers and guides is undergraduate students. So many of the smaller graduate institutions (like my own) and research establishments, which have the best resources, many research students and might well be good places for you to study, are not included in many tables. If there are only around 97 institutions on a list, then it covers only large institutions with undergraduates.

Second, a central problem for research students is that the two audits precisely separate research and teaching, as if they were distinct activities. However, in fact the traditional universities dominate the top reaches of both tables.

Third, some versions of RAE tables aggregate the results from all the subject areas into an overall score for the university as whole. This may not reflect your discipline's standing. Some good universities have duff departments, and vice versa. This applies especially to the former polytechnics in large cities like London, Bristol or Manchester, which have long been able to recruit excellent staff – because they want to live in London, Bristol or Manchester. Some have a few 5* research ranked departments.

Fourth, the single subject RAE score itself is an aggregate of all the members of the department who are 'research active'. Plus it doesn't tell you if the department is getting stronger or weaker (unless you look at past scores and allow for the rules having changed and people having been bought in specifically to increase the scores). A reputation can rest on everyone being very good, or on a few 'stars'. It does not tell you much about the department as a centre and context for research, let alone for research students. But it does strengthen the position of some departments against others in that university, and the funding system means those doing well already are likely to be supported more in future too. Heads of department can decide not to 'count' some people if their 'research productivity' is low. A potential supervisor could be such a person – and demoralized because of this.

Fifth, after the results of the 1996 RAE appeared, a number of alternative tables were produced as vice-chancellors struggled to dream up formulae of ratings and research staff numbers which put their institutions higher up the rankings. Also some independent alternative versions have been produced which supposedly give a better picture. There is a league table of research funding (produced by the Higher Education Management Statistics Group, see *Guardian* (Higher Education) 6 October 1998: i) which compensates for universities' different subject specialities. (The sciences attract large amounts of funding and institutions with little science suffer because of this.) This puts four of the post-1992 universities into the top thirty research fund earners.

Finally, interpreting the Subject Review is even more difficult. First, because the QAA has concentrated on undergraduate and Masters provision (in the first instance) and has not (yet) included doctoral teaching in its inspections. Second, because the figures go out of date. (Sociology departments, for instance, were inspected in 1995–6 and had still not re-viewed by 2000. There have been lots of comings and goings in between. Education was hardly done at all until 2000 and so for years the one department which *had* been assessed appeared to be the only one judged 'good or excellent'.) Third, the commonly presented overall figure for each subject is an aggregate of marks (currently out of 4 for six separate areas, a total of 24, but changing). You need to find the disaggregated SR figures, because the scores for staff to student ratios; library, computer and facilities expenditure; and the quality of teaching accommodation *are* important to you, whereas the scores for undergraduate teaching and for Quality Assurance mechanisms are much less so.

Books and journal stocks in university libraries are in a parlous state, according to the latest figures released by the Library and Information Statistics Unit at Loughborough University . . . In the old universities, book expenditure per student fell in real terms from £57.05 in 1986–87 to £34.93 in 1996–97, a drop of 39 per cent. Periodical expenditure fell even more sharply from £131.19 to £57.91, a decline of 56 per cent. New universities had much lower levels of spending in 1986–87: £26.12 in books per student and £41.31 in periodicals, but even here expenditure has fallen to £19.15 and £16.27 respectively (27 per cent and 61 per cent)

> ... [The Labour] Government, which took office in May 1997, [gave] an
> enormous boost to school libraries ... [but] University libraries have
> not received that sort of assistance and are facing increasingly severe
> problems in meeting students' learning needs ... The contrast between
> provision at some universities and at others is very stark ... those uni-
> versities that are regularly shown to be achieving the best results, like
> Cambridge, Oxford and Imperial College, are also among those that main-
> tain the highest spending levels on their library collections ... Basically,
> universities are adding to stock less than two books per student per year
> and barely more than one periodical article. Local and remote electronic
> information systems are being introduced into university libraries but
> currently these amount to less than 10 per cent of spending and have some
> considerable way to go before they become ubiquitous ... The recent
> survey of student attitudes to books undertaken by the Council of Aca-
> demic and Professional Publishers indicated overwhelmingly they remain
> dependent on books and printed matter as the main tools of learning.
> (Advertisement by the Council of Academic and Professional
> Publishers, *THES* 28 May 1999: viii)

You might be well advised instead to use other indicators of prestige or
quality, such as whether or not a department is eligible to supervise students
holding research council grants (since they require rigorous assessment of
adequacy of provision of formal training; of arrangements for supervision;
the presence of a good research environment; adequate through-put of students; and satisfactory thesis submission rates); how many doctorates it
awarded last year according to HESA statistics; or by talking with professionals in the field that interests you and enquiring of the national professional
association for that discipline. If you visit the British Council abroad, they
may not tell you about the relative prestige of departments, since they represent the UK as a whole, but they will at least say which are the particularly
popular places among past students from your country.

Differences of ethos

Within disciplines, there are also differences between the culture or climate
of different departments. Each has its own shared assumptions, traditional
modes of thinking and behaving, and there may also be subcultures within
a department which are at war with each other. These envelop and shape
a student's graduate career. They are rarely studied in academe, though the
organizational climate has consistently been found to be associated with
job satisfaction and productivity in other workplaces. There can be variation in the extent to which members are integrated into the group – and

both doctoral students and women tend to be outsiders and most need a centrifugal pull. There can be differences in departments' theoretical allegiances and preferred types of methodology; in how much they focus on postgraduates as against undergraduates; and in the facilities they provide. (The last overlaps with differences between universities, see next section, but within one university different departments or research centres can have accumulated different resources.)

Some of these differences are attributable to the individual departmental research tutors and committees, who may choose just to supervise admissions and organize a cheese and wine party at the start of the academic year; or alternatively may try to establish an effective institutional focus for research students. This can include a buddy system for new research students; regular seminars and/or social meetings; joint outings to professional association meetings and conferences; perhaps even retreats – all of which enhance opportunities for students to get to know each other and staff, and to form networks and support groups.

Other differences relate to location. There are big differences between departments in cities, with large enrolments of part-time students with outside jobs; semi-rural campuses, where everyone lives in the same small town, and many research students have jobs connected with the university; and departments using new modes of delivery, including information and communication technologies where most learning is at a distance. Of course location is not determinate: sometimes in small towns students will band together for reading groups and seminars, while in others they are reluctant to do so for fear of seeming in opposition to the faculty and because of cultural norms of 'doing it on your own' and a strong sense of competition.

Finally there are differences in the absolute numbers of research students in a given department, and differences in friendliness towards (what are seen as the contributions of) women and international students. The term 'critical mass' often gets used to suggest that the number of active researchers, funded research projects and research students, and the degree of coherence in the departmental research programme, need to reach a certain scale to work well. However, discussions of critical mass are entangled with political pressures to concentrate postgraduate research training into 'centres of excellence' which get 3 and above on the RAE and have sufficient 'size'. Universities which would then lose their research students fight back because they don't want to 'fall' into being 'teaching only' institutions (see pp. 40–1). How important the 'mass' of a department is to you depends on the academic culture and mode of organization of your academic discipline. Research in the lab sciences does need large groups and a dense sequencing of generations and continuity of research to facilitate the repeated cascading down of intellectual capital and research problems to the students who pass through and are enculturated in it. Big money is required to sustain equipment and technicians and to pass on theory and practices. Size matters less in the social sciences and humanities, where there is more often a succession of one-to-one supervisory relationships. Here you might prefer to be in a small department and to feel 'special'.

We could also talk of a critical mass of *women* staff and students not being reached in some departments because of the gendered identity of the discipline (see pp. 66–7, 179–80). Accounts of other workplaces have shown how different the environment can be when there are just one or two women, as against say one-third of the staff women. A visible and strong women's presence can also ensure that departmental financial resources are equitably distributed, especially in the less well funded professional schools, humanities and social sciences; and that the mechanisms for distribution are 'transparent'. This could mean you are more likely to get financial support from the department to attend conferences, and encouragement to present and publish papers. Otherwise student 'stars' and faculty pets are usually men – especially in the physical sciences.

Where there is a sizeable number of research students in a department or lab, and a high proportion of women (and Black and overseas) students, it is also easier to establish peer groups and networks which can improve minority participation. Even though a high proportion of women students does not mean women will dominate seminars, or even that they will get an equal share of resources, there are still differences in the experience of being in a very small or in a moderate sized minority. It certainly helps to avoid the terrible visibility/invisibility of being, say, the *only* overseas or Black woman student. Being given special attention and put on a pedestal can be almost as difficult to cope with as being patronized, disparaged or ignored. High visibility often means being asked to speak on behalf of your group, to answer questions about anything that happens in your country or to be responsible for everything done by its government; to be the token on all the committees; or to catch lecturers introducing a mention of gender or homosexuals or your country or race only when they catch your eye in a seminar. All are ways of stressing that what people see when they look at you is, above all, your sex, sexuality, nationality or skin colour. It means you are never allowed to forget you are a woman or whatever. In such situations you find you constantly stand out , but equally your needs are never central to the main agenda. A 'critical mass' of women can mean our concerns are 'normalized'.

Similarly, the presence of a reasonable proportion of women on the staff with some in high positions is helpful to women students. The possibility of finding this varies a lot by discipline: only 8 per cent of all professors in the UK are women, but this ranges from 0 per cent in veterinary science and agriculture and related subjects, through 1.4 per cent in engineering and technology (14 out of 981!), to 19 per cent in education, 20 per cent in subjects allied to medicine and 29 per cent in librarianship studies. It also varies between universities: the worst have no women professors at all and nearly two-thirds less than 10 per cent. The best are post-1992 universities with small science departments: Robert Gordon, East London and South Bank universities with more than 30 per cent (HESA Staff 1997/98, in *THES* 28 May 1999: 21).

> Just 4 per cent of economics professors are women
> 11 per cent of readers and senior lecturers
> 17 per cent of permanent lecturers
> 28 per cent of fixed term lecturers
> 32 per cent of PhD students (Booth 1999).

What you should look for is not *a* woman on the staff to provide a 'role model' (though this is how it often gets expressed when appointments are being considered – and conversely it is said that 'we don't need another women' when there are already one or two). Rather, it is helpful for women students to have a range of women staff around, and ideally some with experiences of working in different cultures. These women teachers (and welfare advisers, counsellors, health and sports centre staff) also need *time* to be available to offer help, both when there is blatant misogyny and more routinely, when women students feel easier talking to a woman. But time is something they often do not have, because what they are expected to do pastorally is unrecognized and done routinely on top of their other workload.

The presence of a good body of women students and a large number of overseas students, especially of women students from one or two particular countries, and/or good provision for students in wheelchairs or with visual impairments, might seem 'selling points' worth mentioning in the brochures of appropriate universities. But they never are. So do *ask* institutions about the numbers and proportion of their women students, and about other facilities, and so help future generations by getting the importance of this recognized and supported. Post-1992 universities have generally a much better track record of providing high quality support. If British universities and governments were serious about providing what students want and need, gender and other specific needs would be taken into account – and existing women faculty would get run less ragged.

Differences between universities

When looking at possible places to study, there is now certainly no short-age of information – in individual institutions' advertisements, brochures, websites and videos, some of them wonderfully glossy; and in general government and commercial guidebooks and databases on CD-ROM. The former are of course (increasingly) advertising materials – sales documents – creating, promoting and distributing an education product for tangible returns (see pp. 13–14, 26–7). So 'read' advice in the context that it is no longer as disinterested as it used to be in the past; and find more independent sources to place alongside the full colour pictures of improbably sunny parts of Britain. This could include student union websites, which can be revealing (as can the ease with which you can/can't link from them to the university's official site!).

There has never been parity among universities in Britain (nor indeed in any other country) and as Chapter 1 (pp. 40–1) stresses, there is an increasingly graduated hierarchy, which is at base social class related (Halsey 1992). Britain has never had women's universities (unlike the USA) – only colleges within a few coeducational (formerly men's) institutions – and hardly any of these colleges remain single sex. 'Top' universities never seem that good when you are actually in them, and they may be snobbish to boot, but they do have kudos. There is also a great difference in size (ranging from 6000 to 15,000 students) and disparities in who they recruit.

There are currently striking differences in the student profiles of different HE institutions:

- 80 per cent of those going to Oxbridge, Edinburgh, Nottingham and Imperial College London come from middle or upper class families against 40 per cent of those going to East London, South Bank and Thames Valley.
- 70 per cent or more of first year undergraduates at Thames Valley and South Bank universities are mature (over 21) – but under 10 per cent at Bath University.
- 70 per cent of first year undergraduates at the London Business School and 67 per cent at the London School of Economics are from outside the UK against 3 per cent at the University of Derby. (The national average is 14 per cent.)
- 45 per cent of those at the universities of North London and East London are from minority ethnic backgrounds, against less than 1 per cent at the University of Plymouth.

Gender breakdowns are more consistent across the universities, though at some business schools and technological universities there may be only 20–30 per cent women, while 60 per cent of new undergraduates at Keele are women.

(*THES* 2 October 1998: 5; *Guardian* (Higher Education) 12 January 1999: iii)

You can do a doctorate in most of the universities in the UK, even though people commonly differentiate 'teaching' and 'research' universities.[1] (Half of all SERC research grants went to just 11 HEIs in 1989–90: Hogan 1994: 38.) But your choice is clearly not simple. How do you choose between a research centre with established areas of specialism in a low status (probably, but not only, a 'new' post-1992) university, charging lower fees (see p. 129), where the general facilities will be poor and the fabric tatty; and a more prosperous 'brand name' with many research students but different foci of interest? Especially since the former is also likely to have a higher proportion of women faculty, and Black and women students?

Graduate provision

The advantages of elite institutions lie not just in their reputations, but also in their resources. Oxford and Cambridge, Imperial, UCL and King's College London have incomes of £10,000+ per student, while Thames Valley and Luton universities have just over £3000 (*THES* 3 March 2000: 1). The former are based on past benefactions and current incomes from research and its spin-offs (patents, consultancies, science parks, and so on) and allow for such facilities as new laboratories and expensive equipment; specialized and copyright libraries; better staff–student ratios; more interesting visitors from abroad giving public lectures; wonderful sports facilities; subsidized accommodation; more computers and space given to research students; and post-doctoral fellowships in the humanities and social sciences as well as in the sciences. These can tide you over past the end of your grant while you complete and until you get a job.

To try to improve facilities in universities which don't have a history of postgraduate teaching, and to support the increase in graduate student numbers against the even greater increase in first degree students, the UK Council for Graduate Education (see p. 24) recommends a clear recognition that postgraduates have different needs from undergraduates, and that research students have different needs from those doing taught postgraduate courses. The former should not be subordinated to the latter.

> [M]any research students are seldom seen around their departments.
> [But] if all research students were to have at least part of an office and
> access to academic and common rooms, many would chose to raise their
> profiles . . . and, by increased participation, they will be offering more to
> their departments and university community . . . Many institutions are
> in serious danger of becoming commuter schools, with students coming

in only for lectures and the library and returning to their flats, halls and homes at all other times. Attendance at speaker meetings and social events is falling, as has the pride people take in being a part of the whole. This unravelling of sense of community is a large part of the 'isolation' . . . [which] is difficult to measure or remedy but [which] remains very much a problem . . . Some of this isolation is unavoidable, but research students are lone scholars only to a certain extent. The rest of our isolation is quite treatable, as it arises largely from neglect.

(Gross 1994: 23)

To counter isolation and keep up morale and general inspiration, research students need ideally:

- access to the building, computers and photocopier after hours to facilitate a working pattern of 52 weeks a year and 24 hours a day, and library and departmental facilities (and nursery and childcare arrangements) open during vacations and weekends, as this is when part-timers especially need them most
- courses to be repeated at varied times: in the evening and on Saturdays; plus some self-paced/contract and distance learning
- a research library (with single copies of many books and journals, not multiple copies of textbooks) and access to other specialist libraries; borrowing periods longer than is usually needed by undergraduates
- a home-base location in the university in which to work: an office, possibly shared, which is pleasant, well ventilated, not too crowded, with a desk, good chair, lockable filing cabinet, bookcase, and a telephone for local and research related calls, and a post box to make being accessed much easier
- postgraduate accommodation, including provision for couples, for children and for wheelchairs
- facilities to organize meetings or do some teaching, i.e. they need to be able to book and use departmental rooms and to have some way (say a pigeonhole and phone number) for other students to contact them (see p. 141)
- social common rooms in the department and institution wide, plus educational trips and talks and social events, so as to develop a postgrad identity and to mix staff and students to exchange ideas
- a postgraduate students' society or association and a postgraduate officer in the student union (with special concern for research students)
- university newsletters aimed at postgraduates
- specialist student support services: health, learning skills and counselling, and

- computing facilities for word processing and data analysis, email and using the web, with machines reserved for postgraduates (which do not get booked for teaching purposes) and access to software and printers, training to use the programs, and no hidden extras of massive costs per sheet for printing and photocopying.

Computing provision is probably worse than for most other resources, not just because of the increase in student numbers, but also because of the exponential increase in the variety and amount of work people want to do using computers, and younger students' familiarity with machines and software. Some universities are now putting computer access points in all students' rooms, so you can use your own machine there (but this can be isolating).

Above all, a department should not take on a student unless it is able to ensure that adequate facilities (be they scientists' need for lab space, expensive equipment which can have long delivery times, library resources, bibliographical and archival materials, expenses for fieldwork) are available to allow the student to complete the research.

A research student working in Australia on early women travellers discovered only late in her research the paucity of resources she had had previously, when she could finally make a trip to the British Library. She then had to fight with her university to get them to fund microfilming of several books. Should she have been allowed to undertake the topic in the first place?

Woman (and other) friendliness

The limited, liberal commitment to Equal Opportunities of universities in Britain (see pp. 32–6) generally consists of a policy statement (covering gender, race, disability rights), with a committee meeting irregularly, and occasionally a part-time officer – who is really only able to cope with casework, not to be proactive; together with tolerance of some teaching and research on women/gender (see pp. 180–3).

The UK is way behind the USA – though what was vibrant in the USA in the 1980s is now often routinized and depoliticized, or disbanded. However, in its heyday, a team lead by Florence Howe of the Feminist Press produced and published an *Everywoman's Guide to Colleges and Universities* to describe what would be ideal for women, and what was actually happening at different colleges.

Many US universities do still have a women's centre and an office of women students, with paid administrator or leader, running various events. These are recognized as important in attracting women to the campus. A survey by Charlotte Kunkel selected out a number of instances of good practice.

> The Women's Center at the University of Virginia seems ideal. Started three years ago by the director of the Women's Studies Program, the center has moved twice to larger spaces and its staff has increased from five mostly part-time to 22 paid staff in 1992 . . . A task force appointed by the President of UVA in 1986 to assess the environment for women at the university and make recommendations for improving their status, issued a final report in April 1988, that among other things, recommended that a women's center be established and funded, 'which would provide supportive services to female faculty, staff, students, and community members, as well as educate the University community about women's contributions to scholarship and the need for equality among women and men' . . . The entire philosophy promotes educating the community so that it will welcome women's changing status . . . Established for the 1989–90 academic year, the center currently publishes the journal, *Iris*, and a local newspaper, *In Our Own Words*, provides services and resources, promotes an artists and scholars series, and sponsors specialized task forces. Some specific programs and activities I thought impressive are a child-care referral, a legal clinic, a committee on women of color, a committee devoted to lesbian concerns, and a women's international network. Over 8,000 people are estimated to have been served in 1991–92 . . . The center, however, still has concerns about limited funding (their spending is estimated at $187,000, of which the University provides $126,400). They meet the additional expenses of their goals through fundraising, grant writing, donations, and shared departmental commitments.
>
> (Kunkel 1994: 23–5)

In the majority of UK universities, if you ask questions about the needs of women students or teaching on gender issues, you will be met with a blank stare, or aggression. There may (but will not necessarily) be verbal commitment to equity from the leaders of the institution, but there is no encouragement to routinely consider gender in course contents, no specialist counselling, no friendly woman to speak for you about course scheduling or accommodation problems, no concern with non-Anglo women's issues, no special mentoring, and no social programmes for women. At best you will be constantly directed to the women's studies programme and to named individuals. Which is to say, the issue is generally not taken seriously, most people do not know, and do not care, about it, and zilch resources are devoted to it. Indeed some women's units in student unions are even being closed because of opposition from religious fundamentalist groups.

A Nigerian student found she was required to share shower facilities with men. She hadn't realized this was a possibility before she came. When she asked if she could be moved to a room on a single sex corridor, she was told that she was old-fashioned and that she would find no one in Britain would support such an attitude any more. Even when the matter was pressed as an issue of religious (Muslim) belief, the warden of the hall of residence would not budge. Only when she hesitantly raised this in a seminar during her course, did she discover many British women would support her, and that this was an ongoing dispute the feminist faculty had been having with the hall in question for several years. She then extracted a promise from the warden that when another room became available, she would be moved, which took months to materialize. But she felt better having at least been given validation.

The best there is in the UK are a number of university research and teaching women's studies or gender centres, some with a paid director and a few attached staff, together with women's officers in the student unions. But these centres do not include formal positions for women's advocacy and they are only informally (voluntarily) central clearing houses for women's issues on campus. They may run special events for International Women's Day and Women's History Week and represent women's issues on university committees – and continue wearily to argue for woman and Blacks on governing bodies. They can sometimes offer information and referrals on women's health, childcare and rape crisis, and run courses on women and leadership. When there is an enthusiastic cohort of women or lesbian students, they may run safety campaigns (for safe places to study, to make a phone call, have lunch, park a car; for freedom from fear of assault, rape and harassment) and training programmes for support, health, porters and teaching staff on sexism and racism and/or produce a newsletter or a website of staff and research students with gender research interests. But this is all sporadic and depends on individuals and their time and motivation.

The Women in Higher Education Network (WHEN) was founded in Cambridge University but coordination moves around the country. It is a national network, spanning all sectors of HE in the UK and bringing together academics, administrators, students and support staff from all disciplines. It aims to further the position of, and to improve the climate for, women in higher education. It has held an annual conference since 1993 in different locations and also seminars around the UK, and published collections of papers from these meetings (Davies *et al.* 1994; Morley and Walsh 1995, 1996; Malina and Maslin Prothero 1998).

Britain is also well behind some other countries in provision and advocacy for overseas, disabled, and minority ethnic group students – so do similarly check each university's brochures and website, and ask questions if you go to visit. Do they have an international centre, not only dealing with international student's admissions, student exchange and study abroad, but also providing help with settling in, schools for children, where to find certain foods, and support for accompanying partners? Can they say how many other students have come from your home country and what they have done when they returned home? Can they put you in touch with any alumni to talk to before you leave? Do they have visiting and permanent members of staff from other countries? How good is the stock of books in the library in languages other than English and on countries other than the west?

It is particularly worth asking what efforts are made to introduce home and foreign students (and students with special needs) and to include formal teaching about other cultures (see also pp. 203–4). Just having different groups present on campus does not ensure contact: students tend to congregate separately, within their own ethnic groups and have only superficial contact. Mutual learning is more rhetoric than reality, and it is international students who tend to want more intercultural contact than British students. The latter may initially not be that interested. The institution itself needs to take positive steps to facilitate the rewards of symbiotic relationships. It must not only challenge negative stereotypes, but also develop the regular curricula and pedagogy to be sensitive and well informed, encourage equal status contact, monitor organizational processes, and establish tasks to promote cooperation. This requires involving and training both staff and student leaders (and both these groups should include non-British individuals) and using volunteers to help make accompanying partners and children feel at home.

Further reading

Experience of doctoral research in different disciplines

For physics, biochemistry, economics, sociology, history and modern languages:
Becher, T., Henkel, M. and Kogan, M. (1994) *Graduate Education in Britain*. London: Jessica Kingsley.

For biochemistry, artificial intelligence, earth sciences, physical and human geography, town planning, area studies, development studies and social anthropology:
Delamont, S., Atkinson, P. and Parry, O. (1997) *Supervising the PhD: A Guide to Success*. Buckingham: SRHE and Open University Press.
Delamont, S., Atkinson, P. and Parry, O. (2000) *The Doctoral Experience: Success and Failure in Graduate School*. London: Falmer.

For education and psychology:

Acker, S., Black, E. and Hill, T. (1994a) Research students and their supervisors, in R. Burgess (ed.) *Postgraduate Education and Training in the Social Sciences*. London: Jessica Kingsley.

Acker *et al.* (1994b) Thesis supervision in the social sciences: managed or negotiated?, *Higher Education Review*, 28(4): 483–98.

Salmon, P. (1992) *Achieving a PhD – Ten Students' Experiences*. Stoke-on-Trent: Trentham.

For sociology:

Allan, G. and Skinner, C. (eds) (1991) *Handbook for Research Students in the Social Sciences*. London: Falmer.

Hockey, J. (1994) New territory: problems of adjusting to the first year of a social science PhD, *Studies in Higher Education*, 19: 177–90.

Hockey, J. (1995) Change and the social science PhD, supervisors' responses, *Oxford Review of Education*, 21: 195–206.

Hockey, J. (1997) A complex craft: UK PhD supervision in the social sciences, *Research in Post-Compulsory Education*, 2: 45–66.

For political science:

Burnham, P. (ed.) (1997) *Surviving the Research Process in Politics*. London: Pinter.

Choosing a supervisor and developing the relationship

The websites of the research councils and universities' own handbooks include formal accounts of what is expected of supervisors (see also pp. 157–61).

Several of the books recommended in previous chapters give helpful advice:

Delamont, S., Atkinson, P. and Parry, O. (1997) *Supervising the PhD: A Guide to Success*, Buckingham: SRHE and the Open University Press, Chapters 1 and 2.

Graves, N. and Verma, V. (eds) (1997) *Working for a Doctorate: A Guide for the Humanities and Social Sciences*. London: Routledge, Chapters 1 and 5.

Phillips, E. and Pugh, D. (2000) *How to get a PhD: A Handbook for Students and their Supervisors*, 3rd end. Buckingham: Open University Press, Chapters 2, 8 and 11.

Supervisory styles

Cohen, D. *et al.* (eds) (1999) *Winds of Change: Women and the Culture of Universities*. Sydney: Equality and Diversity Unity, University of Technology. Well-produced two volume set of proceedings from an important conference, so possibly difficult to find in libraries. Worth seeking out for examples of innovative and 'feminist' supervisory practice in Section 9.

Johnson, L., Lee, A. and Green, B. (2000) The PhD and the autonomous self: gender, rationality and postgraduate pedagogy, *Studies in Higher Education*, 25(2): 135–47. Reports some of the findings from a three-year Australian Research Council project on the pedagogy of graduate supervision.

Pole, C. J. *et al.* (1997) Supervision of doctoral students in the natural sciences: expectations and experiences, *Assessment and Evaluation in Higher Education*, 22(1): 49–63. Based on interviews in nine universities with students and supervisors in physics, mathematics and engineering science.

Supervision for international and NESB students

Channell, J. (1990) The student-tutor relationship, in M. Kinnell (ed.) *The Learning Experiences of Overseas Students*. Buckingham: SRHE and Open University Press. Reports on research in two universities on what staff see as the 'problems' posed by overseas students and how they try to respond to them radically and positively in order to improve learning and teaching.

See also two previously recommended titles:

McNamara, D. and Harris, R. (eds) (1997) *Overseas Students in Higher Education: Issues in Teaching and Learning*. London: Routledge, Chapters 5 and 11.
Ryan, Y. and Zuber-Skerritt, O. (eds) (1999) *Supervising Postgraduates from Non-English Speaking Backgrounds*. Buckingham: SRHE and Open University Press, Chapters 3, 4, 6, 8, 9, 10 and 13.

Differences between universities and departments in Britain

You can find universities' self-presentations on their websites and in brochures, but for more objective and comparative accounts try some of the various annual handbooks or CD-ROMs to be found in public libraries or any British Council office abroad. These will tell you about the size, location and something of the history and culture of each institution, as well as the ratio of men to women, proportion of mature and overseas students, and their teaching and research ratings. But do recall the shortcomings of the various indicators (see pp. 99–101) and note that because most lists are undergraduate focused, they leave out many graduate institutions with excellent facilities and a large proportion of research students.

The Times Good University Guide (annual). London: Times Books/HarperCollins. Also available on the *Times Higher Education Supplement* website www.thesis.co.uk. Profiles only 97 universities and lists the 'top 20' universities for more than 40 subject areas.
The PUSH Guide to Which University (annual). Maidenhead: McGraw-Hill Publishing Company. This prides itself on offering the student perspective – atmosphere, entertainment, accommodation and sports. Researched by a team of over fifty recent graduates who visit every university campus.

Better to seek out the full lists in:

ACU (annual) *British Universities' Guide to Graduate Study*. London: Association of Commonwealth Universities.
CRAC (annual) *Postgraduate: The Students' Guide to the Development of Graduate Studies*. London: Hobsons.

If you are interested in gender, the Women's Studies Network (UK) produces a biennial national handbook on women's studies courses and centres, and has a website. Or see the Fawcett Library website http://www.lgu.ac.uk/fawcett.htm

Studying abroad

If you are thinking of studying abroad, help is available from most countries' cultural sections equivalent to the British Council. *Study Abroad* from UNESCO (1998/9) gives details of opportunities in all parts of the world and possibilities of financial assistance.

For study in the USA, see the rankings in *US News and World Report*. Washington, DC: US News and World Report Inc. (www.usnews.com/usnews), based on universities' resources, research activity, student selectivity, and two measures of reputation. Or see the National Research Council's survey conducted every ten years (which questions deans or top faculty practitioners and 5000 students in each field). Supplement these with the National Women's Studies Association's (NWSA) annual *Guide to Graduate Work in Women's Studies*. College Park, MA: University of Maryland (www.nwsa.org/grad2000a.htm).

For Australia, see the renowned annual publication by Dean Ashenden and Sandra Milligan, *Postgraduate and Career Upgrade Courses and Campuses*. Melbourne: Mandarin, which includes subject by subject information on graduate enrolments, greatest research student concentration and highest graduate overall satisfaction.

If you are interested in studying elsewhere in the EU, speak to a university's European Liaison Officer (or the Association of UK Higher Education European Officers – HEURO), supplemented by DfEE (1999) *The European Choice: A Guide to Opportunities in Higher Education in Europe*. Nottingham: DfEE. This gives brief details for each country on the organization of its higher education, admission and registration, level (tests) of required knowledge of the language of instruction, financial assistance and scholarships, entry and residence requirements, social aspects, and areas of specialization of all universities. It also has information on the European University Institute (Florence) and the College of Europe (Bruges).

Note

1 While the pre-1992 universities gave priority to permanent faculty (appointed to teaching jobs, even if they then give most of their attention to research activity), the reverse is true in some post-1992 universities. To try to improve their research rating, the latter have piled undergraduate teaching onto a few individuals and put any research money they received as a result of good scores on the RAE into 'releasing' the 'research active' and buying in new researchers.

4 | FINDING THE TIME, MONEY AND SPACE

Whatever the motivations for wanting a doctorate, the central problems facing any potential student are having or finding the time and money to undertake the work, and not only the research project itself, but also attending courses, seminars and conferences so as actively to participate in the research culture. If you do a doctorate full-time the problem is mainly money; if you do it part-time, it is time. Either way, there are also problems of reorganizing domestic life, and for many a change of location. Whichever comes first for you, finding a supervisor and university and issues of time, money and space are inextricably linked; and there are few more gendered phenomena than time, money and space.

As already noted, the training perspective has reinforced the idea that doctoral students should be like the idealized young lab scientist: able to work full-time on the research and to live on a grant, that is without a job and with no major domestic responsibilities, and so able to complete quickly. It hence has exacerbated some of the effects of gender since, as is widely recognized (except in relation to students), women's financial, time and geographical constraints are systematically different from men's. Students of both sexes experience enormous changes in their first year of graduate study if they give up a well-paid job, but for women income and job status are particularly important because we get little respect without them, especially in later life. Also our time and space are not unproblematically our own.

Everyone has to find within themselves ways of working on their own piece of research which both fit with the rest of their lives and – at least at times – bring about a sense of progress. All this is very difficult. The creative process is itself notoriously capricious. Most PhD students, additionally, have both work and family or domestic responsibilities, leaving only limited time and energies available for research. In the case of many women students in particular, there are often inner barriers against a confident claim to spend time on their personal work. Yet given that, for most students, their PhD project represents their first experience of independent research, it is at this stage that a personally viable mode of work needs to be discovered.

(Salmon 1992: 22)

Finding the time

Time for the thesis means cutbacks elsewhere

As stressed in Chapter 2 (see pp. 77–8), carving out the time to do a doctorate means some radical cuttings back. To find the equivalent of two days a week if studying part-time, or to maintain a steady pace in unstructured full-time study in humanities and social sciences, or to run experiments, means putting in the hours regularly every day (and sometimes at night). Don't think you can catch up with ten hours on Sunday. All possible aspects of employment, social life, voluntary or political work and domestic commitments have to go on the back-burner (though bubbling gently as you need support, and there is a life after the PhD). So anyone contemplating a PhD obviously needs the support of family, friends and bosses for substantial changes to relationships for somewhere between three and ten years.

So how to start? Initially just start. Just jump. Later on, if you find the going hard, you can try some time-management exercises (or go on a – short! – course).

Doing a day course on time planning is more fun and possibly more useful than reading a book on the subject (of which there are many) because it makes you set time aside to concentrate on the subject and to develop a plan of campaign. Either way it will include exercises to make you aware of how you actually spend time, what time is available (once you allow for travel, domestic life, job, exercise, etc.), and how to use the time which is available well, by cutting out your own particular 'time vultures'. It will also probably consider time management accessories, such as appointment diaries, electronic lists and other programming aids. Having done a course, you need to repeat the exercises from time to time, because we all slip back into old habits.

Start by assessing your existing work patterns – where does the time go?

- Use a time log.
- Recognize your displacement activities.
- Distinguish between the active positive tasks which achieve the objective of finishing the thesis from reactive tasks (the things that come across one's desk; requests to do things).

Identify your own barriers to effective use of time: external and internal

- What routines do you already have? Do they work?
- What is your prime time? Are you using it effectively? When do you feel tired or find your attention lapsing?
- How organized are you (your work space, your filing)? How much rubbish do you hoard?
- Do you filter phone calls via a machine in your prime time, and save your post and emails for when you are at a low ebb?
- Are there other, personal reasons why you are not getting the thesis done? Do you actually enjoy being a student (see also pp. 230–3)? Decide what can done about these blocks.

Get organized

- Set your priorities by classifying tasks as: important and urgent, important but not urgent, urgent but not important, and not urgent and not important, and ignore the last entirely (see also pp. 156–7).
- Establish realistic targets for specific periods ahead: the next day, the next week or two, the next six months. Develop better judgement about what you actually *can* achieve. There is nothing more depressing (literally) than never getting to the end of the list for the day, especially when the end of the thesis itself is so far ahead.
- Set aside blocks of time for active positive tasks and leave defined spaces for reactive things. Don't let the latter overlap into the former, thus allow just half an hour per day for your post.
- Use target completion dates as your own deadlines, rather than 'real' deadlines.
- Build in some slack since there *will* be some unforeseen activities which disrupt your plans.

Behave assertively

You need to make judgements and decisions about your own use of your time: to establish your own priorities and a timetable to suit *your* pattern. Put on your own pressures. Don't (only) react to other people. This will get you respect: people won't hate you. Compromise – don't give way.

Start by taking a couple of days to sort out your work environment

File and file again, cut back lists, throw out rubbish.

Domestic commitments

Research on adult (mainly undergraduate) students notes that 'family' rather than time clashes with 'professional activities' are the main constraint mentioned by both sexes. But most such research then moves on to focus on women with dependent children, in or out of relationships with men, and so overlooks other groups who also have specific problems – women with grandchildren or sick or elderly dependants, and young or older women on their own or in lesbian relationships (and also differences of circumstance between men).

> married women dart to class and to the library and then home to keep childcare costs down . . . But . . . the monetary costs of buying time may be far surpassed by the professional costs of isolation, including lost intellectual and informational exchange as well as lost opportunities to build useful networks of acquaintances.
>
> (Aisenberg and Harrington 1988: 43–4)

However, if we start with the 'normal' presenting issue of women with young children, then the literature suggests that although preschool children may be less keen, older ones can be proud of their mothers studying and become more independent: happy because their mother is happier, more committed to their own schoolwork, and more responsible at home. Also, arguably, academic life can combine quite well with childcare – better at least than some paid work. Combining employment *and* children *and* studying is, however, obviously more difficult, and universities' general lack of sympathy with childcare problems is probably well known to you from your undergraduate and Masters degrees, or your own past experience if you work in education.

Helen, a single parent, and others visited campus two weeks before the start of a new academic year to enquire about seminar times. On realizing that none of the times fitted with the school day, the women successfully negotiated with the Sociology staff to alter them. Joyce discovered that the culture of the Politics department was rather different. In making a similar request to change the time of her seminar she was told by a lecturer: 'we don't want to hear anything about child-care arrangements. If you can't fit in, just do not come.'

(Bourgeois *et al.* 1999: 127)

My own institution (which has only postgraduates) would argue that it has primarily to fit in with the needs of the majority of – employed – students, and so has to hold most research seminars in the evening or at weekends because we don't unfortunately have the staff to run the same course twice at different times – though we are trying to do this. Timing is perhaps less of a problem for doctoral than for other students, since there are few courses after the first year or so, and supervisions can be timed flexibly. On the other hand, some experimental sciences demand not only regular lab hours but also at some points in the project, visits during the night; some fieldwork involves long periods away; and in all subjects, much of the 'research culture' is build up outside of 9 a.m. to 5 p.m.

The actual provision of childcare within higher education institutions has certainly been very poor in the past and for years it was not an eligible use of central government funds. (Car parks were.) Ideally for research students childcare should be accessible 5 days a week, 15 hours a day (7.30 a.m. to 10.30 p.m.) for children from 6 months to 14 years, on an irregular basis. But many campuses manage just three regular days a week in the morning for 3–5 year olds. Some may want parents to volunteer x hours a week and costs can be substantial. There is also likely to be little public nursery provision available in the locality, since the UK is invariably in the bottom three European countries for childcare, and what there is is focused on children who are socially or emotionally deprived. For the rest you have to rely on your own resources with some help from the student union and advice from the university welfare office on the quality and entrance procedures for local private nurseries. There is almost no help at all with older children after school, children who are sick, or during half-terms and holidays.

An African student suggested not only that universities should give much more help by providing family accommodation and with finding children's schooling, but also that rents should include payments for 'babysitting' help at home in the evenings. Alternatively, she suggested student unions could organize paid childcare as a form of work for other students (such as under-graduates from abroad who otherwise do a variety of illegal work). She had noted that many women students save money for childcare by cutting back on food, which makes them susceptible to new diseases. She wanted better social support for students from cultures where women's social life is family based, including events over long public holidays. In her view, these are not optional extras for a difficult group of students, but necessities if this group is to prosper in their studies. Otherwise, she said, women just stay in their rooms.

Some men also may not be enthusiastic about the idea of their partners doing higher degrees and they can actually prove a bigger obstacle than children (see pp. 228–30). Some may enjoy, participate and even emulate your interests; but others who appear supportive can keep finding 'essential' extra things for you to do; and others may be (or become) strongly opposed. So too can parents and in-laws, especially where (as for international students) the issue is long periods away from home. Even liberal husbands who do not overtly contest the division of domestic labour or begrudge their wives' fees, may still pull the plug if they are not properly (including emotionally) serviced. Wives are more likely to support their husbands through the uphill struggle to complete a doctorate than husbands, who may threaten or instigate divorce.

There were those who delighted in [my] development and in my growing courage to express who I was, rather than merely to facilitate others. Others did not find it so easy, including my husband. On the surface, he actively supported my progress. But, sensing his gradual withdrawal, I would often express my concern that he was holding back things that could only damage us in the long term. I used to plead with him to be open, and not to let us go under for the sake of 'just a PhD'. He continued to assert that no, everything was fine. He continued to take the greater share of household tasks. But as he said to a friend, several months after we split up, he realised how much responsibility I had taken previously for the 'real work' of our relationship. During those last two years of the PhD, I was suddenly not there in the same way. And instead of allowing us space to work through what we were both experiencing in terms of our relationship, and to make informed choices about our future if that were necessary, he chose to find another woman on whom to lean. Who was just starting on her career.

(Salmon 1992: 61–2)

If you reverse the sexes in this account it is not impossible but certainly less credible, which makes clear the continuing difference of 'labour relations' between men and women in marriage.

Commentary on the family . . . has so emphasized the labour women perform 'for children' that at times it has virtually excluded the work they do for other family members and specifically for [husbands]. This . . . reflects both the dominant ideology of the family in the West today, which is increasingly child-centred, the commonality of experiences and problems households share in providing quality childcare, and the age group to which many . . . researchers belong, which makes them acutely conscious of childcare issues. It is also a middle class bias, for housework has been rendered invisible in the middle class home. It has gone underground, transmogrified into a 'leisure' activity, and 'positive learning experiences with children' during the 'quality time' their mother spends with them. The work which wives do for their husbands' occupations, for men's leisure activities, and for their emotional and sexual well-being, gets completely lost sight of [until it is withdrawn] because it is so varied, so personalized and so intimate.

(Delphy and Leonard 1992: 226)

Gill Dunne's study of same-sex partners with small children found the very contrary of the butch/femme stereotype which suggests that lesbians follow heterosexual patterns. Rather, all the couples she interviewed, and who also kept time diaries for her, sought a balance between employment and home lives for *both* the women. They welcomed their freedom to negotiate a relaxed and equal division of labour and, except where there was an extreme difference in their hours of paid work (30+ hours a week), the division of household chores was more or less equal. Since childcare was seen as a valuable job in itself, if either partner reduced their hours of paid work to do it, this was not seen to justify that person also doing most of the household chores. Moreover women's skills at noticing and anticipating emotional needs was an advantage in such situations. None of her informants reported they were doing any training (or a doctorate) – and maybe this was not seen as feasible when they had small children because, although they stressed the importance of both partners having an identity beyond the home, none of them justified long-term relinquishing of household responsibilities for long-term pursuit of employment opportunities. Indeed they often favoured both partners having part-time employment. On the other hand there was great flexibility in such relationships and being a birth mother did not predict one would be the one to do the childcare, nor that one would have the lower paid of the two jobs (Dunne 1998, 1999).

Even women without partners of either sex, and without dependent children, are still not 'free'. We are often seen as having all the time in the world and as being selfish if we don't spend it helping others. I have known many single women students in their twenties who have found themselves required to devote weeks to taking care of relatives who have come to London on holiday or to attend hospitals. Divorced older women can also get put upon.

> The family are supportive up to a point. They still do not help with the housework. It is a big issue in our house. I am constantly screaming and yelling but they just say, 'oh mum is psycho'. Nobody listens. I just get accused of being selfish if I try to make time for myself and my studying. It is a real battle to have time for myself. I just fall out with the kids most of the time to make my point. My eldest daughter had a baby last year. She moved out of the house after Christmas. She was coming back every weekend which I did not mind but it put pressure on me. She would turn up with the baby and come for a rest and it was giving me more housework . . . In the end I had to tell her and we had a big argument. I told her that she could not keep on doing this. I have got to find time to get my studying done. She did not like it, so consequently we hardly speak to each other. In her eyes I am a bad mother. She said some awful things to me and I want an apology. She said that I am not there for her.
>
> (Merrill 1999: 157–8)

Paid work

Common sense suggests, and research confirms, that it will take you longer to complete your doctorate if you continue in full-time employment, especially in a demanding job (see pp. 141, 230). But paid work does have its advantages: money obviously (which may buy you out of domestic and some routine caring responsibilities), but also access to resources (such as computational) and possibly useful contacts. You may be able to strategically choose a research area or topic which your employer would be willing to pay you to research, or at least to cover your fees and expenses, or which could attract funding from elsewhere. Moreover, doing a project for someone (for cash or time out) might look good on your CV. Or you could take on a new job locally and turn this (or your existing job) into a base for a research project. This is particularly likely to be possible with professional doctorates – it is partly what they are about – and also favoured by the various partnerships developed by the Department of Trade and Industry (DTI), DfEE and others and administered through HEFCE, such as 'HE Reach out to Business' or the Community Fund (HEROIC).

If you do continue to work full-time, try to buy yourself some time out for some periods (or to cover some of the rest of your income if you work part-time) by getting some small grant money (see pp. 142–4) or by being adamant that research is part of your role and that you should have staff development funding for it. Make an EO issue out of this (especially if you have a job in the education sector), citing reports on how a pattern of not getting small grants handed out in a grace and favour way systematically disadvantages women. Also that junior women have less control over work demands than men and so have to work as long or longer hours than their colleagues – and this lack of time to prepare major research grant proposals holds women back. Point to your job experience as an indication of your project management and budgeting plus writing and access skills. And watch the men to get smarter at ducking aspects of your job, which sometimes means just not volunteering for them. Failing that, set your priorities and take time off, including unpaid leave.

Finding the space

Location

If you are a part-time student you may feel you have little choice where you study: your university has to be conveniently nearby or within commuting distance. Similarly if you are relocated to a particular city because your partner is posted there, you may think it sensible to study close by, especially since some universities now encourage partners to study, especially spouses of PhD students who are present for long periods, so as to help the adjustment and domestic stability of their students and also to increase their student numbers.

Most 'accompanying spouses' are women. Moreover, women have only had the same legal rights as men to have their spouses and dependent children accompany them under UK immigration restrictions since 1995. The requirements remain stringent, and same-sex partners are not recognized. This is reflected in sexist elisions of 'students' with men, and 'wives' with 'non students' in the literature, and uncritical acceptance of men's accounts.

A large proportion of the [overseas] students surveyed [at Nottingham and Loughborough universities] were married and had families, and many of them wished to have their partners and families accompany them to Britain, especially research students who would be resident for more than one year. However, both universities advised against this due to a lack of suitable accommodation . . . Some male students found they had difficulty in catering for themselves and had sent for their families so that their wives could undertake time-consuming domestic chores. [However] Wives were lonely and isolated, often with no English and with young children obstructing the opportunity to learn, [so] male students found themselves solely responsible [*sic*] for shopping, overseeing schooling, rent arrangements, transport, medical matters and similar, all interfering with studies.

(Lewins 1990: 92–3)

Constraints on women travelling alone, and expectations and social pressures to remain with their families, have been stressed as key reasons for the small numbers of foreign women coming to Britain to study at graduate level in the past. Certainly the requirement for mobility for the long periods required for a PhD used to, and can still, present invidious choices for women who are forced to choose between marriage or higher education, and/or between studying overseas or remaining with elderly relatives and young children; and this can hit those from poorer countries and backgrounds hardest, since return trips to these countries are usually more expensive and they are also the ones most affected by immigration restrictions and grant limitations.

But even if you are not free to chose your location, there are often several possible universities to choose between in urban centres; and if you are prepared to do some travelling, you can look further afield. Especially if you are doing a humanities or social science degree, you may find you need make the journey only one day a week or in blocks, and that you can get access to another nearby library, or borrow books from your 'home' library by post or access them through the worldwide web. (But note pp. 162–72.) The concern to increase overseas student numbers and the increasing availability of information and communication technologies has meant alternative modes of delivery are being considered, and universities are changing their previously rigid residence requirements. While it helps to spend some time physically in the university, some courses may be delivered by video conferencing, some supervision may be by email, student contact can be continued through teleconferencing and internet chat rooms, and there may even be some alumni conferences organized in your home country. Flexible course delivery has been shown to attract women at first degree level, not only because of location but also because the pacing of study makes it easier to get the necessary family and cultural support mechanisms in place (especially before travelling overseas), and also if there are several exit points with a qualification. We need to make women's voices heard more in such debates at postgraduate level too.

Despite its problems . . . the [United Nations Educational and Training Programme for South Africa] has qualities that approximate the ideal scholarship programme . . . students study predominantly in low-cost Third World countries [not necessarily their own]. The result is that more students benefit from the allotment than would be the case if they were to study in high-cost countries. Furthermore, the majority study in environments that approximate the life conditions of the vast majority of fellow citizens in their home countries. The latter offers the opportunity to consider ways and means by which social, economic and political problems can be studied and possible solutions considered. Alienation is kept at a minimum. The multilateral character of the programme with its scattering effect minimizes the magnitude of a single-country influence over an inordinate number of student participants. Ideal scholarship programmes should reflect mutual understanding and respect between the parties concerned.

(Nkomo 1989: 140)

Even if you are a home student and planning to study full-time, you may still want to live in or close to a particular place so as to remain in contact with friends, partner or family; to be in a place where you can get part-time work; or because of what the city (or local countryside) has to offer, be it theatres or access to the Lake District. Alternatively, you may want to be where there is a comfortable, sizeable, visible population of your particular ethnic or sexual group. On the other hand, you may be one of the women who positively welcomes travelling to a new place to study – as perhaps the only available or acceptable opportunity for such travel – whether for personal growth or to escape home pressures (which can include not only pressures to marry, but also to escape a previous relationship or to re-enter the mainstream after a past life involving illegal activities).

Accommodation

For research students it is especially important to have a space where you work regularly. You may be able to have a shared office or workbench in the university, but if at all possible you should also have space at home, especially if you are working in the humanities and social sciences.

David Sternberg (1981) argues strongly that you should set up a base organized exclusively for the project, not only for practical reasons but also to demonstrate the change in your social and psychological priorities. He stresses it doesn't have to be luxurious, but it must be private. Ideally it should be a separate room devoted to thesis matters. Failing that, it can be a space carved out of a bedroom or sitting room or top of the stairs, using some sort of room divider (bookcases or a screen). Everyone else in the household must stay out of it during your dissertation working hours. You do not want to be interrupted, especially not when work is not going well and you are wandering around or easily distracted. It is essential also that it is not used for many other office purposes (marking pupils' homework, paying bills, or for children to use email). You must be able to leave work out between sessions without risking a file getting lost, and not have other work on hand to deflect you. If you already have a study, he advises having a separate thesis corner, with a table and files devoted to the dissertation (Sternberg 1981).

Such space is especially important for women, even if it is less available to many of us as women because, if we share accommodation with family members, we are expected to put our husbands' 'needs' first, our children's second and our own interests last. If space is limited, you may think you have to work on the kitchen table or in a spare room – to which you lose access whenever there is a visitor. Having Virginia Woolf's famous *Room of One's Own* can mean making children share a bedroom for a few years, or not having guests to stay – but maybe that is what it takes. Since it is normally a woman who is responsible for 'keeping the house quiet' while others are working, having a door which can be shut, and even locked, is really helpful.

> The Brontë sisters may have written great novels, but it was their brother who had the study. The women in the family had to clear their books off the dining room table for every meal.

The privacy of the office signals to you and to others that they must respect the importance of your new independent project; that it *is* a new project; and that when you are engaged with it, you are single-minded. It will always be waiting for you when it is your scheduled time for work or when you feel you want to put in some extra hours. There are no diversions for you there: you are up against the task. All you need in it is a good sized desk, one or more bookshelves, a computer with ideally a modem and a printer, a filing cabinet (building up files is essential to organizing yourself), possibly a small tape-recorder or dictaphone (so you can record ideas at any time of day; or if you are stuck, so you can record yourself trying to explain your ideas to someone else; or to take notes when reading) and/or a whiteboard and pens. It is also a bonus if it has got a pleasant view, is nicely decorated, and has good music. But provided the room is private and exclusive, doing it up elaborately can be a displacement activity (Figure 4.1)

If you are moving home to study, then your choice of housing is especially important because, as a research student, you are going to be living in it for some years and will spend more time working at home than an undergraduate. (As a woman, you will probably spend even more time there than a man student would.) Obviously, living close to the university saves money on fares *and* time, and you may want to go into the library or labs at odd hours. But if this means living on a campus away from a town centre it can get very claustrophobic during term and isolated during vacations (when external conferences dominate). Moreover, some student accommodation (whether rooms in student halls of residence or shared houses in student 'villages') requires you to move out during the summer vacation so it can be rented to higher paying guests. This is energy and time consuming. On

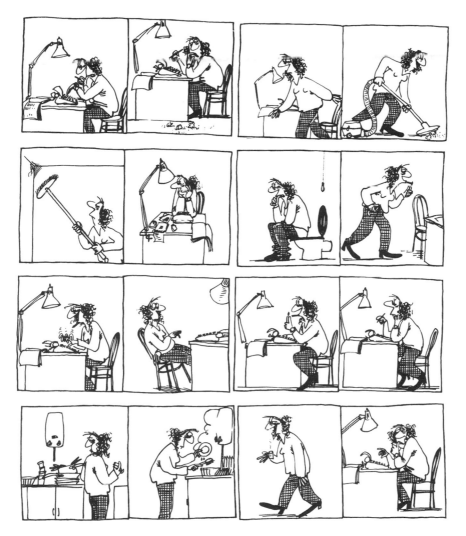

Figure 4.1 'Creation', cartoon by Claire Bretécher
© Claire Bretécher and *Le Nouvel Observateur*

campus it is also hard get away from work-related people and venues, especially if you are reliant on public transport. There is little choice of places to
eat, and relatively expensive supermarkets. Halls of residence may be good
initially, until you have made some contacts, but equally you may meet
mainly overseas students and the price may include meals which turn out not
to be to your taste. You do want to be able to do some of your own cooking

– and to be able to get appropriate ingredients – since a complete change of diet can itself be a source of stress. In any event there is certainly a lack of good university provision and a real shortage of family accommodation for students in all British universities.

> A student from Malaysia said she chose accommodation in a student hall of residence so as to have contact with people, but she found the relationships unstable.
>
> They can be close, but they come and go. I thought one or two were friends, but it stopped as soon as they left. As a woman I'm learning a [new] way to socialize with people here. At home I know when to start and stop and how to get along with my friendship. Here people think you are easy maybe. There is the barriers of my language also – how to express myself. My character may seem quite different from back home: how people may see me.

Your university welfare office and/or your student union or postgraduate student society should have an accommodation officer (and an adviser to overseas students) who can help you find somewhere to live in the area and give you an idea of the range of provision and rough costs you are likely to incur, for example what is a reasonable rent if you share with other students. But you'll find that universities see themselves as having fairly limited responsibilities in this area, especially for research students. They should, however, have leaflets on safety issues (such as those supplied by the NUS Welfare Unit) covering everything from landlords' responsibilities for annual checks on gas appliances, through getting household insurance against the distressingly frequent burglary of student accommodation, and how to use Victim Support if you have emotional and practical problems after such events. These leaflets may, but more likely will not, specifically mention issues for women students – like how safe it feels walking around a district you are considering living in at different times of day and night; not going to look at flats on your own or without telling someone where you are going; making sure there are good locks on doors and windows; and renting with other women students for security. If you do have difficulties later, your student union welfare officer can also represent you in a small claims court regarding evictions or harassment or repairs not getting done. If you have problems with sexist or racial harassment by landlords you can call the Commission for Racial Equality or the Equal Opportunities Commission. Discrimination against gay men and lesbians is not illegal, and it is hard to get action on lesbian-bashing, but you can get advice and support from Lesbian and Gay switchboards. Other alternatives are lodgings – living with a family, and getting some meals included – and living with relatives, which may be unbearable, but it can be supportive and cheap! The cost of living in many northern, Scottish and Northern Irish towns is up to 50 per cent cheaper than in London and the south of England.

Finding the money

Last but not least, can you get a grant? Can you face living on the low income a research council grant gives you for three or more years? Can you be self-funding (or family funded)? Alternatively, can you live on Social Security benefits? Or 'work your way through college'? Let's look first at the likely costs and then some possible sources of income.

Costs

At undergraduate level, charges for UK higher education are a rigged market (see pp. 11–12) and the fees that all universities have charged for similar types of courses have been the same (though this may change). At postgraduate level, on the other hand, universities have been free to set their own 'home' and 'overseas' fee levels, and there is considerable variation. So check the fees in all the places you are considering. You do get roughly what you pay for, if not in quality of supervision then in resources and prestige. But remember, fees may change (increase) over time (and will vary for international students if your home currency goes up or down against the pound), so budget for some fluctuation. The gap between the cheapest universities and the most expensive widened in the late 1990s, and fees increased 10 per cent from 1998 to 1999, at two or three times the rate of inflation. Fees for part-time home (and EU) students are markedly less well below half those of full-timers. But even the lowest – those for part-time, home, arts research students – are still likely to be around £1000. And there may be additional fees in certain heavily resource dependent or prestige subjects like medicine and business.

Studying full-time at a medium cost university in a medium cost part of the UK will cost around £8000 to £13,000 per annum:

fees	£1500 for a home student, £6000 for an overseas student
rent	2300
heat and light	600
travel	400
books and paper	200

clothing	250
food	2000
personal	1500

£8250 but, unlike the USA, few medical costs.

On top of this, as noted in Chapter 2 (see pp. 78, 126), you should allow for the cost of a computer, books, postage, phone and stationery, and perhaps a tape-recorder. You may be able to borrow some or all of these (and other equipment like video recorders and transcribing machines) from the university, but only for fixed periods, which may well be inconvenient. There can also be lab costs or fieldwork expenses, which may (or may not) be covered by the project you are working on, and travel costs. You should also budget for going to conferences (see pp. 151, 169, 244) since these are an important element in becoming a member of the disciplinary culture. Academic meetings usually offer cheaper rates to students, but they are still expensive – say £200 for registration plus accommodation, plus travel. If your grant covers these it is an important 'hidden' benefit. You should also not skimp on childcare, because you need undisturbed time.

Ingrid Moses (1990: 35) argues that mature women students in particular really need to have scholarships or study leave from their employment so that they can study full-time, and to have money in these grants for the care of children under 12 years of age. Otherwise graduate study is difficult if not impossible. However, a colleague at the Commonwealth Secretariat suggested to me that

> There is a worrying trend amongst many donors arising from general funding cutbacks. The argument goes that if we reduce the allowances then you can maintain current numbers or even increase the flow. Of course the allowances which are generally first to go are for spouse and children. This impacts, of course on the male, but it's worse for the female. If she can't take her spouse/children she may not want/be able to take up the scholarship. And if she does take the scholarship, particularly if she is a mature age student, she may encounter [other demands on her time which] could manifest in not finishing studies on time and we try to take this into account when dealing with requests for extensions . . . (By the way every extension, of course, reduces the pot of available scholarship money so there is a good argument that taking away family allowances is a false economy and counter-productive anyway.)

Possible sources of income

Unlike undergraduate courses, there is no statutory entitlement to financial support for UK students for any postgraduate study (except teacher training). The differences between science and engineering, and humanities and social science doctorates already noted (pp. 61–4) include differences in the funding needed to conduct projects (for equipment and consumables) and in the number of grants and salaries available for research students. In SET, it is relatively easy to get a research studentship and in some cases (for example on Wellcome Foundation funded projects) research students receive an income equivalent to starting academic salaries. Whereas in the latter two, even modest sums for research are hard to come by and there is fierce competition for awards. Even getting one's fees paid is a huge advantage. So while the first possibility to consider for UK domiciled (and to a more limited extent, other European) students are research council studentships, you should also look for individual universities' studentships and bursaries, for studentships attached to projects or employer's grants and awards, and at support from NGOs and charitable trusts. You will find advertisements for such sources in the *THES* and the weekly education supplements of the *Guardian* and *Independent* (and their websites) from mid-February onwards, but the advertisements can be rather confusing. Universities are each touting for the best doctoral students for their own programmes, and when you enquire, you may find what they are proposing are scholarships they *will help you apply for*, not ones they are free to give. Some of the more wealthy universities do, however, have their own bursaries – but then the question is, are they really open to all?

Consequently, less than a quarter of 'home' postgraduate students hold an award and the majority of women students rely on personal savings or their parents and/or partner, and opt for part-time registration combined with paid employment for support – if not at the start, then certainly in the later stages of doing their doctorates. This applies *a fortiori* when theirs is the pay cheque which is vital to a household: where women are on their own, or their partner is low earning, or they are single parent and/or have other dependants.

Funding for non-EU students is also very limited and generally 'development'/overseas aid related. However, without such support most students can't contemplate study in the UK – so not surprisingly, nearly half of such postgraduate students have a scholarship or grant of some kind from their own government, or their employer, or UK funding. This is one important reason why there are more 'overseas' men students than women.

The quotation from Ingrid Moses (1990) in the previous box argues women student need grants to replace their domestic responsibilities. I would add, they need them *more* than men, not only because they have greater domestic responsibilities, but also because research on the sociology of the family shows women (throughout the world) do not have the same right as men to call upon 'family' money for their own 'personal' spending.

Whether you get a grant or not, you may want also to pick up some casual or hourly teaching or research within the university, as much for the experience and to put it on your CV as for the money. It is worth also looking for small grants for specific expenses from professional associations and charities; again both for the money and for the kudos.

I'll say enough about each of these sources of income, and about employment in academe and loans and social security, to give you a flavour. But in this area things change quickly and it is essential both to know the current situation and to read the small print. So seek advice from specialists. Many universities have financial advisers (and there is a national Association of University Financial Advisers), or, if you are living outside the UK, ask the British Council for help and they will know of any awards from your own country's government. In addition, try to find and talk to students who have already got money from these various sources and ask them how they did it. The NUS also produces useful advice sheets. Supervisors may or may not be helpful on this score. But whomever you ask, if you are not happy with the answers or confident of the person, do try again. Be convinced you deserve financial assistance, and persevere in your efforts.

Research council scholarships

There are now effectively seven research councils (see p. 19), covering all fields of academic inquiry. To be eligible for an individual studentship you will need to have a first class or good second class honours degree from a UK university, and you need to have been resident in the UK for the previous three years (not just in the UK to study). EU nationals who don't meet the residence requirements can apply for a 'fees only' award. In addition there are a number of special schemes, such as CASE (Collaborative Awards in Science and Engineering – including social sciences) with the public, private and the voluntary sector, and PTPs (Postgraduate Training Partnerships in SET) with currently funding for one hundred a year.

The systems for applying for studentships vary and you need to check with the relevant council. The Engineering and Physical Sciences Research Council allocates the majority of its studentships directly to departments (based on an algorithm of the EPSRC research grant income to the department) and the departments nominate the students they want to take on. Academics can also apply for research studentships to be attached to project grants and they make the appointments to these posts. You therefore need to locate an appropriate place (possibly using the ESPRC research grants portfolio analyser) and apply directly to the department. The ESRC's individual studentships, on the other hand, are directly competitive and the actual procedure for applying is complex and time consuming. You have to apply through the department where you want to study, which must be approved by the council for the receipt of awards – and by no means all are. (It depends on the quality of the methodology teaching they provide and their PhD completion rate: see pp. 22–3, 41.) It helps to have postgraduate study experience (a Masters or to have done some research part-time and self-funded) and you must include a well-thought-out research proposal and supporting statements from your potential appropriate supervisors. It is quite likely a department won't support you unless they think you have a good chance of success, because of the work involved for them and because they get criticized by the councils if they put in weak candidates. But, conversely, if you do get such a grant it is good for your CV and for the university, so you may get some preferential treatment. Once you have an individual grant, you can move and take it with you (subject to the ESRC's agreement) if you don't like the institution after all, or discover a tutor you prefer, or if your tutor moves university.

In 2000, the EPSRC website shows it allocated 1220 standard research studentships to departments, 45 attached to special schemes and others attached to research projects. In addition it funded 100 EngDs.

The ESRC website, in contrast, reported that its studentship competition had 1161 eligible applications and made 541 offers.

The science research councils provide only 17 per cent of the awards available to research students, whereas the ESRC provides 44 per cent of those in the social sciences (NPC 1995b).

Studentships attached to projects and employers' awards

Most science and engineering students join a team working on a funded project. This may be a directly funded contract; or one of various schemes of collaborative research between one of the research councils and industry or commercial research establishments (in which case you probably get some extra money from the external partner on top of your grant). Alternatively it may be for 'collaborative research' associated with a particular university department's established ties with industry, where a student works in the commercial organization and registers for an MPhil/PhD, subject to an agreement between the university that they will conduct research for a substantial part of their time and be released to visit the university for the rest. In the last case, a supervisor is appointed in the organization in addition to the university one, and the organization, its facilities and the topic for research have to be approved by the university prior to registration. Some arts and humanities, and many of the business departments in post-1992 universities (the former polytechnics) also have similar research links with local employers.

If you work in science and engineering or local government, or for the health service or a new university, your employer might also be willing to pay your fees for part-time study more informally, either from the staff development budget or if you do research which is useful to them. This might apply especially to work for a professional doctorate that includes research on a problem which needs solving. Or if you were really enterprising and have some past research or consultancy experience, you could look at the worldwide web (including the *THES* weekly listings of 'research opportunities'), or the local press for invitations to tender, or follow up personal contacts, and suggest doing some research for a funder, while you register for a doctorate.

A colleague, who as an LEA advisory teacher had written resources for careers education in school, later got a job in a university education department and wanted to do a research degree. She was approached by a charitable foundation on the basis of her past work, and asked to do a study of Black high achievers as the basis for a popular book. This involved considerable time and travelling, but she was later able to use the data she collected as the basis for a PhD.

EU funding

There are some funds available for research students from EU sources, but these are not easy to tap into. The programme 'Framework 5 for Improving the Human Research Potential and the Socio-Economic Base' allowed networks of universities in several different member (and associated) states to bid for funds to establish research links to promote training-through-research. These could include pre- and postdoc level training (for individuals under 35) within the frame of collaborative research projects. If there is an appropriate project network in your field, you might be able to travel to the UK to join a team or go to one in another country. Alternatively, you might be able to get money 'to study techniques and make contacts' in the UK, especially if you come from a part of the EU where there is as yet little by way of research infrastructure. However, arrangements change from time to time and you need to check specific and up-to-date information with a European Liaison Officer in a university (or through HEURO, see p. 114). This is a long shot, but worth investigating.

Women's International Studies Europe (WISE), supported by Dutch government departments and the EU, has produced a useful booklet by Margreet van Muijlwijk (1999) on *Funding and Private Resources for Women and Gender Studies*. This has helpful chapters on the skills of getting grants, knowing where to look, foundations and their typologies, perspectives for women, and 'life after the application'.

British government grants and awards

Those domiciled outside the EU cannot apply for UK research council grants (unless they have refugee status), but there are specific Department for Education and Employment, Foreign and Commonwealth Office and Department for International Development funds, some of which may cover students wanting to undertake postgraduate studies, including research, in the UK. These are relatively generous. They want especially to encourage students from low to medium income countries, and (as noted on p. 37), they have to a considerable extent taken on board feminist concerns and World Bank arguments about the importance of the role played by women in developing countries. Following research on *why* women were so under-represented among those travelling to Britain for training, they now routinely monitor by gender, and officials may require women to be among those nominated for grants. They have also begun to tackle some of the specific problems for women students, such as visa restrictions, allowances for (women's) dependants, and adequate cover for childcare. In my experience they are also helpful if students need to go home in an emergency, such as illness or death in family, or following national disasters (earthquakes, war, bombs, coups).

Although 'domestic restrictions' are the usual reasons cited for the smaller number of women among overseas students, there are also a number of academic and 'employment and international relations' related reasons. These include:

- Women's low representation in education generally in a number of countries.
- The priority the British (and often the home) government gives to project-related training: the tendency to offer postgraduate scholarships in the

sciences, technology and engineering, agriculture, veterinary, forestry and other 'development' subjects as part of the British overseas aid effort.

• Candidates being selected from among the employees of institutes and government administrative departments. This militates against women who have less opportunity for public sector employment and difficulty in achieving senior or specialist technical jobs and/or a long service record.

• Perceptions by those in authority that women are a 'poor risk' for awards.

• Women not receiving information about training availability.

• The fact that British agencies do not themselves 'nominate the people for awards, for that is up to the Government of the Country (GOC) concerned. The British can only make known their interest that GOC should consider nominating more women for awards' (Holden 1988; Threfall and Langley 1992: 28).

The available grants include: British Council Fellowships, British Chevening Scholarships, Commonwealth Scholarships and Fellowships and Overseas Research Students Awards – the last give just partial fee remission (you will be charged only the 'home' fee asked by that university in that field of study).

Individual universities' studentships and bursaries

Many universities or departments or colleges have a small number of studentships or bursaries. These are usually advertised in the national educational press and therefore technically subject to open competition; but my sense is most go to insiders (especially in Oxbridge). They vary enormously. Some are limited to a narrow range of disciplines or to students from particular countries, some only 'waive' fees, some are only for part-time study, or to provide board and lodging, or just for books. But some are like research councils' grants, with the advantage that they can continue for more than three years. The wealthier the university (or Oxbridge college), the more such studentships they are likely to have.

These scholarships may help some worthy students, but their main purpose is to cream off the very best candidates and more generally to act as 'loss leaders': to encourage people to apply, or to start to think of that as a possible place to study. If you get such a grant, you will of course have to study at (and so to move to) that institution; and if the grant is attached to a specific area of interest, you will also be limited in your choice of topic. Do check also if/how much teaching is required as a condition of tenure of any studentship, and the hours, pay and nature of the teaching. You don't want to end up with what is effectively an underpaid teaching assistantship (see pp. 139–41). Where institutional studentships or bursaries are open to overseas students, the fees may be paid only at the home rate, so you might have to make up the difference.

Employment in academia

It may be possible to get a job as a research assistant or a teaching assistant in a university and do your own research alongside. Sometimes this is a way for universities to attract good candidates who otherwise couldn't afford to do a PhD, and it may be easier to get appointed to such a job than to get a research council grant. But, cynically, with the massification and marketization of higher education, it is more often a way to get good researchers for projects, and cheap, casual teaching, often with minimal support for the workers and little concern for their career development. It has yet to become as established, organized and regulated as 'working one's way through college' in North America. British postgraduates face a wider range of different working conditions and opportunities.

Colleges in the USA offer under- and postgraduates help in putting together a financial package to cover all or part of their costs. These are very varied. At first degree level, there are expensive private schools (two-year colleges) and private four-year colleges and universities, as well as state community and junior colleges, state colleges and state universities (with enormously varying costs). Middle class parents will normally expect to make provision and help with their children's education – which is a tax deductible expense. The financial package to supplement this, and for those from poorer backgrounds, can involve:

- US (federal) loans – direct or guaranteed at a bank; and grants based on financial need (so called Pell Grants) and state grants which must be matched from other sources.
- Work-Study, a federal employment programme that pays students an hourly rate for work done on campus or in local non-profit enterprises.
- Cooperative education, where students work during terms or in the evenings, in a job related to their major, and get credits for it.
- Also some input from the local college or university, depending on its resources, its philosophy about supporting poor students, and how it interprets federal requirements (the budgets given to state colleges vary, local costs of living vary, the school's expenses vary, and fees vary for local residents and outsiders).

For graduate schools, there are loans, scholarships and grants from private organizations and foundations. Again, the graduate school will help design a package which may include a fellowship or a job obtained through the student's department; and for years the USA has used postgrads as teaching assistants (or graduate student instructors) for undergraduate teaching (tutorials, first year marking, demonstrating in science, and to support students with special needs) and as research assistants (RAs) or graduate student researchers (GSRs). While there are complaints about departments not necessarily being even handed, or about blatant favouritism in the allocation of such work (see pp. 166, 227) , and there have been struggles over pay and student unionization (see pp. 28–9), there is usually plenty of such work available – though graduate students expect to end up with very substantial debts to pay off.

Working as a research assistant

Short-term research posts are advertised regularly in the education press. They place you as a salaried member of staff, on a higher income than you would get on a research council grant, and (it is hoped) with office space, computing and admin support, attendance at some conferences paid for, and full departmental membership. Tuition fees are usually waived if you register in the same university.

However, in the humanities and social sciences, most research assistantships are for from six months to two years to work on a particular project. (This is part of the increased tightness of funding referred to on pp. 9–12, 40–3.) You will usually have to work full-time on the project to which you are appointed, though you may be allowed/be able to negotiate one day a week for your own research. However, many find the project research so demanding that it leaves no time at all for their own work; and you would need to secure work on more than one project sequentially to give enough time to complete a doctorate. Each will advertise and recruit independently so this route is financially insecure. You will also have no choice in the university you go to, nor in the research topic you are paid to work on – though you are unlikely to be appointed if it is not 'in your field'. In the sciences, the tradition of team working and the greater availability of funding mean that it is easier to work on a project for the whole length of the (usually shorter) doctoral period, and it is more accepted that you will have part of the project cut out as the basis of the work for your own PhD. There are thus fewer tensions between your project director and your supervisor for your time. However, either way, if you are looking to a future academic or policy research job, such paid research experience alongside your doctorate would give you an excellent start, especially if your name is included on the reports produced by the funded project. (In the sciences it will be automatically – the issue is the order of the names.)

Even if you have another source of funding (your savings, a grant or whatever) you can ask to be put on a list of people looking for temporary research work (interviewing, data processing, transcription, literature searches) in your own or neighbouring universities – though you may need to be persistent to find and get yourself put onto appropriate lists. Or you may be able to pick up work from in-house advertisements. It is useful for your CV also to be able to say that you did fieldwork, programming or coding for X's project. You may also make useful contacts.

> A young Canadian moved to Britain to study with a particular supervisor whose work she had admired. She started on a self-funding basis, but half-way through the first year got a half-time six-month research assistant's job doing literature searches for someone in another department who advertised in the university's internal newsletter. After this, she got a similar job at another nearby university by word of mouth.

Teaching

Once people know of you (in the university where you are registered, or by meeting you at conferences, or by asking your supervisor for a recommendation), you are likely to be offered casual, hourly teaching. Someone will phone up and ask if you are interested in running some tutorial groups (alongside the large lectures they are giving), doing some demonstrating (in science), accompanying field trips, or giving a series of lectures for someone who is on leave. This can be terribly flattering, especially if they also smarm up to you; and it is probably worth doing for the experience. But it can disguise blatant exploitation.

> One student who had a research council grant was asked to do some teaching by a man at a neighbouring university in the same city. It emerged this involved two courses, both in her field, which she agreed to undertake. However, it was in fact half the (quite senior) man's entire teaching load, and included marking essays which formed part of the undergraduates final degree assessment. Moreover, the man concerned gave her very little help with course planning or delivery, was slow chasing up the payment of her fees, and was generally unavailable. ('He was on study leave.') He later tried shamelessly to shift the blame for some complaints on to the student in question, even though she was valiantly trying to cope and give the students a fair deal, including substantial pastoral support. She was also expected to attend relevant administrative meetings. For this she was paid a total of less than £1000 – very poor money if worked out on an hourly basis, especially given her inexperience and how much preparation she needed to do. It occupied most of the first two terms of her three-year grant, and greatly annoyed her supervisors, who were worried about getting her to complete within four years.

Practice is certainly very disparate. It can also vary in an ad hoc (or is it systematically biased?) way between individuals 'employed' within the same department. But even in the best cases, you can end up with a lot of out of class responsibilities ('other duties when needed') – expected to attend course meetings, to hold office hours, and (as a woman) to give informal counselling on both individual work-related queries *and* personal problems – for free and/or at a time when you need to concentrate for a period on your own research. If you have a choice, US research suggests being a research assistant is better (in terms of effect on time to completion) than being a teaching assistant – but women are more likely to be offered TAs than RAs, and also to receive less financial support generally. You certainly need to guard against finding yourself locked into doing so much teaching and giving so much pastoral support that you can't complete your own doctorate.

A survey in 1995 found the rates of pay for casual employment (in old universities) actually averaged out at £3.79 per hour for lecturing, £4.40 for tutorial work and £6.22 for demonstrating (where the total hours worked before and after each hour of face-to-face contact are fewer) (AUT, NUS and NPC 1996).

Getting teaching experience as a postgraduate does have its positive sides, however. It is desirable (indeed essential) to get some appropriate teaching experience if you want to get an academic job. If you apply for an academic lectureship, you want to be able to show your ability to teaching the range of courses the employer wants filled. You may anyway be interested in doing some teaching because it encourages wider reading in your subject area, and nothing clarifies one's ideas like explaining them to someone else. Being able to make presentations and run training courses is also a useful skill outside academia (see pp. 58–9).

Certainly reasonably paid TA positions would seem ideal during the writing up phase of a thesis or to provide a newly graduated PhD with a first job as a full member of teaching staff. (Something Oxford and Cambridge colleges have done for years, with 'Junior Research Fellowships' which provide rooms and food in college, a small income, book grants, and some required teaching until you land a proper job.) So we can guardedly welcome the introduction of formal graduate teaching assistantships – fixed-term, renewable contracts in return for a bursary broadly equivalent to a research council grant, with fees waived – resulting from the combination of heavier undergraduate teaching loads, more postgraduates with little funding, and general pressures on faculty. Of course, the other side of this coin is that this means a diminishing of the permanent jobs available for newly qualified individuals wanting to embark on an academic career.

An Italian woman studying in a shire counties university was awarded funding for four years as a teaching assistant. Her fees were paid and she got £2000 a year. But she had had to co-fund most of her attendance at the conference where we met. 'Nothing is paid for by the university if it is not joint.' She said she liked to get involved in departmental issues, but lecturers get a lot more money for the same hours, so she had started to say no. The lecturers accepted this, but they put pressure on her: 'They keep saying it would be *nice* if you *could*'.

Some formalization is clearly needed to protect both undergraduate and postgraduate students. NATFHE argues all teaching should be done by teaching staff on lecturer pay scales and conditions of service; student bursaries shouldn't require teaching; and if postgraduates do teach, it should be on proper hourly rates. The AUT is not opposed to TAs in principle, but does worry about the exploitation of graduate students and the undermining of undergraduate teaching and postgraduate research. It proposes that teaching assistants should only *help* an academic, for a limited time each week, their pay should be clearly related to academic pay, and there should be a written contract, for a minimum of four years. Also the terms and conditions should include as much support (office accommodation, access to post and telephone, including a pigeonhole where students can leave messages, ability to book teaching rooms, and attendance at conferences) as is given to students with research council grants. There should also be adequate training for teaching (TAs should been able to join the Institute for Learning and Teaching: see pp. 93–4) and continuing support and supervision. The mechanism for distributing such work should be 'transparent': it should not be handed out informally by professors.

If you have a research council award you are not supposed to undertake teaching which exceeds 180 hours per academic year (six hours a week) – but this includes preparation and marking in a ratio of 2:1, a total of two hours face-to-face teaching a week. This is probably a good guide to the maximum anyone should take on. US research shows teaching can increase the time it takes to get a PhD *more than other work* (sometimes to ten years or more, see pp. 197–200).

Work as an administrator or other support staff

Although few of the guidebooks mention it, maybe because it is a woman's job, it may also be possible to get a job as a part-time secretary in a university while undertaking a higher degree. Like TAs and RAs, you will probably get your fees paid and find various academics acting like mother hens, trying not to exploit you, to help you get round red tape, and to make useful contacts. On the other hand, the formal staff development system in most universities is not good at recognizing the skills or ambitions of administrative staff, nor providing them with career development. However those employed as senior administrators or 'academic related' staff are increasingly finding it helps to have a higher degree, even a doctorate, if they want to progress. A final possibility to consider is becoming a warden of a hall of residence, which provides living accommodation and a small salary.

NGOs, charitable trusts and small grants

A whole variety of organizations, including special educational charities, general international philanthropic organizations (like Rotary and Swedish International Development Agency – SIDA), churches, trade unions, private companies, and parts of the United Nations provide money for higher education studies. Serious money is mainly for students from specific countries (such as Fulbright between the USA and others; the Canon Collins Trust for students from South Africa moving to the UK); and more is again available in engineering, mathematics, science, business administration and agriculture than in other fields, though there is some for education, medical and paramedical fields, public administration, transport and communication, and natural resources management. Some agencies say they are currently 'backing off PhDs' because this involves putting too much money into one candidate, when they would rather support several individuals with more certain and practical returns, but you could be lucky.

Information on these larger grants and also a host of smaller grants can be extracted by determined use of registers and directories in reference libraries, or through personal networks if you are well connected. But they are now much more easily accessed through websites and search engines. Again it obviously helps to have expert specific advice, especially since particular countries and particular fields are priorities at different times. This applies *a fortiori* to the small pots of money which exist to fund very specific things. In any event, you need to plan at least a year ahead if you do want to try and get some money: find out about deadlines and allow six months for the review process and the funds to be processed. You can almost never get funds retrospectively.

US research students are more geared up to apply to foundations, agencies and their own university for small-scale support for elements of their project and for travel (to a particular library, museum, region, lab with individuals, to solve a problem posed). Workshops are run on campus to make sure students locate and apply to appropriate sources in the right way; and/or there is a fellowship office in the graduate school. Such workshops always stress being realistic, asking only for things which the fund specifies it will support, and showing how the money will enable you to do things that are important but impossible without the funder's support. If your university in the UK doesn't run similar sessions, ask them to do so.

Most small grants are for very specific purposes and it is a waste of time to put in a general request hoping for the best. It helps a lot to talk to someone with a good track record with each particular fund and to have looked at some past successful applications. You need to search for cues as to current priorities in the blurb and (if you can) from committee members. If it says that methodology and dissemination strategies and policy implications matter, be sure to stress clearly how your work will contribute to each and every one of these things. Be very specific so as to show you know what you want, and that it will be obtainable with this amount of money, and also about what you will (realistically) deliver. Even if the sum you get is small, do write any required end of grant report and, if it is a charitable foundation, acknowledge them in subsequent publications and thank them personally. It takes those administering them much (often voluntary) time to raise the funds, and they are interested in those they support.

Examples of the diversity of small grants available in the UK

The AL Charitable Trust will assist postgraduate students with small grants for travel, interviewing, and writing up costs. Specific preferences vary from year to year, but there is generally a preference for PhD students and women.

The Royal Society Industry Fellowship Scheme is for individuals wanting to go between academe and industry for periods on full or part secondment.

There are scholarships from Rotary and various business and professional women's clubs, for re-entry women.

The British Federation of Women Graduates has a fund for final year women research students to help them have time to complete their degrees.

The Economic and Social Research Council Postgraduate Training Board has money for developing specific methodological skills which will allow you to study for a month in another university which specializes in what you need, or to attend specialist workshops and seminars.

The Nuffield, Wellcome, and Royal Societies all give small grants (under £15,000) for consumables, travel, and equipment in their fields. The British Academy small grants can give up to £5000 to cover consumables and the costs of preparation for publication, such as permission fees and preparation of illustrations.

The British Sociological Association has a support fund for members living in the UK who are unwaged or have low paid part-time work (without grants) for travel to and subsistence at its conferences; for research and/or fieldwork expenses; and for typing and binding theses.

Existing academics might be able to get a six-month fellowship from Leverhulme, the British Academy, the ACU or a Nuffield Science Research fellowships to work on their research.

The British Association of Irish Studies will support postgraduate research in Britain on Irish topics with four bursaries of £1000 each.

The German Academy Exchange Service (DAAD) distributes its own funds and also gives advice on other organizations' funding, including short-term research grants for research students to carry out work in universities, research institutes, libraries and archives in Germany.

The European Doctoral College offers a limited number of research grants 'to enable talented students of European countries to prepare a PhD in two different European institutions': one in Strasbourg and the other in a European country of the student's choice (other than France).

Above all, even though it sound obvious, do check what your fees and grant statutorily entitle you to! This might include a desk, locker, lab space, photocopying allowance, books, local phone calls, equipment and consumables (chemicals, paper, floppy disks). Also note any discretionary opportunities. Can you call on technical assistance from the department or centrally? What travel money can you apply for to pay for fieldwork or conferences (especially if you give a paper)? Can you borrow a laptop or audio equipment? Can you get your thesis bound for free? Does the university or its student union have a hardship fund and/or can it make short-term loans? Also do you get a student card, even if you are part-time, and ask places if they do student discounts. A surprisingly high number do, but many don't advertise the fact. So ask!

Finally, note there are funds allocated to individual institutions from central government to be distributed to individual 'home' students 'whose access to further or higher education might be inhibited by financial considerations or who, for whatever reason, including physical or other disabilities, face financial difficulties'. There is a separate fund for postgraduates, though in practice universities often merge it with their undergraduate funds. Within the category of eligibility, universities can determine how they distribute this money. They often choose to target specific groups like single parents, students with disabilities, and mature students with dependants; but it is also often used to help part-time students who lose their jobs and self-financing students who run into financial difficulties half-way through their course. It cannot be used for studentships or postgraduate bursaries but it can contribute to the costs of travel, childcare, books and equipment. Ask the student advisory service about the specific local conditions at your university.

Part-time employment and loans

Obviously some financial planning is necessary before starting a PhD. Try to liquidate debts and build up savings. This of course means it is increasingly difficult to go straight on to do a PhD after an undergraduate degree and Masters because you will probably have an existing heavy burden of debt. Although repayment can be delayed till employment after the PhD, interest continues to accumulate.

> Midland Bank research showed that by the time they reached their third year, the average UK student in 1998 had amassed debts of £3,800 and expected to take up to five years to pay them off (*Guardian* 15 August 1998: 6).

If you are planning to return to do a PhD, do all the overtime you can, carry as few monthly bills as possible, and negotiate to pay interest-only on loans for a while. You must allow for grants arriving late. If you are registered full-time, you may want to get a part-time job from time to time. This should be as skilled and highly paid as possible, and/or useful for your CV later, but it should not too demanding, so you keep your mental energy for academic work. Those with grants are allowed to work for only a specified number of hours per week. 'Overseas' students can also now (legally) take on part-time or vacation employment in the UK if they wish, following the abolition of restrictive visa requirements in 1999 (see p. 13).

> Even before the relaxation of visa requirements, many Japanese women students in the UK found part-time jobs in Japanese related services, especially in London – Japanese bookshops, language teaching, waitressing in Japanese restaurants and serving in shops and hotels catering largely to Japanese tourists. Information circulates through the free Japanese language newspapers published in England and available in such locations. (Habu 2000: 54)

There is a relatively new DfEE scheme in partnership with high street banks to provide career development loans for vocational education or training for UK students. These cover full-time study – up to 80 per cent of fees and living expenses to a total of £8000. The DfEE pays the interest while you are studying, but thereafter you are liable for the repayment, and interest at commercial rates. If you are unemployed on graduation, you get five months' grace. Not many use this for financing a PhD, because the study has to be job-related and only two years of study can be supported. Moreover it is an expensive route. But it is worth considering in the later stages if nothing else is available.

Social security benefits

Social security is, of course, a complex and fluid arena and set up so as to minimize entitlements. Most full-time students are disentitled from claiming benefits from the first to the last day of a course/registration. But if you are a student with disabilities, a full-time student single parent, or part of a student couple with dependent children, you should seek guidance from your university's student advisors, or the NUS, and/or look at the Child Poverty Action Group's publications to see if you are in fact able to claim means tested benefits (Income Support and Housing Benefit). Disabled Students Awards (DSAs), which have provided relatively better financing for full-time undergraduate students since 1990, are unfortunately not available for postgraduate students.

If you are a full-time student and don't fall into any of these categories but you become ill, you should make a claim for Incapacity Benefit, and submit medical certificates to the Benefits Agency if the illness looks likely to continue for a long time. Even though you won't qualify for Incapacity Benefit (unless you have the requisite National Insurance contributions from previous employment), you will be eligible for Income Support or Housing Benefit after 28 weeks, when you become classed as a disabled student. You can receive one-twelfth of the amount of your grant monthly. It is however worth doing this because, with limitations on time to completion, it allows you an extension.

If you have a research council grant and you become pregnant you are entitled to four months' paid maternity leave and an extension for the same length of time at the end of the three years. If you are employed, you have a right to time off work for antenatal care and to 14 weeks' leave, but not necessarily to be paid during this time. If you have paid full National Insurance contributions for 26/66 weeks before the baby is due, you are eligible for Maternity Allowance for 18 weeks. Check your position with the Citizen's Advice Bureau, the Benefits Agency, the EOC Employment Policy Unit or the Maternity Alliance. Various of the science research councils have instituted 'family friendly' policies and issue guides for their employees.

All research students should get an AG1 form from an optician, dentist or DSS office to get free prescriptions, eye tests and dental check ups. The form seems designed to put people off, but persevere and fill it in. It could save you a lot of money.

Further reading

Time

Personal accounts
Significantly none of the study guides for doctoral students considers the issues of balancing study, employment, personal relationships and domestic life. The best resources are still personal accounts.

David, M. and Woodward, D. (eds) (1997) *Negotiating the Glass Ceiling: Careers of Senior Women in the Academic World*. London: Routledge Falmer. This includes more than twenty accounts with a longer term view.
Salmon, P. (1992) *Achieving a PhD – Ten Students' Experience*. Stoke-on-Trent: Trentham. See p. 82.
Vartuli, S. (ed.) (1982) *The PhD Experience*. New York: Praeger. This includes 'In and out of relationships: a serious game for the woman doctoral student'; 'The impossible dream: the PhD, marriage and family' and 'Grandma! What big plans you've got! The older woman's PhD experience'.

General guides
General guides for women professionals and managers together with the work of organizational psychology gurus may be also be helpful.

Cooper, C. (1990) Coping strategies for managing transitions, in S. Fisher and C. Cooper (eds) *On the Move: The Psychology of Change and Transitions*. New York: John Wiley.
Steiner, J. M. (1990) *How to Survive as a Working Mother*. London: Kogan Page.

Overall project and time planning
Blaxter, L., Hughes, C. and Tight, M. (1996) *How to Research*. Buckingham: Open University Press. This describes the context and processes of research, including combining it with other work, and has extensive annotated bibliographies.
Delamont, S., Atkinson, P. and Parry, O. (1997) *Supervising the PhD: A Guide to Success*. Buckingham: SRHE and Open University Press. Chapters 2 and 3 discuss designing a manageable project, timetabling and planning; and Chapter 6, problems with work habits, motivation and isolation.

Space

There are many sources of information on handling a move to live in Britain and its costs. The British Council produces materials for those living abroad, for example Education Information Service Sheets (free at any of their offices or on their website) which have regularly updated information on immigration, customs, accommodation, medical treatment, public services and so on. UKCOSA: the Council for International Education produces publications and runs courses for university support staff and students, and has a good website.

Cryer, P. (2000) *The Research Student's Guide to Success*, 2nd edn. Buckingham: Open University Press. Has good advice on going around your institution when you arrive and locating people and resources within it, as well as on establishing your workplace and choosing a computer, software, access to email and internet – even what music to play while working.

Lewins, H. (1990) Living needs, in M. Kinnell (ed.) *The Learning Experiences of Overseas Students*. Buckingham and Bristol: SRHE and Open University Press. Gives realistic accounts by overseas students of arriving, settling in and working at Loughborough and Nottingham universities.

NPC (1995) *Guidelines on Accommodation and Facilities for Postgraduate Research*. Troon: National Postgraduate Committee. Describes what work space and other facilities universities should ideally be providing.

Unterhalter, E. and Green, D. (1997) *Making the Adjustment: Orientation Programmes for International Students*. London: UKCOSA. This includes a critical overview of the literature on 'cultural adjustment' and takes a more postcolonial approach to what both sides have to contribute to international relationships.

Money

The NUS has a Welfare Unit which produces information sheets on student finance to send out to member student unions. Although largely undergraduate focused, it does have advisory committees for mature students and postgraduates (see p. 29).

Sims, A. (1997) Financing a doctorate, in N. Graves and V. Varma (eds) *Working for a Doctorate*. London: Routledge and Kegan Paul. An article by an NUS staff member which is an excellent source of information, especially on funding humanities and social science PhDs and on welfare benefits and loans.

Information on sources of grants or other funds can be searched for with keywords on various websites, including those of your professional organization, relevant research councils, the *THES* weekly listing of 'Research Opportunities', REFUND: a newsletter published monthly by the Research Services Unit, University of Newcastle and *Research Fortnight*. You can also access directories of research grants such as *The Grants Register*, the *Educational Grants Directory* and the Charities Aid Foundation *Directory of Grant Making Trusts, Charities and Foundations* in public and university libraries and on the web.

Help with writing grant proposals

Locke, L., Spirduso, W. and Silverman, S. (1993) *Proposals that Work: A Guide for Planning Dissertations and Grant Proposals*, 3rd edn. Newbury Park, CA: Sage. American focused, but a good general guide to producing proposals and managing projects, with Chapters 6 and 7 on seeking large and small scale funding. The second half consists of four complete sample proposals with boxed commentaries on what the writer is seeking to achieve in each section of the proposal.

Research work

Short-term and part-time research work is often advertised in internal university newsletters, but full-time work has to be advertised nationally, usually in the *Guardian* or the *THES* (see their websites). On the terms and conditions you can expect as a part-timer in higher education, and those you ideally should have, see:

Open University (2000) *Support for Part-time Teachers of Sociology*. Milton Keynes: Centre for Higher Education Practice, Open University. A full account, including case studies, of good practice with fixed-term contract and part-time university teachers, much of which is also applicable to most disciplines and to research assistants. Funded by HEFCE and will be sent free to any university department or library. Short guidelines available at http://www4.open.ac.uk/sociology

Reay, D. (2000) 'Dim Dross': marginalised women both inside and outside the academy, *Women's Studies International Forum*, 23(1): 13–21. Describes the positioning of women, especially those from working class backgrounds, as contract researchers within universities. The phrase 'dim dross' was used in an attack on educational researchers (notably women) in 1999.

5 | GETTING OFF TO A GOOD START

As has been stressed, few people fail a doctorate, but many give up before completing. Research by Ernest Rudd (1985) suggested the main reasons were that individuals allow too little time, because the reality is different from what they expect, and/or because they don't have the flair or the dedication needed for research. For women, however, we have suggested there are also issues of not understanding the rules of the game as well as men, and lack of confidence. However, assuming you are able, well informed and have an (at least) competent supervisor, how do you get going?

Prior to starting

Although you can usually begin a PhD at the start of any term, there is much to be said for beginning in October at the start of the academic year if you can, so you do courses in the best order and pick up on any formal induction sessions. With professional doctorates you will probably be expected to start at a particular point in the year. If you have some time to wait before you start a course or join a project, it will help to do the following.

First, set up your study and get back into regular studying. Refresh your study skills, especially if it is some time since you did an academic course. This is not just a question of sprucing up on how to read a book quickly, or note taking and effective use of the library. There are also issues of computer literacy. You must be able to word process – which may be a new skill if you have been used to secretarial support. You can type with four fingers, but it is better by far to (learn to) touch type. There is no excuse nowadays for making your supervisor read handwriting, and more importantly the possibility of drafting and redrafting and editing allows a whole new mode of writing. You will also find invaluable software for footnotes, bibliographic databases, spreadsheets which produce graphs and tables, and statistical packages. You will need eventually to give papers, so presentation skills and use of audio-visual aids will save members of of your future audiences from boredom. Get your 10-year-old niece to teach you how to use the world-wide web if you don't already know.

Second, talk with your supervisor(s) about initial background reading, which can include looking at what is on their course booklists and their own work in your field, so you know their background. From now on you will want to pay particular attention to the context of production and the methodology, as well as the findings, of every piece of research you look at: what did they do and why? And does it prove what they say it does?

Third, if English is not your first language, it is worth taking courses if you need to improve. Many universities now run sessions which are cheaper than commercial services. But, more importantly, they teach not general language, but rather 'academic literacies'. These can be useful for home students too (see pp. 245–7). This is a well-developed academic field, fed by composition studies, sociolinguistics, work on discourse and textuality, and critical ethnography. It considers what counts as learning, how to frame a good argument, and the politics of writing style in the various specialist fields and disciplines, and in different countries. It can therefore make you aware of your specific *habitus* (see pp. 69–70) and how to develop various genres, and so help you to write not only for your examiners but also in the future for academic journals and educated lay people.

> Whether an individual text is recognized as 'argument' or not is . . . largely a matter of cultural or disciplinary criteria. Thus, in some educational contexts, students' written argument is expected to match a certain well-defined generic pattern . . . while in others 'argument' is used much more broadly to include recount and even narrative form. Consequently . . . lecturers across a range of disciplines in which the required modes of textualization are very different can all state that they expect students to produce 'argument'.
>
> (M. Scott 1997)

Fourth, do join the professional association for your subject area, and its postgraduate section (and possibly its women's caucus), and attend relevant day meetings and conferences. There are usually very reduced rates (and some benefits) for student members. If you are planning to go or return to another country once you have your doctorate, it would be worth joining the appropriate organizations in both places to keep in touch with events. Also add a North American or European professional society to stay in touch with developments in other countries and to find out about grants and awards. You may want to join a few selected email lists and to check the research councils and other websites for current and recently completed reports. It is helpful also to join the listings pages service run by the publishers of relevant journals (usually via the publishers' web pages).

Finally, your university will probably hold various orientation courses, including quite extensive ones lasting for a day or a month for international students, and some social events. You should be sent an information pack beforehand. Some of these are excellent, others are mind-numbingly boring but perhaps a necessary ritual. You should at least get from them a chance to know the geography of the campus and its resources, including the non-academic services (like sports facilities and health provision), to meet people from around the world and to make a few friends. They may or may not consider specific issues for women, or for students from particular countries.

UKCOSA runs courses for people in charge of international students' welfare and has published an overview on what does and doesn't help in induction courses, with outlines for good practice (Unterhalter and Green 1997). Should your university not provide what you think you need, become a student representative and make them change their practice next year.

Starting the research

The process of finally getting started will obviously vary with your field and source of funding. For the lab scientist and some social scientists, it means joining a team and getting to grips with a given problem which is part of a larger funded project. For someone working on, say, artificial intelligence or physical geography, it can involve catching up on computer modelling which has been done by a predecessor so as to move it on. For an anthropologist, it requires reading all the literature on and learning the language of a given society and arranging for a field trip; for an historian, reading and exploring possible sources; for a sociologist, possibly a whole year deciding upon a research question and appropriate methodology.

These all have in common that the first stages of a PhD especially can seem slow and frustrating. But the very diversity suggests the worth of reading both the research on disciplinary differences (see pp. 61–5, 83, 111–12), and some of the accounts which seek to demystify the research process, especially the ones by research students themselves (see the further reading pp. 172–3). Professional doctorates help precisely by having courses which urge you along and break up the path into stages. But in either case, do push ahead as fast as you can. Things will speed up later, so it is important not to waste time in the first term, especially if you have time-limited funding.

There will also doubtless be many 'straight' textbooks on research methodology which your supervisor can recommend in your field or which get referenced in the taught element of your course, especially if it is an area where there are many competing paradigms and ethical dilemmas. Most of them start at the point in the research process we have reached here – four chapters into this book. 'Beginning research' textbooks are also helpful about keeping records, referencing and noting page numbers, on filing, backing up disks, and keeping successive drafts. I would also recommend Delamont and colleagues' (1997) advice book for supervisors (see pp. 70, 83), which both outlines the phases of research and helps you see the process from the supervisor's perspective. You could use it as the basis for talking through your working practice with tutors (and as a delicate means of improving their practice if necessary!).

For a PhD/DPhil in any discipline you will have to fulfil the common requirement to produce an original contribution to the field (see pp. 64–5, 238–40 for definitions of these terms) – something between a Nobel prize contribution and your little mite – and you will always go though stages of defining the topic, designing the project, gathering material, processing and analysing the data, writing up, and revising the final draft, followed by submission and the viva voce. Beyond that, there can be no formula for progress if it is a creative project (as opposed to a research exercise).

In his classic account of supervising sociological study, Bob Connell (1985) stresses the dialectic involved:

> an argument between the general conception and particular investigations, a back-and-forth between data and theory, between formulation and critique. This dialectic has to follow its own logic. If we knew its course in advance, the research would not be worth doing. A good research project opens new questions up as much as it answers questions already posed . . . So there can be no formula for PhD supervision, no fixed course of events. The 'curriculum' cannot be planned in the way it is for undergraduate courses. At the same time, there are 'moments' in the dialectic that are common to most research projects. And the higher degree framework imposes some tasks that have always to be done. [So students can find it helpful to be told that] such and such a development can be expected.
>
> (Connell 1985: 39)

In professional doctorates the stress is on applicability rather than 'pure' research – the production of knowledge within the profession – and a range of elements have been included in the assessment by different universities. The structure is still basically academic, but the proportion of coursework to thesis varies, and coursework can involve 'structured research tasks' in the workplace, or reflections on required conference attendance, or publication in professional journals. There is, however, almost always a more or less lengthy thesis, and a viva.

In whatever field, I hope your research will make a substantial contribution. I am worried that some influential textbooks strongly advocate 'safe' research projects. For example Estelle Phillips and Derek Pugh in *How to Get a PhD* (2000: 50ff) distinguish research which is 'exploratory' from that which is 'problem-solving' or 'testing-out'; and because their stress is on *getting* a PhD as quickly and securely as possible, they favour the easiest –'testing out'. At times this seems like just getting through a doctorate. This was perhaps a necessary corrective to the inflation of social science and humanities PhDs at the time when their first edition was published (1987), but today I think academics should be leaning in the opposite direction: *against* the over-rationalization and curtailing of research (see pp. 41–3).

My preferred differentiation is between 'classic' academic research, where the focus is on producing an original contribution to knowledge; 'policy' research, where the concern is to solve a practical problem; and forms of 'activist' radical research, where the issue is not only to 'understand the world but also to change it' (Table 5.1). (Of course these are 'normative' types and actual practices are much less ideal – academic research is full of personal aggrandizement and people keep results secret for personal and pecuniary advantage: see p. 92.) Good PhDs should, however, be primarily concerned with the first – with scholarship – and professional doctorates near to applied or policy concerns. But both can profitably combine elements of the academic with policy and/or activism (and vice versa).

In thinking how these various categorizations might apply to your area, read some recent theses; think also of their 'originality', 'contribution', disciplinary competence and literary worth. It is also never too early to be thinking of the immediate audiences for your own work, who might be examiners for the thesis; and about subsequent publication. Plan ahead how your topic can fit your subsequent career, in or outside academia. Be trendy, but not so much as to go out of fashion. Be wary of (but don't dismiss!) 'sensitive' or 'political' topics. Be marketable: consider where the topic may help you to get a job. But consider also whether you can bear to be focused upon and considered the expert on this topic for years and years. This may help to guide your choice of topic, the debates you consider, and how you

Table 5.1 Types of research[1]

	Academic research	Applied or policy research	Activist research
Problem formulation	Original Making an important contribution to knowledge	Commissioned Solving a practical problem or with a practical application	Empowering Understanding the world in order to change it (so as to help the less powerful)
Context	Universal What could be changed	Local What can be changed	Politically engaged What should be changed
Role	Detached Public intellectual	Hierarchical Values and responsibilities from top down	Participatory Democratic decisions with participants
Methodology	Rational, sceptical Concerned with epistemology and methodologically correct practices	Expert Hired to provide information, on time and under budget	Standpoint Ideas come from political struggle Empathetic and ethical concern for subjects
Presentation	Communal Stress on freedom to publish worldwide	Proprietary Knowledge owned by funder Evaluated by effectiveness	Accessible Accountable to a specific constituency

might analyse your results and present your findings (all of which are obviously open to change). It should also give you some estimate of time (how much to allot to each step) to get a sense of the scale of the whole and make sure it is not too vast. Make sure, too, that it is researchable: the texts are available, you can get access to the field (and at the time when you want to do fieldwork), the equipment is available, the project will be stable for the required length of time (even if the director moves on), and it does not present insurmountable ethical difficulties. This makes you focus on the material you actually need to answer your research questions, and stops you wandering off to look at lots of other 'interesting' data you will have no time to use. It lets you judge if you are working hard enough – not against others but against your self.

David Sternberg (1981) likens completing a doctoral dissertation to a long distance run, and advises padding along on an agreed path without constantly looking at the finishing line.

- Set yourself a steady pace. Sternberg quotes the editors of the *Paris Review* (Plimpton 1977) who interviewed over fifty writers who had been successful over more than twenty years, and found the important common feature among this very diverse group was that they maintained a virtually invariable daily writing time: from two to four hours, five to seven days a week, at the same time of day (mostly in the morning). Authors may present themselves or be stereotyped as 'unpredictable', radical or flamboyant, but professionally they are nearly always systematic and business-like. (Denis Lawton (1997) makes a similar point, citing Somerset Maugham.)
- Agree a time-line with your supervisor which gives the marking off points along your own route.
- Get a handle on the scope of the work and manage the project. Keep an overall view but break it down into manageable sections (Sternberg 1981).

Managing time is especially problematic for those in the humanities and social sciences who don't spend fixed hours with a team in a set place. But in science too you need to establish a firm schedule of hours to work on the project each day. This applies especially if you are full-time and your time is your own and particularly to women, because, from a different perspective, our time is not our own: it is less under our control. Build in some slack, and try to stay ahead, but don't slow down if you are ahead. Analysis is faster with computers, but it still takes ages; and writing (especially in the humanities and social sciences) takes far longer than you expect. Paradoxically, limit your research time, at least in the initial and middle stages, so as to keep a balance in your life. Work on it when you are at your best – which may mean getting up (and going to bed) earlier, unless you are a night owl who wakes up at 11 p.m. and works in the quiet of the night. Or alternatively, if you have a job, consider staying on at work (or going home via the library) for a couple of extra hours and do it there. But in the early and middle stages at least, work your agreed hours and then stop so as to be keen to get back to the research the next day.

Progress on a dissertation comes with day-to-day involvement, with keeping it constantly at the front of your mind. It is better to put in five two-hour sessions, or five one-hour and one five-hour sessions, than to think you will do one ten-hour session at the weekend. You will find not only that you frequently can't do a full ten hours because of things that happen (or that you have no time for shopping and seeing family and friends), but also that you spend much of the session catching up and reminding yourself where you left off. So you lose time. On the other hand, don't curtail your set hours on a particular day because you 'lack inspiration'. Tough it out and maybe an idea will come. Or do some routine filing or read an article. If you travel away from home, take a laptop and work on a chapter which needs redrafting. Even when you are spending time out in the library or doing fieldwork or experiments, come back to your desk or laptop to touch base and sort things out, write up fieldnotes and hunches, and plan the next day. If you have a job, try to take occasional days off to work on the thesis to give it a boost. (You may need to have days off sometimes anyway to collect data, so negotiate for this to be an acceptable possibility with your boss.) Don't burn out.

If, in time-honoured time management fashion, you divide your tasks up into

important and urgent / urgent but not important

important but not urgent / not urgent and not important

your thesis is more than likely to fall into the 'important but not urgent' category. The sad reality of life is that 'urgent but not important work' takes precedence over 'important but not urgent' work *every time*. The trick is to find a way to move the thesis into the 'important and urgent' box. Use your supervisor or a study group (see pp. 165–6) as people you 'have' to present material to at regular intervals – as deadline setters, within an overall tough but realistic time-line. Agree to give some seminar presentations to raise your adrenalin. Eventually you have to, and will, reach a point where just finishing the task, without it being perfect, is all you ask. It will mean giving up some important things – but for a limited time, rather than dragging the thesis around like a ball and chain for years.

Developing your relationship with your supervisor(s)

Concern with low rates of and long times to completion lead research councils, professional organizations and universities to focus on improving supervision (as noted on pp. 23, 39, 87–93) – 'effective' supervision being now defined as 'that which propels students to present their thesis in under four years'. The councils all started producing guidelines on postgraduate supervision from the mid-1970s, followed, from a more student perspective, by the National Postgraduate Committee and the various how-to-do-research textbooks of the late 1980s and 1990s. It is likely your institution has also produced its own variant of a list of the joint responsibilities of staff and student, and that this will be included in the information sent to you before you start. It is now a required aspect of Quality Assurance following the Harris and Dearing reports.

It is worth reading these 'responsibilities' through (and seeing what the research council and professional association for your area have on their websites). You can then discuss these with your supervisor to get a sense of where you each stand on different elements. You could also discuss the various modes and metaphors for the relationship suggested earlier (see pp. 90–2) and see which ones you both feel comfortable with.

You can expect your supervisor minimally:

- to see the relationship as professional and contractual
- to behave with integrity and friendly detachment
- to be interested in supervising
- to be at least moderately interested in your subject and with adequate knowledge of the field
- to have the respect of other faculty (and generally in the field), as this will help your thesis to be taken seriously.

Your supervisor should help you select a thesis topic and develop a proposal and/or to get experiments going. You should meet regularly to discuss your progress and for specific comments on any problems with what you are doing, and advice on correcting them. Your supervisor should know their own mind and stick to the decisions you make jointly. They should not be forgetful or wishy-washy and wavery (even if a very nice person).

You should get prompt feedback on the material you submit. This includes:

- your papers read within a reasonable time after submission
- constructive criticism, with ample comments and suggestions
- your supervisor being accessible and friendly
- and giving you an appointment before hell has frozen over.

They should give you recommendations to talk to other members of the department about your and their work; and guidance on becoming a professional in the field, including introductions to other scholars in the discipline and on joining professional organizations.

Your supervisor should help you prepare your first talks at scholarly meetings (and if possible attend the event) and read drafts of articles for publication, and/or publish with you. They should read and help you develop your applications for grants and your applications for posts. Finally, they should write you references for fellowships, grants and jobs – and meet the relevant deadlines.

It is up to either or both of you

- to initiate meetings
- to establish a schedule for the project
- to keep to deadlines.

How often you see your supervisor(s) varies over the course of the thesis process. It also depends upon your personal needs and whether there are other doctoral students, postdocs and technicians, or members of year group on a professional doctorate who you can call on. There are times when you need to meet quite frequently (at the start, in a crisis, if you have a deadline for a paper); and times when you need to meet less often (when it's best to wait till a particular phase is finished or a chapter written).

Even when you arrive to start your degree thinking you know just what you want to do, you may need frequent guidance and reassurance, with your supervisor giving encouragement and suggesting techniques, reading and divergent thinking. You need help if you feel lost; or to let you know when it is time to push towards closure. When you are designing what you plan to do, you want your supervisor's technical knowledge and criticism; and when you at last get things working in the lab or on the computer program, or go out into the field or into the archive, you need your supervisor to keep in touch and listen to your stories of triumphs and occasional disasters – to help when you have difficulties in getting access, or to catch mistakes, and in the event of major disaster when everything goes pear-shaped (equipment non-delivery or breakdown, access to a key institution being withdrawn), to help you swiftly redesign and escape the problem.

During data processing, analysis and writing up, when it is hard to stick at the task, you want support to keep the overall process moving and to reassure you the whole thing is not a waste of time. Once you have a first full rambling draft, you will again need to meet frequently to decide if additional sections are needed or new books and articles should be included; but also to put limits on the job – referring you back to your original plans. You need your supervisor to confirm you are up to standard on presentation and meet the formal requirements of your particular university. Finally, you have to rely on your supervisor to suggest a suitable short list of examiners. Even afterwards, you can look to them to provide help in getting published or otherwise feeding back your findings and 'to put in a word for you' to relevant parts of the outside world.

The advice books talk a lot about 'handling' your supervisor, but, unlike the US committee situation, in Britain a supervisor is committed to you and your project on a personal, continuous, serious basis; so you should feel free (and confident) to negotiate the degree and sort of support you want, especially as time goes on. Some students like a personal relationship, others more professional distance. Some enjoy thinking of metaphors to express what feels comfortable (see Cohen *et al.* (1999), p. 112).

In the difficult task of evolving a personal way of working, a supervisor who is delicately attuned to the student can be a real help. One aspect of a personal, rather than an impersonal, supervisory relationship is that it entails an acknowledgement of the student as a person in the round. Discussion of the work includes a recognition of the life situation of which the research project is part. Non-academic matters do not have to be discarded at the office door; supervisor and student can together mull over the absence of a room at home to work in, the demands of a young child, or the fact that ideas seem to come only at impossible moments and never when research time has been set aside (Salmon 1992: 22).

This a point where gender is key. Researchers have noted that women have in common that both they and their supervisors are more likely to focus on their non-academic lives when talking about 'problems' or difficulties with their research. This does not mean that their 'private' lives are actually more problematic for their progress, merely that they are seen to be relevant, rather than 'noise' to be excluded. It is however probable that women fit the system less well, given it was set up for men's strengths and possibilities.

Even if you are close friends with your supervisor, or see them every day when you are a research assistant on a project, do keep a degree of formality in your supervision. Schedule regular meetings, even a regular time, to discuss your work so as to establish a good rhythm and to get feedback within a reasonable length of time. Either fix a series of meetings for the term ahead, because it helps your supervisor to have it written into their diary, or fix the next meeting before you leave each time. A minimum frequency of meeting is an hour of face-to-face contact for a full-time student four times a term – which may, paradoxically, be especially important when you see your supervisor regularly anyway. You need scheduled time to discuss *your* progress. Confirm when you need to hand in written work for your supervisor to have time to read it beforehand. Give a note in with it to say what you want focused upon, and where it fits into your work. But meet for a short time even if there is little progress to discuss. Some ideas always come up. Don't wait till you hand in a vast tome. It will get read superficially. Keep in touch with your supervisor even if things are going badly – indeed *especially* if things are going badly. They need to know what is going on and can often help.

Arrive on time and don't stretch the appointment out unnecessarily. Avoid appointments late in the afternoon when you are both likely to be tired. Both sides should treat meetings seriously, giving each other full attention (with no callers or answering of telephones). Let's hope that your supervisor will structure the time well, with a negotiated agenda and space in each supervision to say how you think you are getting on and what you think you are doing. (If not, take control!) Make notes. I write on self-carboning paper and give the student a copy and keep one in my own files, but if your supervisor doesn't want this (or in addition) make your own notes, especially of decisions made, dates agreed, topics discussed, problems noted. You could do this on an email and send a copy to your supervisor and one to yourself.

Stages in a research supervision	
opening	establishing rapport
review	establishing the current context
definition	scope and purpose of present meeting
exploration	problems, results, progress
clarification	decisions needed
goal setting	decisions taken, next tasks identified
conclusion	evaluation, summary and disengagement
recording	notes on supervision made and filed

(Brown and Atkins 1988: 133)

If things do seem really wrong, remember you can expect basic courtesies and you are not obliged to accept your supervisor's advice. If you feel you are not getting what you want, try first to direct your supervisor to the professional organization's guidelines (or Delamont and colleagues' *Supervising the PhD*) and/or talk to the departmental research tutor. If it can't be resolved at department level, go on and talk to the Director of Studies of Graduate Students or equivalent. But start sooner rather than later, when massive resentment has built up; and take it step by step. Think perhaps of getting someone else involved and having joint supervision. But if all else fails, change supervisor. (See also Chapter 7.)

Building support for yourself

Within the university

Women often feel isolated and alienated by a 'chilly climate' in their own departments, so it is doubly important for us to build up support in and outside the university. This also helps to reduce making unreasonable demands on your supervisor (especially on women supervisors). While the books and articles listing the ways in which women are made to feel 'not quite first-class citizens in the academic community' can be very heavy (and will be looked at again on pp. 201–9 on what can slow down your progress) we are, after all, used to the following kinds of things in the rest of life and have some strategies for resistance:

- people paying less attention to what women say; interrupting us; and picking up points only when they are made by men;
- the few women in prestigious positions being always visible, scrutinized, and expected to speak on behalf of women (but people then sighing 'she is off again . . .') – with the many women in support roles semi-invisible;
- being expected to take on caring roles and having our time less valued.

It's sad that universities are not different from – that is to say, they have the same sexist micropolitics as – many other institutions, despite their liberal front and pretensions. So regrettably we do need to set up ways of countering the effects of sexism; and also to note for future reference those women who either use and/or contribute to their own and our positioning, or who personalize intellectual differences.

> I got hurt badly by a woman when I first started here because, as she so sweetly put it, 'you don't help the competition'. That was a good lesson for me. I had always thought that women helped women. Well, honey, they don't! Not always.
>
> There are some [women] who are committed to women, but who will only go so far to support you. They won't upset the situation. And you can also upset really important feminists, who might otherwise support you, if you critique their work or dismiss postmodernism in three lines. People jump on you from both outside *and inside* feminism.

Establish good relationships with the departmental office, the graduate school staff, librarians, and student union personnel. You are not likely to find much structural support for women's concerns in your university: there will probably not be a women's centre, and if there is, it will be poorly funded; there will be little specifically women's preventive health care or sports provision, and limited childcare. But with luck there will be some women's or gender studies taught (see Chapter 6), and an EO office, probably mostly run by women low in the hierarchy and/or off the teaching or administrative career path (see pp. 33–5). But many women's faculties do have a sense of mission about helping women students, so identify your friends (women and men) before trouble arrives, especially since pastoral support has been one of the first areas to decline with cuts in costs. Let individuals get to know you by being friendly all the time and give them your support throughout – not just opportunistically, when you want something. There are plenty of attacks on such 'feminists' – or use of the attribution of being a feminist (or a lesbian or just simply a c . . . t) – which are part of a general putting women 'in their place' (see pp. 209–17). Know the grievance procedures on EO and harassment just in case you need them – and who you should talk to first and who would be an advocate.

If your department is well run it may have a buddy system whereby a third-year student is assigned to help a newcomer through the first terms. They will also provide a first friendly face and tell you when and where people meet socially. You can also use the compulsory taught courses and optional seminar programme strategically – to make contacts as well as for their content. If you plan to take some optional courses, plan ahead and sign up for them (drop a note to the teacher) early. Some get very full and you may not have the same rights as, say, Masters degree students. If there should be difficulties, do *not* be the nice woman who volunteers to leave! You need and have a right to peer stimulation and support as part of varying your use of time, and for companionship. (It may be the main reason for the expensive childcare you were encouraged to set up.) Make time for cups of coffee and learn a lot serendipitously about other related fields. Also find out about researchers on projects in the department, and visitors on sabbatical leave who may have more time to talk. This is part of your essential involvement in the research culture of the discipline, and also how academics build personal networks.

> All the research on PhD students has found that isolation, both social and intellectual, is a frequently mentioned problem . . . in one way isolation is essential. Once an original thesis project is well under way, the student has to be intellectually responsible for it and has to become the expert in the field. *Intellectual* isolation is necessary and desirable. However, there is no reason for this . . . to be accompanied by social or emotional loneliness. Indeed, students need to realize that the former is impeded by the latter . . . Seminars on how to get published, build a CV, prepare for the viva or apply for jobs can be slotted regularly into the academic year, in addition to seminars at which students present their work to each other to provide occasions to meet.
>
> (Delamont *et al.* 1997: 96)

In general, when you want something, be prepared to hustle a bit, even if this goes against your grain, and even if you think it comes easily to socially competent middle class, 'home' students, but not to you. Don't take no for an answer, but do do your homework (looking through official guidance or grant directories, for example) before making a formal appointment. Don't just drop in on senior people. Make an appointment or use their office hours, take the necessary documentation with you, and have your questions written down. Value your time equally – but don't demand more of women staff than of men (see also pp. 90–1, 98).

You can also of course seek support from specific groups of women who share your background.

A recent PhD graduate told me that, as an older woman from a poor back-ground, she would never have stuck at her PhD at this large university were it not for the constant support of a charismatic woman in the re-entry pro-gramme. She went to almost all her classes, year after year, including ones on leadership, giving conference papers, fundraising, and computing skills. The women's centre had innovative curricula and a room she could use to chill out in. It also provided counselling. In return she made occasional contribu-tions to its courses.

Associations for different groups of overseas students or home minorities may, however, be more problematic. While giving you the warm comfortable feeling of home, they may also be sexist. Indeed some student unions in England have withdrawn funding from women's groups in the last few years at the behest of such groups which have become dominated by religious fundamentalists. Women are always positioned differently from men in the role they are expected to play as bearers of their home culture – as 'keepers of the hearth' – being required to be more conformist in dietary, clothing, cultural and religious mores, and not expected to have fun. I have had women students who came under enormous pressure to 'represent' their home country and not to accept feminist ideas – one to the extent of giving up her studies and returning to Japan.

I'm quite used to [British] society because at home my male friends said 'You don't have to be so independent – so strong!' Here people can accept me more easily. They don't expect you to be gentle. You don't have to pretend to be incompetent. But yes, I'm part of the Taiwanese community. We have a national network and a branch here [in this locality]. But the chair is appointed by the ruling Party and he has a military [college] background and will go back to work for the govern-ment. Taiwanese men are quite conservative. They wouldn't assume men and women are equal. They will come to help you: you don't have to ask. They will pay even if they are not your boyfriend. It's true you make a choice between career and marriage. My parents said that to me. As did the guy I was seeing. The better I adjust myself here, the more I'm going to get into trouble, to have problems adjusting, when I go back. Some live here as Taiwanese and have little to do with foreigners. They just say: 'foreign customs' [to distance themselves]. When I went back after the MA, people at home thought I'd be a completely different person. A BIG contrast.

This is of course no different from what happens to women routinely, but it is harder to cope with if you are already feeling fragile and isolated *or* rediscovering an identity. Equally some lesbian, gay and bisexual student groups constantly 'forget' about women and have to be equally constantly reminded. If the sort of group you would like to join does not exist, set one up, or set up a women's section within an existing association, even if you get initial antagonism.

You should certainly also consider joining or establishing your own study support group. The aim of this is not only to get away from the cut and thrust of some academic seminars to a small group where people listen and give constructive criticism, but also to make you feel you *have* to report to the group and so can use it to pace yourself.

Self-help groups are probably best made up of four or five members, all of whom are in roughly the same field and at the same stage, but possibly from different institutions so there is less rivalry and less chance of being seen as a threat by faculty and other students, and greater confidentiality. The small size ensures that if you meet weekly and each meeting is reserved for one or at most two people to present their work (distributed in advance) and/or to discuss their feelings and problems, you still get around to each person regularly and keep up with the details of each other's work. You could usually meet centrally but occasionally in each other's dissertation offices, which helps each person review their arrangements and reduces isolation. Members must make every effort to attend all meetings and confidentiality must be discussed and agreed. All successes should be celebrated.

(Adapted from Sternberg 1981)

Every element of the above prescription can of course be varied to suit. I would strongly advocate an all women's group, since the dynamics of mixed sex groups are different. You might want a Black women's group, or all lesbians, but variety also has advantages and it may be you have to go with what you can get! You may want to start with more than five people, in case some drop out. You don't necessarily all have to be at the same stage and the group can include hourly paid lecturers, research assistants, librarians, and women on temporary contracts as well as (or they may themselves be) research students – though you should be wary of carrying over power relations from the mainstream institution. The group can certainly include some consciousness raising, but probably not much psychotherapy. You may decide it helps to have one person in charge of organizing it, and if members include those with jobs in higher education, you might even get some staff development money for the convenor and for photocopying and postage, and even for joint travel to some conferences. Schedules can be altered to help particular people who have problems; and outsiders can be invited occasionally. It is worth trying such a group – and if you do, don't give up on it too easily. They often go through early rocky patches, but later prove invaluable.

Within the wider discipline

The links you make through your study support group can be also graced by the term 'networking': they forge productive and cooperative contacts which provide information, advice and moral support to help career advancement. Networking is acknowledged as an integral part of men's career trajectory generally, and men academics rely, consciously or unconsciously, on using professional networks for information about current developments and to increase their own visibility. Only latterly has the great significance of women's exclusion from men's friendships, homosociability and formal organizations been given serious consideration. It constitutes an actual structural barrier so the response has been to encourage the potential of women's own networking for our professional enhancement.

With this has come also recognition of a specialist network link – having a mentor. There is now quite a literature from management specialists about what 'a mentor' is, with hotly contested definitions, and attempts made to measure the effects of having or not having one. This is put forward as *the* key to success for the fast-track professional woman – or at least of keeping on some sort of par with the men.

> Those homosocial senior mentors, adept at placing their proteges in desirable educational and occupational posts, act as gatekeepers to important positions. Even without formal rules and regulations barring women from the highest ranks . . . the informal practices of the 'old boy' network manage to reserve the lion's share of the roles for their own and their colleagues' proteges.
>
> (Lipman-Blumen 1984: 148)

There are least two broadly different versions of mentoring: one is a mentor within your own workplace, who is set up in a relationship with you by the institution as part of a staff development programme (such as the buddy system referred to above or a mentor provided for your first term of teaching). Such a relationship is hierarchical and often directive. The other sort of mentor, which I am advocating here, is a more informal relationship, chosen and worked out between the two of you. This is both instrumental and emotional. It is essentially a friendship which has been established with an experienced and smart person, often your senior, often from outside your workplace so it can't be seen as favouritism, who is interested in supporting your career. It involves his or her giving you advice, coaching and sponsorship to increase your visibility, and also giving protection if you get attacked. Your mentor can raise your self-esteem and encourage you in non-traditional attitudes and assertiveness, including giving suggestions about arguing for pay increases, taking promotion possibilities seriously, and with applying for grants. It is a long-term, may be a lifelong, mutual relationship, but with someone you don't necessarily see all that frequently. (It may be better that you don't meet all that often in case it should end up feeling constrictive rather than developmental.) It expands the influence of the mentor, so the protégée is usually someone who follows and promotes their ways of thinking.

> People ask me about my mentors, my feminist role models – well, a lot of the women I look up to are much younger than me.
> (Hon. Justice Sally Brown, Family Court of Australia, quoted in Trioli 1996: frontispiece)

A mentor can be a man or a woman, and there is nothing to stop you having more than one. You want them to be well placed and close to your background and interests. Men are useful, especially in very masculine fields, because their voices are more likely to be listened to, they let you know what a man would expect in a particular situation, and also because, since there are so few women to go round, senior women are overburdened. But a woman can be especially helpful with her experience and knowledge of difficult career progression and of the problems in balancing work and domestic and social life; especially if she comes from the same sort of social class or religious background as yourself. Some people use their supervisor as a mentor, and some women have husbands who are aghast at the ways their wives get treated and encourage them to push back and who open up their social network. But both supervisors and spouses or other partners are *parti pris*, and it helps also to have someone else who stands more apart from things.

A mentor would point out to a woman in science, for instance, that women do not routinely get the same sponsorship to attend high status research (as opposed to teaching) universities, to participate in conferences, to collaborate on scholarly work, to enter the professional network, or to get the better jobs, promotion and salaries (Cole 1979). They would suggest the need for some self-promotion, and when and how to make some perfectly legitimate demands for equity – which might be against the self-interests of a supervisor (or indeed a husband).

A mentor could help you recognize what Judith Lorber refers to in academic medicine as the 'Salieri' phenomenon. In Peter Shaffer's play *Amadeus*, the court composer Salieri is the gatekeeper to musical patronage from the emperor. He pretends to be a benefactor to Mozart by recommending him, but he makes sure his salary is low. So the talented but socially graceless Mozart feels gratitude to Salieri and doesn't recognize how Salieri is blocking rather than advancing him. Lorber suggests that academic women are often similarly constrained by an inner circle of dominant men. The women are recognized to be talented, but found not to measure up in some way. They are not kept out, but rather limited to a low level of advancement by people who present as their supporters (cited in Clark and Corcoran 1993).

You can also chose someone as a mentor to supplement your supervisor's gaps – someone from another university and/or back at home if you come from another country. You can then tell your supervisor what your home mentor says about, say, issues of research design or the type of publishing you need to do in order to make what you do in Britain acceptable as a basis for job applications on your return. Your examiners will probably also help in this capacity later. But it is up to you to ask for help – and to make it easy and pleasurable for people to give it.

Your chosen person(s) need to be alert to feminist issues and tied into professional organizations and the job market network in ways that will help you. They need to push you to be that bit more ambitious and to recognize how women get overlooked, or have to be doubly as qualified to be considered for grants and consultancies. Your mentor should urge you to apply for opportunities, discuss strategies with you, coach you and give feedback, write you a letter of recommendation (or if possible actually be on the relevant committee), and help you over tough spots.

After noting that women were only half as successful as men in the competition for postdoctoral fellowships from Sweden's Medical Research Council, Weneras and Wold got a court order in 1997 to obtain the (officially public) peer review scores. They found that women applicants had to be 2.5 times more productive than the average man applicant (on six productivity variables) to receive the same competency score. It also helped to be a colleague of a member of the review committee (Weneras and Wold 1997).

However, although this study is much quoted, UK national research funded by the Wellcome Trust, which followed it up, including a major study of applications by academic staff to the six main research councils (i.e. nor postdocs), found that women who applied were as successful as men. However, women were less likely to apply – because of their lower and less secure status in their institutions, because they had less support, because of their professional profile and because of family circumstances (Blake and La Valle 2001).

You could establish your own specialist research and professional network (maybe even your personal study group) initially through your professional association and its study groups and postgraduate sections. (You can put a notice into their newsletter.) You can then develop these contacts by attending conferences and workshops, and talking to a few people and volunteering yourself to give papers at seminars. (I am not denying how stressful this can be. But the person sitting next to you in a session at a conference is *surely* likely to have similar interests? And people in the audience for your talk could include a future mentor.) It is very helpful in getting your name known to help organize some of these events – or if there are no appropriate existing working groups or conferences, to volunteer to establish and run one (see my own experience, p. 177). Also, get your own website and contribute to email discussions (see pp. 244, 256–8).

Networks and contacts with mentors need to be maintained – but women ought to be well placed to do this, given our greater skill in 'emotional work'. None the less, a study of men and women in psychology found women had in fact fewer collegial ties to their previous institutions than men (Rose 1985).

Coping with stress

Sue Vartuli's (1982) early edited collection on *The PhD Experience: A Woman's Point of View* has a whole chapter on stress, concentrating especially on the first year and the comprehensive exams (in the USA) but looking also at more general issues of loss of status, lack of money, the need to build a new support system, and the physical effects of changed patterns of diet and exercise, recreation and socialization. Changes are obviously most marked for those who move home and culture, who may be disoriented initially by studying in a new environment while missing people and things which are a long way away. A lot of the writing concerned with international students is certainly around welfare issues (but note that the research on which it is based often used samples with 70 per cent or more men respondents without looking to see if there are differences between the sexes, Wright 1997: 99). Questionnaire surveys drawn up by British researchers may also not be aware of the issues which actually concern students themselves. It is assumed the issue is one of 'adapting', but autobiographies more often explore the *opportunities* opened up by travel. A period studying for a doctorate may be less stressful, or chosen for more complex, reflexive reasons than is dreamed of in much of the current literature.

> When I was working on my Doctoral dissertation, which finally became this book, I was thinking of the woman – myself – that came to the USA in May of 1988. At that time, I was carrying with me the tiredness of seven years of teaching within a sterile theorisation locked in the discourse of methods. I was still full of the fear and the anger that a long period of political repression in Argentina had imposed on people as an everyday experience. At the same time, I hoped to find new spaces of reflection, a language to articulate my lived experience, and the means to articulate my theoretical baggage. By doing graduate studies at an American university I do not mean 'visiting dream land' in an uncritical perspective. Rather, I intended to gain some material and emotional distance on my immediate context, to think not only from a different location, but from one that makes more explicit power relations – in the sense of being positioned as an outsider thinking with others.
>
> (Hernández 1997 quoted in UKCOSA 1998)

Philips and Pugh (2000) suggest the first year can produce a loss of sense of balance in life, especially in disciplines where the work is less structured and potentially isolating, and a feeling of especial unease in the first six months because of being in many ways in a privileged situation and feeling you should be doing better and enjoying it more. But this is something common to most projects. In doing a doctorate, however, the emotional rollercoaster doesn't go steadily up and then down. It can switch back and forth from day to day and for a long time. Certainly for those who find this stressful, the effects can be harmful – anxiety, irritability, accidents, aggression, use of alcohol, depression – and a vicious circle of less leisure, less exercise, sleeplessness, and lack of concentration, leading to working longer hours. There can also be physical stresses: risks of repetitive strain injury to one's hands and arms, and damage to one's eyes from hours in front of computer screens. 'Stress' is also often tied in to contemporary overwork and it frequently gets commented upon in the popular press. We can see it all around us. However, 'stress' is not a new experience, despite the headlines, nor is it simply equatable to escalating external demands.

It is now [1949] sixteen years since my first book was published, and about twenty-one years since I started publishing articles in the magazines. Throughout that time there has literally been not one day in which I did not feel I was idling, that I was behind with the current job, and that my output was miserably small. Even in the periods when I was working ten hours a day on a book, or turning out four or five articles a week, I have never been able to get any sense of achievement out of the work that is actually in progress because it always goes slower than I intend, and in any case I feel that a book or even an article does not exist until it is finished. But as soon as a book is finished, I begin, actually from the next day, worrying because the next one is not begun.

(George Orwell in Bott 1958)

Doing a doctorate is stressful, in so far as it is, because of changes and trying to make sense of situations, because of worries over one's abilities and having straitened finances, because you are trying to work on a long-term project when other aspects of life demand immediate responses (with breakfast meetings, mobile phones, faxes, email, and children's routines); and because we have to be 'present' for long hours at work to show our keenness. The very fact that we now have a word for it, and specialists in 'handling' it, make it both visible and experienceable.

But an alternative approach is to see 'stress' as a new 'expert knowledge', a therapy and media discourse, which makes it seem that the distresses we feel are chiefly a function of ourselves: of our approach to life. We grab on to accounts of 'stress' because they seem to explain us to ourselves, and we actively participate in them when we understand ourselves through them. We believe that 'stress' is an outside, scientific and objective fact of modern life (or of doing a doctorate), and that the solution is to organize our time better and to think more positively to avoid feeling bad. But the stress discourse (and occupational therapy gurus) see the stressed person as an apolitical, decontextualized 'autonomous person', instead of seeing individuals in relation to codes of required emotional restraint within private, public and organizational settings and in relation to the power relations between superior and subordinate, men and women, employer and employee. From this alternative perspective, 'stress' in doctoral studies is better handled by getting an understanding of the process of disciplinary socialization rather than by 'time management'; by recognizing that one has been put (back) into an apprentice position, and coping with this through negotiating a more equal relationship with one's supervisor; and by establishing solidarities with others in the same situation, rather than by retreating into one's room and adjusting one's head.

While men with stress turn to their spouse or parents, all the writers in the field emphasize the importance of female networks in providing not only support but also solutions – and fun – up to and beyond doctoral level study for women. We may indeed find it easier to 'settle down' and work if we are *not* with partners, not only because we then do not have to look after another person's emotional and physical needs, but also because we can be more independent on our own and mix with different people. Both academic and welfare staff should encourage and facilitate women's support groups, including contacts between 'home' and international women students (compare pp. 111, 203–4). Ingrid Moses advocates research groups to maintain women's confidence and connectedness, while Phil Salmon suggests using mutually supportive (mixed sex) group meetings facilitated by the supervisor, rather than (or in addition to) one-to-one supervision. But again, of course, the possibility of establishing such networks depends on the physical presence of a fair number of women in the institution. It is difficult to establish women's groups if most women students are part-time, or if there are not many postgraduates in your field (say in social work or architecture). It also does help if the initiative came from the institution, because students then experience less harassment from their peers and compatriots for being 'feminists'. But with or without staff support, do organize yourself support.

Further reading

On trying to demystify the actual process of doing research

Bell, C. and Roberts, H. (eds) (1984) *Social Researching*. London: Routledge and Kegan Paul. One of the early and very readable accounts of 'real' (as opposed to textbook ideal) research. Includes discussion of the politics of funding of research and some of the possible problems of interviewing (when people tell you too much or are more powerful than you) and of publishing your results.

Delamont, S., Atkinson, P. and Parry, O. (2000) *The Doctoral Experience: Success and Failure in Graduate School*. London: Falmer. Gives full accounts of what it is like to do research based either in laboratories or involving fieldwork, and the different ways in which research students acquire the specific 'habitus' of full members in different disciplines.

Devine, F. and Heath, S. (1999) *Sociological Research Methods in Context*. London: Macmillan. Critically evaluates eight key recent (mainly gender-related) studies in core areas of sociology (work, education, family, and others). It looks at the choices made, including compromises and constraints, and how these shape the findings of the research.

Knorr-Cetina, K. D. (1999) *Epistemic Cultures*. Cambridge, MA: Harvard University Press. Documents disciplinary differences in scientific cultures of high energy physics and molecular biology and pays explicit attention to the role of doctoral students.

Stanley, L. (ed.) (1990) *Feminist Praxis*. London: Routledge. Combines discussion of feminist methodology and detailed accounts of research in practice, especially the use of women's, including the researcher's own, 'experience'. It includes some accounts of major problems and 'failed' research projects. (You might wish to reflect on whether it is advisable to publish such work, and/or at what stage in your career you can afford to do so!)

On developing support within your university

Butler, A. (1998) Creating space: the development of the feminist research group, in D. Malina and S. Maslin-Prothero (eds) *Surviving the Academy: Feminist Perspectives*. London: Falmer. Describes the establishment and issues within a study group which included staff and students (and got staff development funding to cover its costs).

Hatt, S., Kent, J. and Britton, C. (eds) (1999) *Women, Research and Careers*. London: Macmillan. A similar theme to the above: a collection of chapters by women in a social science faculty at a new university describing how the support they gave each other helped each of them develop their own research agenda alongside various other (heterosexual) domestic and employment demands. The second half is a 'self-help tool' for you to use to evaluate your own situation and needs.

Keeling C. and Coe, E. (2001) *Setting Up Peer-Mentoring With Postgraduate Research Students*. London: SRHE and THES. Describes a successful scheme in the science, engineering and medicine graduate school at the University of Manchester. This offers free, high standard training in mentoring techniques to postgraduate mentor volunteers.

Russell, C. L., Plotkin, R. and Bell, A. C. (1998) Merge/emerge: collaboration in graduate school, in E. Peck and J. S. Mink (eds) *Common Ground: Feminist Collaboration in the Academy*. Albany, NY: SUNY Press. Three ecofeminists credit collaboration with broadening their learning opportunities, increasing their willingness to support unpopular positions and helping their commitment to 'honouring a multiplicity of voices'. Part of an interesting collection which includes reflections on sharing an office, sharing teaching, reconsidering and challenging the Romantic and academic ideals of single authorship, and former lesbian partners writing together.

Stacy, H. (1999) The law, policies and ethics: supervising postgraduate NESB students in an era of internationalization, in Y. Ryan and O. Zuber-Skerrit (eds) *Supervising Postgraduates from Non-English-Speaking Backgrounds*. Buckingham: SRHE and Open University Press. Not so much how to develop as how to insist on support. The author suggests what an aggrieved (home or international) student can threaten to do if they are conceived of as 'customers' or 'consumers'. She considers using legal challenges on the basis of 'educational negligence', 'misrepresentation' in advertising, and 'vicarious liability'.

On developing wider support within your discipline

Blaxter, L., Hughes, C. and Tight, M. (1998) *The Academic Career Handbook*. Buckingham: Open University Press. Chapter 4 is an excellent guide to networking:

how to use conferences, seminars and societies, and getting involved in journals and newsletters. It also discusses mentoring and establishing writing and teaching partnerships.

Segerman-Peck, L. (1991) *Networking and Mentoring: A Woman's Guide*. London: Piatkus. Particularly focused on mentoring for career development. Expert guidance on what to look for in a mentor, how to select and approach one (or more), and getting the most out of the relationship, as well as considering some problems that can arise. Contains case histories.

Note

1 The first two columns derive from ideas by Robert Merton (1957) on 'cosmopolitan' and 'local' professionals developed by Ziman (1991, 2000), to which I have added a third column.

6 | HOW TO ACCESS WORK ON GENDER WHEN YOUR SUPERVISOR DOESN'T KNOW WHAT HE (OR SHE) DOESN'T KNOW

Most people have an area of interest in mind when they approach a supervisor about doing some research. Your supervisor should then either provide an interesting topic as part of (one of) their own projects in the field, or help you sort out what constitutes an interesting research question in an area of your own. Supervisors should stretch you – get you thinking in ways outside your initial mindset on the topic. They should (help you) recognize the things that you say or plan to do which are genuinely new, and suggest ways to develop your insights. They should also constantly remind you of possible audiences for your findings. They must therefore be conversant not only with general methodologies and approaches current in your discipline or area, but also with the specific skills and resources you will need to use, including the relevant journals and recently completed and ongoing research and what you can access in your library (or labs) or elsewhere. In the social sciences and humanities, supervisors do not need to be in exactly the same field as the one you plan to work in (or wherever your focus may shift to); and inevitably your own supervisor will sooner or later know less about your central concern than you do. But they should constantly provide exciting, expanding, relevant possibilities, contacts and suggestions.

Students interested in doing research on women or on men/masculinity and sexuality, or any work which may have a gender dimension to it (which is almost everything), should therefore be warned that many men (and some women) academics have not read more than a sprinkling of the literature in this field despite 25 years of active feminist scholarship. They will therefore *not* be able to stretch research students in this area. Instead many steer away from feminist research because it is too daunting to know where to begin, because they are afraid of saying something foolish and getting attacked by their supposedly dungaree-wearing, lesbian feminist colleagues, or because, misogynistically, they can't believe it can be interesting. They may well encourage you to do the same. Alternatively, some supervisors may, innocently or otherwise, take on students who express an initial interest in gender, thinking their general knowledge is enough to guide students who just need to 'add women in'. Or they hope that through working with a student they themselves will learn about feminist work.

If you are to ask important research questions, however, it is not a question of 'adding women in' but of overturning sexist paradigms in the sciences, social sciences and humanities, and thinking differently. It is certainly not enough for your supervisor to 'send you off to talk to a feminist they know', generally late in the day and certainly too late for it to be helpful to your research project. (It is also not fair to ask extra unrecognized work of such women.) As a result, sometimes neither the student nor the supervisor knows what a thesis is lacking – theoretically, methodologically and empirically – possibly until the viva or until you seek to publish.

> This book itself exemplifies the ignorance of gender of most of the 'experts' who produce mainstream research and national reports on higher education. If you read their work you will see they have no notion of what has been achieved by feminist researchers, either generally or in relation to higher education itself, nor how gender affects any and everything they look at. Of course this ignorance is political: it has an origin and a purpose. But one would hope for better in future, and especially in the guidance given to future women researchers.

So if you do want to do research on women, or on men (as such), or if the field you are interested in has a *possible* gender dimension, do make sure you work with a gender specialist as supervisor or co-supervisor. *At least* attend a good relevant course in your university on women's (or feminist or gender) studies. If you are doing research on another country, find a specialist on gender in that country, since obviously there are important national and cultural variations. Otherwise you will simply not know what you are missing until it is too late – and 'what is missing' is both scholarly insight into your material and the intellectual excitement and sense of solidarity that exists in this rapidly growing field. Some suggestions for further reading are on pp. 194–6, but reading texts is no substitute for the good coaching of face-to-face interaction with a knowledgeable supervisor.

Research on women and sexual divisions

My own entry into feminist research came in 1971 when I was trying unsuccessfully to analyse the data I had collected for my PhD thesis in anthropology, on the rituals of courtship and weddings in South Wales (finally published in 1980). In fact I was not getting very much writing done at all because of domestic circumstances (the care of three small children and social isolation after a move away from the town where I was registered, because of my then husband's new job). A friend invited me to join a group of women anthropologists in London who were discussing the state of the discipline: our place within it, its treatment of women in the cultures it studies, and how we could/had developed better accounts in our recently completed or ongoing PhDs. To this end we read various newly emerging British writing and the already quite large corpus of US work; and to publicize our ideas and broaden our membership we organized a day conference with a similar group which was meeting in Cambridge.

I was also simultaneously a member of the British Sociological Association (BSA) and volunteered to take on organizing one of the study groups I had been attending. This led me to have the luck to be asked by Professor Sheila Allen to help organize the BSA national conference in 1974. It changed my life. The BSA Executive had suggested to Sheila that the theme of the conference should be 'The Family' (why else would they have asked a woman?), but we changed this to 'Sexual Divisions and Society' and recruited everyone we knew working in the wider area to attend and give papers. Some of the conference contributors were only marginally 'sociologists' (they were historians, anthropologists, or social work and policy analysts). But the conference was well attended and buzzing as a result of the emergent Women's Liberation Movement; and the two books of papers we subsequently edited became a turning point in the social sciences in Britain (Leonard Barker and Allen 1976a, 1976b; Leonard and Allen 1991). Two working parties on the position of women and on curricula in sociology were set up at the AGM at the conference, along with a women's caucus which continues to this day (Allen and Leonard 1996).

Similar things were happening in a number of other disciplines, notably history and among members of the National Association for the Teaching of English (NATE) in the mid-1970s in Britain, and several new academic as well as popular journals and specifically feminist publishers were established within the next few years (p. 257), while similar work also blossomed in North America and elsewhere in Europe. Looking back, one can see these conferences and publications as together constituting a first phase of *recuperation* by the second wave of feminism in Britain (de Groot and Maynard

1993: 4): initiatives to assert the importance of including women on the agenda of scholarship and in the academy; of challenges to the silences and misrepresentations around women; and of collecting and disseminating empirical evidence in social science, history, literary criticism and also in science. But with the recovery of our own history, which has been an important part of feminism, we also now appreciate that this was just the latest phase in a long history of concern with the situation of women. Collectively and individually we have worked since then to develop a specifically feminist perspective, and the concepts needed for this (such as, in the 1970s, 'gender', 'sexism' and 'patriarchy').

I am distinguishing a feminist perspective from Equal Opportunities (see pp. 33–4) while recognizing there are a number of different positions within each.

Work with an Equal Opportunities (or equal rights) perspective
- believes there are differences between men and women which need to be changed because they are disadvantageous for both sexes (though especially for women)
- sees these differences as especially to do with women's responsibilities for child (and other) care and access to paid work
- focuses on differences between men and women as the attributes of particular sorts of individuals
- tackles race, class and gender discrimination as separate issues
- sees politics as being to do with the public but not the private sphere
- is ambivalent towards any organized form of feminism (women working together as women for women's rights), seeing it as unnecessarily 'extreme' and 'off-putting'.

Work with a feminist perspective
- stresses the relationship between men and women is one of inequality
- tries to connect the various elements of women's position in society, including (hetero)sexuality and violence against women
- understands that to change sexual divisions involves fundamental change in a wide range of social relationships, including aspects of class and race inequalities (and vice versa)
- acknowledges that the power which operates in personal relations (parenthood, marriage, informally with colleagues at work) is also political
- sees relations between the sexes as also to do with masculinity and male-defined structures and cultures
- has a clearly articulated commitment to women as as a political group and to autonomous women's action (including academic study and research) to allow issues which matter to women to be raised, understood and collectively challenged.

(Adapted from Barry 1993: 54–6)

The first 'recuperation' phase of feminist scholarship in the 1970s was followed by one of *reconstruction* from the end of the decade: of creative reassessments of whole areas of study leading to a re-evaluation and redesigning of the very terms and topics which had structured existing academic disciplines. (See for example the reappraisal of the concept of what it means to be 'professional' referred to on pp. 43–5.) This included looking at how academic disciplines themselves construct and reconstruct gender.

Kim Thomas's (1990) work (see also p. 67) points out that while higher education is generally regarded as a liberal social institution – an arena which allows women to enter in reasonable numbers, and even to succeed – but,

this liberalism is ultimately illusory and allows gender divisions to be maintained and renewed . . . Inequality of achievement is seen as the fault of schools or of society in general or as the result of student inadequacy: never [as] the inadequacy of the individual departments or institutions. [Certain disciplines] are regarded by some of their practitioners as potentially, and even actually, subversive of conventional beliefs about women and men. Yet it is very rare that this subversion of the values of the outside world leads to a critical examination of the practices of the institution [or the department itself] . . . Higher education does not reproduce inequality by actively discriminating against women. What is does is make use of culturally available ideas of masculinity and femininity in such a way that women are marginalized and, to some extent, alienated.

(Thomas 1990: 180–1)

In science men students reconstruct a middle class version of masculinity, bound up with ideas of following a successful career: being clever, competitive, pushy and earning a lot of money. They have an image of a 'successful physicist' which could equally mean a 'successful man'. Studying physics affirms their masculinity, and hence their certainty and self-importance: a mutually reassuring circle. For women science students, on the other hand, choosing to study physics or physical science is an act of non conformity, though not necessarily an act of rebellion since they are often encouraged by single-sex schools and scientist parents. But many feel they have to prove they are 'as good as men', as if men are innately better scientists – which of course women can never do, since men have a head start in the 'being a man' stakes. Women science students therefore feel pulled in various directions, notably because the certainty, single-mindedness and conformity required by physics depends on a negation of femininity, and they want also to be successful as ordinary women.

Most English and communications men students, by contrast, see themselves as non-conformists and rebellious, not only because they are studying a non-vocational, non-boring subject (and so opting out of the rat race) but also because this is how their subject allows, indeed encourages, them to see themselves. '[T]here is nothing easier than for a man to be "masculine" in a subject where women predominate and where individualism, originality and assertiveness are highly valued' (Thomas 1990: 177). Women students in these fields, on the other hand, are caught in a double-bind. English appears to allow women an escape route from an education system where sensitivity, breadth, and femininity are not generally valued. But university English is in fact less about the emotions and subjectivity than about individualism; and the (largely male) staff say women are *too* emotional, *too* subjective, too involved, and so on. Moreover, if 80 per cent of the students are women, who is an individual to be 'different' from? And if a woman opts out the rat race, isn't that what women have always done? (Thomas 1990: 176–8 and 180–1)

Reconstruction in feminist scholarship was joined by a phase of *reflexivity* in the 1980s and 1990s: of self-awareness and self-criticism, with differences and debates among practitioners. This involved serious questioning of the white, western and heterosexual biases of feminism; and of the ways in which knowledge is produced. This has been particularly constructive for discussions of research methodology.

While these three phases occurred sequentially, they have overlapped and each still continues and remains necessary. There is a continuing need for 'recuperation' in those fields which have been as yet little touched (like research on higher education!), and in newly emerging fields (like information and communication technology). There is also a continuing need to fight to retain the intellectual spaces which have been established for feminist teaching, discussion and research (including doctorates). That is to say, for what has been called women's studies.

Women's studies

Courses which provided an 'intellectual space where women's identities, activities and experiences can be explored and understood as worthy topics for serious scholarly attention' (Zmrochek and Duchen 1991: 14) began to be established in the UK in adult education classes and university extramural departments, and as 'options' within courses in sociology, English and history in universities, as a result of student and staff demand in the late 1970s. Degrees in women's studies as such were initially only (and are still largely) offered at postgraduate level – the first being a Masters course at the University of Kent at Canterbury in 1980. That is to say, within the British system, universities would at first accept only a (multidisciplinary) degree in women's studies at a level where people had already been satisfactorily socialized into a 'proper' discipline. This is in marked contrast to the USA, where women's studies developed initially, and much faster, in undergraduate liberal Arts degrees.

With the increasing marketization of British higher education, more and more Masters degrees in women's studies were rapidly established because they 'sold' well. That is to say, later acceptance of women's studies was due not to senior academics and administrators having a change of heart, but to their supporting a general expansion in the humanities and social sciences in the 1980s because these fields are cheaper per capita than the sciences and can soak up, and were popular with, students. Undergraduate women's studies was borne along on this tide. At postgraduate level, women's studies was also welcomed because its enthusiastic students were prepared to pay their own fees. It was cost-effective because it needed, at most, a few new (but cheap, young) temporary appointments; and with luck it simply required the willing redeployment of existing members of staff. By the late 1990s it had therefore become possible to do a women's studies course at a university in almost any part of the UK.

Some people have produced very triumphalist accounts of this increase in numbers of centres and courses and publications in women's studies, and it certainly has provided an important 'address' for those seeking involvement in feminism. Several generations of students have passed through, including many who have now moved on to do doctorates. However, in most universities, with the possible exceptions of Lancaster, York and Kent, women's studies courses are still, after 20 years, institutionally insecure. The subject area does not have autonomy in hiring and promoting staff, it is always short of resources, it doesn't get credit for its teaching and research profile, and there are few doctorates in women's studies as such.

Historically, university women's studies in Britain has been the result of a felicitous, but essentially sporadic and ad hoc, series of encounters between academic women from various disciplines and of various political outlooks, all interested in gender, or 'women', or sexuality, or feminism, or sexism, or equal opportunities, or oppression, or some aspects of culture's dealings with one of the above, and all looking for a legitimate context in which their concerns might be shared, supported and developed. Feminist critique in, and/or of, higher education has systematically demonstrated that, left to themselves, the traditional disciplines are likely to marginalise, misconstrue or altogether exclude women as objects and subjects of enquiry. Hand in hand with this pessimistic dismissal has gone a correspondingly optimistic sense that it is in the engagement between disciplines and in the concerted challenge to their self-sufficiency and integrity, that gender relations, women's subordination and the 'subject of feminism' can be articulated and theorised.

(Broughton 1993: 73)

That is to say, the 'multidisciplinarity' of women's studies has been due partly to a commitment to such an approach, but also largely to force of circumstances – because of who were the available and willing members of staff in a particular institution. Women's studies has rarely been the result of a careful selection of the disciplines which need to be drawn upon to cover carefully selected aspects of understanding and changing women's situation, and each university's course is rather different. Some are arts and others social science focused, women's history stays somewhat apart, and while a few include modules on women and science or technology of various kinds, none is centrally science based. Many women's studies students actually get a smorgasbord of disciplinary courses and are left to make interdisciplinary sense of them for themselves. There are always some 'core' women's studies courses, but what is included even in these can be very different from one institution to the next; and many of the optional courses offered are mono-disciplinary and simply cross-listed with women's studies. All of this weighs heavily on those in charge of women's studies or who are concerned for its survival and the quality of its scholarship. This is also probably why women's studies has come to focus more on its innovative and participative pedagogy, which *is* shared, rather than its curriculum, which is diverse.

Women's studies has been particularly concerned with the dynamics of classroom (small group) interactions. It has sought to minimize the hierarchy between teachers and students so as to create a collaborative and participatory environment to draw women into learning, within which women can talk about their own experiences (without the silencing presence of men) and collectively produce an organic (student generated and action oriented) curriculum relevant to their particular concerns. It has a lot in common with the liberatory pedagogies proposed by various major educationalists (such as Dewey and Freire) and with the progressive pedagogy practised in primary schools and adult education. However, what exists in women's studies mainly grew autonomously out of feminist 'consciousness raising'; and those in women's studies are certainly not generally keen to explore its commonalities with other educationalists' ideas. Women's studies also has a deliberately recognized alternative ideological agenda, which is in opposition to and which problematises the partial interests of so-called mainstream liberal education. The latter is supposedly neutral, but in fact class, race and gender biased. Women's studies also has much in common with other radical critiques of education, though it has been more successful than most of these in recognizing and working with differences among the oppressed group it focuses upon (among women, by class, culture, age, sexuality). It has also been hugely successful in producing transformative experiences for its students. All of which is not to say that it is not also constructed and constrained by being an institutionalized field within educational institutions where teaching is often directly instructional and where students are assessed and issued with credentials.

During the 1980s, problems within women's studies were not too apparent because the subject area was expanding. The competition for students and general postgraduate expansion made any Masters degree which attracted international students and part-time, home, fee-paying students, welcome. Moreover, feminist options were also welcomed by the disciplines at undergraduate level because their intellectual content broadened, updated and generally perked up some tired old disciplinary approaches. But by the end of the 1990s, strains were certainly showing. Many of the modules included in women's studies courses are put on by discipline-based departments and so women's studies centres have little control over what is taught in many of the courses they list. Also (most important in these audit-conscious days), credit for the enrolment of students goes to mainstream departments and any research projects and publications are also attributed to staff's home departments. Students often 'sit in' on women's studies core courses, either because they want some feminist input but prefer their degrees to be formally in one of the traditional disciplines; or because they are research students whose supervisors have sent them to fill in the gaps in the supervisor's knowledge. But they 'don't count' for women's studies when it comes to justifying extra staffing.

On top of this, overall recruitment to women's studies has been going down rather than up, at both postgraduate and undergraduate level, even though feminist options in mainstream subjects are still very popular. This may be partly because of a direct backlash against feminism, though the UK has not experienced the same attacks and counter-exaggerations that women's studies has in the USA. But it is more likely to be because there has been a decline in the size of the general constituency from which women's studies undergraduate majors and Masters students have been drawn. Working class, women, older and part-time students, and especially working class mature women students, are being particularly squeezed by current policy changes on fees and grants, by changes in the labour market, and by ideological pressure to see education as primarily about vocational training rather than personal development and the production of exciting new knowledge.

Moreover, the significantly increased workloads of all staff have made it harder for them to take on the extra teaching or networking 'for personal interest' which women's studies has relied upon. Some faculty are therefore simply withdrawing back into their disciplinary department and teaching feminist courses and doing research there alone. Others are focusing upon themselves and getting their own promotion. A committed few are arguing for a regrouping, with women's studies starting to work *within* the fiscal and intellectual structures of the universities, instead of trying to cut across them (or hovering on the margins) and using the skills and clout of women who are now in high positions. This implies abandoning arguments for full women's studies departments and thinking instead in terms of departments where there are several feminists developing programmes entirely in arts or social science, or in terms of courses *within*, say, law or science degrees. This will make it easier to access resources. Such restructuring could also stress how feminist work is the intellectual magnet that draws (certain groups of) people into universities – some of them groups which the university is encouraged by politicians to increasingly represent on its rolls (older, working class students). It might also help with fundraising and attract external donations from alumni. (Some US universities have received large donations from women's estates.) The contribution of feminist publications and research income would also become more visible if it was recognized as a subsection within English and history (since women's studies research has not managed to get itself recognized as a subject area within the Research Assessment Exercise).

Such national issues show the need for a strong professional organization for women's studies as a whole and for caucuses discipline by discipline, which press not only for research audit visibility but also lobby funders to include feminist dimensions in their evaluation criteria. Such a professional organization is also needed to present feminist perspectives to national commissions and committees on higher education (such as Dearing), to establish national 'benchmark' standards in the field, and to conduct systematic research on women's studies itself, as a subject area.

The Women's Studies Network (WSN) (UK) Association was set up in 1988–9 and has 600 members. It has a website and produces a quarterly *Newsletter* together with handbooks of its members and of women's studies courses available in the UK. It held its first annual conference in 1990 and has published regular edited collections of papers from these meetings ever since. These provide a good overview of the changing field.[1] It has tended, however, to fall between the two stools of being a non-academic network with a friendly annual conference which serves in lieu of a women's movement meeting, and a professional association. It has recently moved a bit more towards being a professional association by joining the new UK-wide campaigning organization, the Association of Learned Societies in the Social Sciences (ALSISS).

More backing is also needed to strengthen the infrastructure for women's studies and feminist research. These have been starved of funds. No library has acquired systematically in this field, although the situation may well improve since the Fawcett Library at London Guildhall University received a £4.2 million grant from the heritage Lottery Fund in 1998 toward an £11 million National Library for Women. The Fawcett Library website and newsletter already provide the best central guide to organizations and events in this field. Nor has any institution done the bibliographic work undertaken by the University of Wisconsin and Northwestern University in the USA and the Dutch International Archief voor de Vrouwenbeweging (International Archives for the Women's Movement) in Amsterdam. Several important UK feminist collections are in temporary premises from which they periodically face eviction, and they rely on voluntary labour. No one has had enough to spend on purchasing, and the archives of the contemporary movement remain scattered and largely unindexed. (The WSN archive is in my office.)

> The European Union supports not only EO initiatives (see p. 38) but also to some extent women's studies and feminist research. It funded a Centre for Research on European Women (CREW) for some years and subcontracted a Belgian/French Groupe de Recherche Féministes (GRIF) to produce an overview of women's studies country by country at the end of the 1980s (GRIF 1989, Zmroczek and Duchen 1989, 1991). Another review of the contribution of women's studies to European integration was produced in the 1990s (Hanmer *et al.* 1995); and a number of overview conferences subsequently (for example Braidotti and Vonk 2000). Several UK women's studies programmes are part of ERASMUS/SOCRATES networks and there are currently two European women's studies associations, one for individual members: WISE (Women's International Studies Europe, founded in 1990) associated with the *European Journal of Women's Studies* and the other for institutions, AIOFE (Feminist Education and Research in Europe, established 1996) run by NIKK (the Nordic Institute for Women's Studies and Gender Research).
>
> WISE is an active and democratic lobbying group with a good website and email discussion groups, a number of specialist networks, including groups focusing on science and technology, racism, and lesbian studies. It also produces occasional guides (like the one on getting grants: see p. 135). However, since relatively few UK feminists speak or read other languages, relatively few are much involved. Also accessing Euro resources feels like penetrating a closed circle – time consuming, cliquey and disheartening.

Vanishing women? Men's studies and gender studies

The reflexivity (self-awareness and self-criticism) within women's studies previously mentioned was largely prompted by critiques of the dominant concerns of early feminist research by feminist lesbians, Black, working class and disabled women. These were later reinforced by women from low to medium income countries. This has been a painful process, but it has led to a focus on the diversity of women, on what we do *not* share, and indeed how some women oppress and exploit others. This has broadened, greatly enriched and internationalized women's studies curricula and research interests, and led to a recognition that structured social inequalities and micro-processes do not just add on to each other but rather interrelate and complexly co-construct each other. Thus issues for Black British women are not just those of Black men plus those of white women, but specific to Black women; and they also vary among Black women according to social class and sexual preference. It is now recognized that women's studies needs to be related to Black studies and gay and lesbian studies, even if it can be hard to form alliances and also hard to maintain a central focus on women.

Identities are now seen as both more fluid and as differently negotiated (and renegotiated) by individuals throughout their lives. Different individuals are recognized as experiencing similar circumstances differently (see Introduction pp. 6–8), which has led to a problematizing of 'experience'. In the so-called 'identity politics' period of the 1980s, what a woman who was working class and a single mother said, was asserted to represent a (if not the) truth about the situation of working class single mothers. But establishing that one has a certain 'identity' (attributes) is no longer taken to guarantee the authority of what one says. It is still accepted that when women talk and share their experience, what each one says needs to be respected and used as a source of insights (as in early consciousness raising). But it is also now seen to need to be 'read' – contextualized and analysed – not taken as a transparent fact.

One paradoxical effect of this is that, just as higher education in general is putting a new stress on experiential learning, women's studies, which developed this form of pedagogy, is back-tracking. Whereas an early driving force of feminism was to get women to challenge the 'experts' by speaking about their own condition from their own position (and so show the positioning of dominant males) – to find a voice and raise consciousness – today we seem tied down like Gulliver. We now put 'experience' in scare quotation marks. It is problematic. Accounts are aimed instead at 'deconstructing' women's experiences, not empathizing with or celebrating them. Issues of 'whose experience?' continue. Who gets to speak? What is reported? What is treated as authentic? Who has the power to provide the analysis? But it is also stressed that is no raw experience. It is always culturally embedded and the very act of speaking constructs and interprets it. So all women's studies can become the study of discourses, and perilously close to the paralysing position that no interpretative analysis of the experiences or stories of others is possible, so we can or should present simply chunks of 'raw' data, or use any old sample, or just write about oneself. I don't accept this. Recognizing the problems with 'experience' should make us wary, but it should not make us forgo systematically investigating our own and other women's accounts and analysing our contexts.

Another paradox is that recognizing diversity had led feminists to question the very category of 'woman'. Can we use a single universal? Or even 'women', which disguises so many differences and tends to be interpreted as referring to the dominant image of women (white, professional, mother, and so on)? I think we can and should, but carefully and with due recognition of complexity.

All these issues were being discussed within general philosophy long before feminism, and within feminist scholarship long before we were influenced by a hyperversion of this problematization in the fashionable philosophy of postmodernism. (Though much mainstream writing on postmodernism does not mention feminism's contribution.) Postmodernists would also theoretically challenge the very possibility of working towards social 'improvement', especially if this attempt is informed by an analysis based on overarching ideas ('metanarratives') of male power, privilege and oppression ('patriarchy'). Such ideas have certainly (but I hope temporarily) undermined earlier bold structural attempts to theorize women's subordinate position. I am glad we no longer have the same disputes between various feminist positions as to what is *the* key factor in women's oppression. Is it our position in the labour market? Or men's violence towards us? Or (hetero)sexuality? Or our unpaid work in the family?) I am also happy to take from post-structuralism and postmodernism the idea that there are multiple and shifting causes for women's position in society. But I am much less happy with other major political and practical shifts within feminist research. Specifically, I want to maintain a concern with the material situation of women and to campaign to improve our worlds, not to be overwhelmed by micro-analyses of cultural artefacts produced by specialized agents (such as studies of Madonna and postcolonial novels and Queer Theory). At times it seems as if feminist research has become largely an issue of epistemology: of what can we *know* and how can we know it; rather than what can we *do*, as academics, with others, to improve what we believe to be harmful to women (and other subordinate groups).

Although feminist scholars usually pay careful attention to the implications of our intellectual work for the politics of gender, race and class hierarchies, what about the politics of our disciplines? ... We claim 'interdisciplinarity', but it is often the case that interdisciplinarity in women's studies is rather like the 'universal' of Enlightenment discourse: seeming to be all-inclusive, [it] too often masks the predominance of one discipline over others. Today, the predominant discipline in women's studies [in the USA] is literature ... and especially that kind of literary studies that has been influenced by the discourses and concerns of philosophy ... Twenty to twenty-five years ago, women's studies programs

> ... just as likely originated in departments of sociology or history as
> literature [but they] are now most heavily influenced by literature special-
> ists ... [This] has affected the construction of U.S. feminist theory. On
> some level, we know that feminist theories are the varieties of thinking
> that aspire to explain women's condition and that we write and read
> these theories in search of presumptions and assumptions that not only
> underlie masculinism but also guide feminists in developing goals and
> strategies. But more and more we use – or we hear others use – 'theory'
> as a synonym for a certain kind of academic philosophical discourse
> steeped in the language of current literary criticism ... Historians and
> social scientists [and scientists] are uncomfortable with and defensive
> about a lot of interdisciplinary women's studies scholarship, often times
> without understanding why ... [They] worry that their particular con-
> tribution to the larger feminist intellectual project is diminishing. We
> set ourselves a worthy goal in aspiring to interdisciplinarity in feminist
> scholarship ... Nonetheless, if we are to manage [it], I suggest we must
> begin by being more, not less, explicit in presenting our disciplinary
> origins, speaking carefully across our scholarly differences [so] that
> others understand the value of our work and that we understand the
> value of others' work to a common project.
>
> (C. Moses 1998: 261–2)

When approaching feminist theories for the first time bear Claire Moses's
comments in mind. Start with work in your own field and not with famous
but prolix writers who use implicit reference to literary and postmodern
philosophical texts you aren't familiar with, and whose language is unremit-
tingly 'clever' and convoluted. (That said, many who struggle and eventually
engage with these writers do later become fans.)

A related shift has been to two new fields: men's studies and gender
studies. The former I distinguish very clearly from the serious study of men
and masculinity undertaken by men interested in feminist work (who sometimes style themselves 'pro-feminists'), which parallels work done by whites
interested in race who study whiteness, and heterosexuals interested in sexuality who problematize heterosexuality. Such reversals of focus, studying the
construction and experience of forms of power and privilege, are long over-
due, and what serious writers produce here is welcome. But this is very
different from some quite anti-feminist work from the so-called 'men's movement'. The latter seeks to 'recover' men's masculinity, wants men to get a
slice of the action in gender/queer studies, and converts men and boys into
victims, blaming women (especially feminists and mothers) for their problems.
Much of what calls itself men's studies is not sophisticated and is stuck at an

individual level of analysis, concerned with issues of subjectivity, socialization and identity: with who men (feel they) *are*, rather than what they *do*. It is certainly not concerned with the consequences of their actions for women. Very little of men's (including gay men's) studies recognizes men's behaviour as domineering, or the misogyny in much of the homosexual community. Nor does it analyse how men hold power over women. It is very much by, for and about men.

Work which calls itself 'gender studies' is more mixed and can include some of the work that I have described above under women's studies, and also pro-feminist work on men and gay studies. So check the grapevine as regards where a text you are thinking of reading or a supervisor you are thinking of approaching 'fit'. It is not that gender studies is about relations *between* the sexes in contradistinction to 'women's studies' which is about 'women', as the title might suggest, since both (multi/interdisciplinary) women's studies, pro-feminist work on men, and feminist work within the disciplines are all about the study of gender. Rather, 'gender studies' has been a term employed by some in the UK with an equal rights approach, and who (a) don't want to be tarred by radical, feminist associations, (b) think focusing specifically on women is unacceptable and (c) have little sense of the *inequality* between men and women. These sort of 'gender' studies, in courses or as the preferred new term for sections in publishers' catalogues or bookshops, tend to undermine feminism/women's studies because their use of the politically uncontentious term 'gender' is alluring. It makes it not only easy to 'mainstream', but also easy to lose sight of women (again) as subjects, actors and academics. For me it represents a failure of political nerve. Feminist and pro-feminist scholarship is about changing the position of women, and I am happy, for the time being, to continue to use a term to study sex/sexual divisions – women's studies – which makes sure we maintain our focus on the marginalized periphery.

Feminist research and methodology

Academic research has been central to the recent 'second wave' women's movement. (The first wave was from the 1850s to 1920s.) In return, feminist research through all the phases of recuperation, reconstruction and reflexivity has made a major contribution to the development of the epistemology, methodology, and ethics of most disciplines. Some scholars may (struggle to) continue the old-established practice of ignoring women; others may try to treat feminist research as a marginal sectional interest, or as simply one of many acceptable topics for research and analysis. That is to say, they may *try* to sidestep the need to rethink the basic concepts, methods and theories of each discipline and the ways in which these construct and validate gender bias and exclusion (de Groot and Maynard 1993: 9). But meanwhile feminism has laid down a foundation and stimulus for intervention within – a challenge to – *all* the accepted disciplines.

Research students have been especially important in these interventions. Many of those who started the new feminist scholarship in western countries in the 1970s and early 1980s were themselves doing their PhDs at the time. This was one reason why the dearth of women research students then was a cause for concern. (Only around 15 per cent of successful PhD completions in the UK in the 1970s were by women, 16 per cent in the USA in 1972, and 14 per cent in Australia in 1977: see Rudd and Simpson 1975; Allen 1994: 15; Astin and Malik 1994: 187.) Our under-representation was both a restriction on women's entry to and advancement within the academic profession, and also a block on the production of new, critical knowledge about women and gender. The emergent women's movement recognized universities as privileged centres for the production and validation of knowledge, and saw it as essential to get more research done on, by and for women within them, if views on women were to be changed.

Some key feminist texts which started as doctoral research include Kate Millett (1971) on sexual politics, Ann Oakley (1972, 1974) on gender and housework, Nancy Chodorow (1978) on mothering, Sylvia Walby (1986) on the history of the labour market, Liz Kelly (1988) on violence against women, Donna Haraway (1989) on primate sociology, nature and the world of modern science, Lisa Adkins (1995) on sexuality and the service industries, and Valerie Hey (1997) on girls' friendships.

Women now comprise 35–40 per cent of all doctoral students in Australia, the USA and the UK, and many of their theses continue to make major contributions to feminist scholarship. Relatively few, however, are submitted in women's studies as such. (The first PhD in women's studies in the UK was awarded at the University of York in 1989.) Supporters of women's studies as a department or discipline in its own right believe it is a failure of nerve not to have doctorates in women's studies. Against the argument that students want PhDs in traditional disciplines because there are few jobs in women's studies, they would assert that the same can be said of university jobs in fine arts or Chinese or Celtic Studies or even in English, but that doesn't mean that people shouldn't do doctoral studies in these fields. Indeed, how many sociology or pharmacy PhDs actually get jobs in sociology or pharmacy? In any case, some posts *are* now advertised in women's studies and many more specify 'gender' as a specialism.

> [The doctorate] is the crucial activity of training new scholars and researchers to continue the field's mission and especially to extend that mission into new domains. The doctorate is related first and foremost to knowledge generation and intellectual development: it is a key way in which the field lays its claim to its domain of expertise – its distinct contributions and insights to collective culture and to improvement or change in approaches.
>
> (Allen 1997: 366)

A more convincing counter-argument is that although feminist research can and should draw on many fields, and women's studies should maintain a balance of disciplinary inputs, the theories, methodology and technical skills of mainstream areas are essential in framing research questions, in analysing data and in constructing written arguments. We need the discipline of disciplines, whatever their current sexist shortcomings. Feminist work isn't distinct because of having specific methods or methodologies, or even epistemologies. Feminists can be found working within positivist, structuralist and interpretativist paradigms, using randomized control experimentation, ethnography or semiotics. Rather, feminist research is characterized by asking questions in a specific topic area and with a specific emancipatory political agenda (see Table 6.1). It is a type of research, and in terms of the classification presented on p. 155, essentially Activist. It seeks to understand the world in order to change it: to improve the situation of a particular constituency – though obviously any work done for a PhD will also have to be academic, focused on making an original contribution to knowledge, and for a professional doctorate, also have applied relevance. (It is worth repeating that of course all three types are 'normative ideals' and that actual feminist research practice, like 'real science' (Knorr-Cetina and Mulkay 1983), can be competitive, for personal aggrandizement, and written in an elitist genre.)

Feminism obviously also favours the emancipatory type of university organization which had a stirring of life with the student, antiracist and peace movements in the 1960s and 1970s (see p. 31). This was supported in the former polytechnics by the New Municipal Socialism of local Labour Party branches in the late 1970s and 1980s.

Starting out

To come to a concern with feminist research for the first time today is obviously a very different experience from the one we had in refashioning the fields of anthropology, sociology, literature and history, and challenging the sciences, medicine and technology in the 1970s. It is equally but very

Table 6.1 Feminist research

Problem formulation	Empowering Concerned to be used by, and certainly not be used against, women.
Context	Politically engaged Investigating what should be changed and how. Challenging conventional methods of research and the Enlightenment claim to 'science' being universal, objective, neutral and disinterested. Argues that what you see depends on where you stand, and for passionate scholarship. Often done with few resources but drawing on sites of struggle for ideas.
Role	Participatory Challenging the 'experts' and trying to give 'voice' to silenced group. Seeking to minimize the hierarchy between researcher and researched, and to maximize the reciprocity. Especially concerned with ethical issues and with democratic decision making within research teams. Supporting individuals doing their own research. Opposed to treating people as 'subjects'/objects.
Methodology	Standpoint Empathetic and holistic concern for those studied. Challenging the dichotomy between reason and emotion, fantasy and reality, objectivity and subjectivity, mind and body, and the devaluation of the feminine elements. Stressing instead alternative ways of knowing and the role of subjectivity in knowledge production. Has contributed substantially to the theory and practice of interviewing, and to a concern for the effects of various topics on the researchers themselves. Hopes to 'learn from the outsider within' (those in marginal social positions: see Hill Collins 1990).
Presentation	Accessible Accountable to a specific constituency outside the university and concerned to make research findings accessible: expressed in simple language and available orally, through the media, formerly through radical magazines and pamphlets and now on the worldwide web, as well as through mainstream books and journals.

differently difficult, and I'm glad I'm not facing it for the first time. Feminist critiques no longer speak from a peripheral, ghettoized position, but rather from a creative liminality, successfully pushing at the boundaries of the disciplines and creating substantial alternatives. Research has moved a long way from simple recuperation: from just anger at the absence or marginalization of women's concerns in every subject from architecture to zoology and attempts to 'put women back in'. Feminist work has re-evaluated and developed creative alternative terms and topics to those which structure mainstream research and teaching, and has deconstructed entire post-Enlightenment traditions of conceptualizing 'the human' as male. It has reassessed notions of 'objectivity', showing these to be male biased.

As a student today you are faced therefore, not with an absence of relevant writing, but rather with a daunting literature. It is all too often verbose and jargonized, littered with inverted commas and diagonal slashes, problematizing seemingly simple words and pairings, and drawing on disciplines with which you may not be at all familiar. Much of this library seems more concerned with understanding the pleasures of popular culture and consumption and the fashioning of identities and legal discourse, than with the economic and sexual exploitation of women. That is to say, with 'words' rather than 'things': with discourses about and meanings of women's lives rather than the material facticity of our subordination. Sometimes the fact (some would even query if it is a 'fact') of 'subordination' is missing; and women's agency is seen to override any contexts or constraints (if indeed any 'real' 'constraints' are recognized).

For the newcomer there are also problems in making sense of the overall history of these ideas. You are faced with trying to sort out a complex tale of different types of feminisms in different countries and different disciplines, each of which has changed over time. Feminism is not, and has never been, a homogeneous intellectual position, and there is certainly not agreement among gender scholars. You are also not helped by some pretty disingenuous accounts. Some introductions are such a parody of, say, the differences between liberal, radical and socialist feminisms, that I want to staple the pages together so no one reads them; or at least to add a warning sticker that 'reading this book may seriously addle your understanding'. In this account I have focused on the UK, and mentioned mainly UK writers, to simplify the tale. Although the UK has been much influenced by North America, the British trajectory has been different from theirs (though few writers make the distinction; and few US writers even mention non-US sources). The same can be said of influences to and from women's studies and feminist research in France and Australia and Germany.

If you are reading this before you have fixed where to study, or are effectively starting on your own because you are interested in women or think there is a gender dimension to your studies but your supervisor is not giving you help, then start with the overviews, with introductory surveys or collections, especially those with good annotated bibliographies and reviews of the different disciplines. Visit the Fawcett Library (now the Women's Library) website (www.lgu.ac.uk/fawcett; which received 67,000 hits a year in 1997–8) or read the WSN Newsletter and *Women's Studies International Forum* for news of conferences. But stick initially to your own discipline and your professional association's women's caucus and relevant study groups. Add your name to the main publishers' mailing lists to be sent catalogues; and join a few email lists. Talk to your librarians and ask for reading list for relevant courses (which will of course include things the lecturer is going to criticize, so be wary) and attend these courses if possible. Librarians may recommend bibliographies, abstracts, computer searches and websites. But, although with computers it is now easy to scan the literature and build up huge bibliographies, how useful much of the material you collect will be is another question. I would suggest using these tactics only once you have a feel for the field and can be selective. You may need to use specialist library or archival collections and inter-library loans because although a lot of published material exists, it is scattered through the many university libraries where women's studies is, or has been, taught. The stock is overwhelmingly in English, and it can be hard to get European publications – sometimes harder than to get those from low to medium countries of the South. Moreover, organizations and their newsletters, and sometimes also journals, come and (unhappily) go, and/or are not able to publicize or disseminate themselves easily. So it can be hard to track down material.

But finally, contact and talk to particular individuals whose work you like, and tell them what you are doing. However, do read their work carefully first, and don't use them as your first port of call. Individual women and men are usually very responsive if it is clear that correspondents are not wasting their time. Voluntary libraries too are helpful but they have even fewer resources for answering individual letters, so be precise; and send them free copies of your work later.

Further reading

Overviews of the history of feminist scholarship

Bulbeck, C. (1999) *Re-orientating Western Feminism: Women's Diversity in a Post-colonial World.* Cambridge: Cambridge University Press. Considers the meaning of feminism to women other than white westerners – their lived experience, concerns and views of western feminism.

Jackson, S. and Jones, J. (eds) (1998) *Contemporary Feminist Theories.* Edinburgh: Edinburgh University Press. An interesting comparison to Spender, 25 years later. It covers a range of social science and humanities fields.

Mirza, H. S. (ed.) (1997) *Black British Feminism: A Reader*. London: Routledge. A challenging collection of 'classic' articles which explore black identities, social and cultural differences and gendered and raced exclusions. Mainly from cultural studies, literature and postmodern sociological perspectives.

Spender, D. (1982) *Women of Ideas and What Men have Done to Them: From Aphra Behn to Adrienne Rich*. London: Routledge and Kegan Paul. An early 'recuperation phase' classic with sketches of the work of women from most disciplinary areas.

Whelehan, I. (1995) *Modern Feminist Thought: From the Second Wave to 'Post-feminism'*. Edinburgh: Edinburgh University Press. A well written and accurate placing of people and accounts of their work, although it doesn't distinguish sufficiently between the UK and US movements.

Overviews of areas and disciplines

Fox Keller, E. and Longino, H. E. (eds) (1996) *Feminism and Science*. Oxford: Oxford University Press. A collection of key articles published over 20 years, including feminist critiques of gendered 'knowledge' in science moving towards standpoint theory and the idea of situated knowledges. Plus detailed analyses of specific scientific fields and discourses.

Griffin, G. and Andermahr, S. (eds) (1997) *Straight Studies Modified: Lesbian Intervention in the Academy*. London: Cassell. Covers education, cultural studies, biology, politics, literature, geography, sociology, film criticism, legal theory, psychology, history, philosophy, health studies, computing and linguistics.

Kramarae, C. and Spender, D. (eds) (1993) *The Knowledge Explosion: Generations of Feminist Scholarship*. London: Harvester Wheatsheaf. Covers medicine, physics and maths, peace studies, Black studies, literary studies, religious studies, cultural studies, women's studies, anthropology, philosophy, engineering, political sciences, history, natural sciences, nursing, sports studies, journalism and mass communication, law, geography, library science, education, sociology, home economics, language, psychology, economics, architecture, music and musicology, and debates on sexual violence, ecofeminism, pornography, reproductive technology etc., with a strong American and Australian flavour.

Robinson, D. and Richardson, V. (eds) (1997) *Introducing Women's Studies: Feminist Theory and Practice*, 2nd edn. London: Macmillan. Includes history, literature, popular culture, sexuality, violence, science and technology, employment, social policy, health, education, family, reproduction and motherhood, race, and Feminist Theory, each with a short annotated bibliography.

Rose, H. (1994) *Love, Power and Knowledge: Towards a Feminist Transformation of the Sciences*. Cambridge: Polity. Locates and traces the history of the feminist criticism of science within both the feminist and the radical science movements and discusses feminist reconstruction of rationality. It includes an extensive and gripping examination of the Human Genome programme, and science fiction.

Wajcman, J. (1991) *Feminism Confronts Technology*. Cambridge: Polity. Very wide-ranging and well-written key text.

Accounts of the growth and development of women's studies

Connell, R. W. (1995) *Masculinities*. Cambridge: Polity. A good introduction to masculinity as field of knowledge and its politics. Connell argues there are multiple forms of masculinity which can (only) be understood through an analysis of gender relations. He includes detailed studies of four groups of men.

de Groot, J. and Maynard, M. (eds) (1993) *Women's Studies in the 1990s: Doing Things Differently?* New York: St Martin's Press. Covers literary criticism, political science, feminist history, postcolonial, critical theory and methodology with writers from UK, Germany and Turkey.

Fallon, H. (1998) *WOW Women on the Web: A Guide to Gender-related Resources on the Internet*, 2nd edn. Dublin: Women's Education Research and Resource Centre, University College Dublin.

Feminist Studies (1998) special issue on 'Disciplining feminism? The future of women's studies', 24(2). Focuses upon the USA, including several articles on the women's studies PhD.

Howe, F. (1997) 'Promises to keep': trends in women's studies worldwide, *Women's Studies Quarterly*, 25(1–2): 404–20.

Munt, S. R. (1997) 'I teach therefore I am': lesbian studies in the liberal academy, *Feminist Review*, 56: 85–99. An account of the highs and lows of teaching in adult and higher education, with very interesting reflections on the relationship of lesbian studies with women's and gay studies.

Women's Studies Quarterly (1992) special issue on 'Women's Studies in Europe', 20(3–4), Fall/Winter. Covers France, Belgium, Bulgaria, Germany, Ireland, Italy, Netherlands, Nordic cooperation, Spain, the UK and various European networks.

Note

1 WSN collections: Aaron and Walby 1991; Hinds *et al.* 1992; Kennedy *et al.* 1993; Griffin *et al.* 1994; Maynard and Purvis 1995, 1996; Ang-Lygate *et al.* 1997; Oerton 2000; Ali *et al.* 2000.

7 | KEEPING GOING AND STAYING THE COURSE

This may appear a somewhat negative and depressing chapter because it concerns things that may trip you up and slow down your progress – but it also contains suggestions on handling them. Non-completion is a terrible waste of student (and faculty) time, money and energy, so remember that despite the long haul, the majority of men and women *do* manage to finish their theses and gain their doctorates.

Completion: rates and times

It is still quite hard to find reliable and up-to-date data on what proportion of people finish PhDs and the average length of time it takes them; and professional doctorates in the UK are too recent to be able to say. Certainly the situation has been drastically altered since the late 1980s, especially in the social sciences, with taught components, improved supervision, tighter record keeping, monitoring and research council enforcement mechanisms (see pp. 22–5). However, even though universities probably now have better information about their students' completion rates and times, this is now 'commercially sensitive' information and not readily divulged to enquirers.

The debate still continues as to what we should be aiming for. What is a reasonable maximum time for a full-time student and what percentage of incoming cohorts should be expected to complete within what time frame? Perhaps 75 per cent completion after six years? Senior people would like higher and faster rates of 'success' than they get. Tardiness ties up supervisors and resources for extended periods and data collected for theses can go out of date. Also, very lengthy prospective periods of study deter students from enrolling and demoralize those already present. However, some long times to completion have to be accepted because of unpredictable experiments and fieldwork and the time needed to analyse and fully integrate theory and data. The pattern of research funding and lack of sufficient financial support for many students, even for those who have got grants and are full-time students, means many have to get jobs before they complete, which spins out the process considerably.

What the studies that do exist agree upon, however, is that there is major variation in time to completion between disciplines, and that the best way to be sure of completing within four years is to do a science-based project.

Recent submission rates at the University of Birmingham show two-thirds of science doctorates were completed within four years full-time or equivalent against half in the arts and humanities. The difference diminishes but doesn't disappear in the longer term: 82 per cent of science and 70 per cent of arts and humanities doctorates were completed within 10 years (Wright and Cochrane 2000). Submission rates for arts PhDs have, however doubled and according to the AHRB 70 per cent were handed in within four years in 2000, against 34 per cent in the early 1990s (*THES*, 5 January 2001: 2).

US studies have been conducted with larger samples and finer differentiation between disciplines than British studies. These show that, for instance in the University of California as a whole, the most substantial differences in mean time-to-[US] doctoral-degree [including Masters degree stage] are between students in engineering (5.5 years) and the natural sciences (6.0–6.2), and students in the social sciences (8.4), arts (8.6) and languages and literature (8.9). The natural sciences, engineering, economics and medicine had not only the fastest time to completion but also a narrower range of variance. Completion rates also vary markedly by major field of study – from 72 per cent in the biological sciences to 39 per cent in the arts and 37 per cent in languages and literature (Nerad and Cerny 1991; Nerad and Stewart 1991).

Such information as does exist suggests there is little difference between the 'success' rates of men and women. Although 'most academics [a]re under the impression that women are more likely to drop out than men, often for domestic or personal reasons', in fact women students who survive attrition in the initial months 'have a significantly better completion record than their male counterparts' even in 'the competitive, strongly male-dominated science environment' (Becher 1993: 141). Women may, however, take a little longer.

So, if success is defined as completing within four years, then probably in the past (pre-1990) fewer women used to be 'successful'. However, since most students simply want to complete reasonably quickly, but not necessarily within four years, and since the circumstances of doing doctorates have changed, it is hard to be certain about the relative performance of the sexes, but such difference as there was is probably declining.

The Californian studies found that among the cohorts entering in 1978 and 1979, only 47 per cent of women overall had completed by 1989, against 63 per cent of men. But these differences varied significantly between the (7) major fields. More women than men completed US professional doctorates, there was parity between the sexes in natural resources, while 2.75 times as many men as women completed in the arts. *Within* each major field, there was no significant difference between men and women in average time-to-degree (Nerad and Cerny 1991; Nerad and Stewart 1991).

Most British studies do not make clear if their findings apply to all or just home graduate students, but the Birmingham study specifically looked and found no difference. The UCal studies record that 'International students, both women and men, consistently [have] the highest completion rates in all fields and all cohorts.' Similarly neither age nor mode of registration seem to have much effect. You are as likely to succeed at any age and whether registered part- or full-time. However, since any group (discipline, sex) which does take longer to complete will obviously have more problems with funding when this is strictly limited to support for three years full-time study, it would be helpful if variance were more often, and more formally, recognized by funders – instead of 'late' completion being seen solely as an individual shortcoming of student and supervisor.

What (existing research suggests) slows down progress

Interviews at Berkeley with students across the disciplines who were seriously thinking of quitting a doctoral programme or who had recently left suggested that there were many reasons for non-completion common to men and women. Those who were thinking of leaving at an early stage had switched field or institution or hadn't checked the current research interests of faculty members (or indeed if certain people were still in post) before they came. It also included individuals who started PhDs but decided to switch to a professional degree, such as law. Those who were thinking of leaving later on in their studies mentioned:

- Not having been able to focus down on a single topic.
- Having a poor adviser–student relationship. This ranged from overuse of students as cheap labour, through students who were over-cautious about talking to their supervisor, to situations where the parent–child relationship was projected onto that between supervisor and student.
- Lack of financial support: those who couldn't get any more teaching work from the university, or in the sciences where the advisor's project ran out of funding before the student's PhD was completed.
- Problems when students were discouraged because they felt no one cared about them, they were wasting the faculty's time, and that research teaching was just an extra burden for staff, done on top of lots of other things.

The last

was one especially salient attrition factor for women. In our interviews, women repeatedly stressed the importance of receiving personalized attention and feedback from faculty in order . . . to have continued faith in their own capabilities. To be sure, we also spoke with male students who were angry about the absences of faculty feedback on their work. In general, however, this factor seldom lead men to question their intellectual capabilities or their capacity to do research, and only occasionally affected their progress towards completion of the doctorate.

(Nerad and Miller 1996: 71)

The UK debate, by contrast, has spent very little time looking at factors inside the university which might influence time to completion – other than the quality of individual supervision. There is hardly any monitoring of whether time to completion is influenced by students' age, sex, ethnicity, domestic circumstances or class background, and if so how – except for the single presumption of 'women's domestic responsibilities'. The play of gender, race and so on in the processes of teaching and learning in higher education are ignored, which is quite remarkable given our knowledge of differential teacher attention and its effects in schools. We need serious studies of how different groups of students experience university in different ways, for this research to be then fed into staff development and advice from the Institute of Learning and Teaching (see pp. 93–4), and for routine student evaluations for Quality Assurance also to be analysed in such a way as to assess overall academic experience and performance by domicile, 'race', age and gender. It is not all an issue of individual students' motivation and error.

The former Science and Engineering Research Council (1992) stressed as 'the main causes of late completion'

- students getting off to too slow a start because of insufficient effort
- students never being satisfied: not cutting back what they do to fit the time available and being perfectionists as regards improving results
- students getting distracted from the main line of enquiry into sidelines which look interesting
- students losing the spur to complete because they were offered the possibility of a postdoc continuation.

(Cryer 1996: 175–6)

Problems within the university

The chilly climate

'Why do you have to be so sensitive? Why bring that issue up all the time? Why do you have to be so Italian?!'

The phrase 'a chilly climate for women' is widely used in the North American literature and derives from a series of papers by Roberta M. Hall and Bernice R. Sandler from a Project on the Status and Education of Women conducted for the Association of American Colleges in the 1980s (Hall and Sandler 1982, 1984; Sandler and Hall 1986; Sandler 1993). These discuss interactions among and between faculty and students in and outside the classroom in which women routinely encounter mild to outrageous academic sexism, racism and homophobia. Often the behaviours themselves are small, and individually might even be termed 'trivial' or minor annoyances – being mistaken for technicians, administrators or secretaries, or immanent mothers and potential lovers, or assumed to be the workplace present-purchaser, peacemaker and harmonizer. But when they happen again and again they can have a major cumulative impact because they express underlying limited expectations and a certain discomfort in dealing with women. In addition, women also encounter a variety of forms of jokes, threats and aggressive behaviour, and sometimes outright statements that they are out of place and not wanted, especially if they are Black, lesbian, middle aged or feminist and especially in those fields where women faculty and students are fewest in number – in engineering, economics, maths and physical sciences. Academia is little different from most other workplaces and has as many formal and informal men's groups, be they Freemasons or 'lager louts'.[1]

The 'chilly climate' involves, for instance:

- Women being called on to contribute less often in discussions and meetings.
- Women being addressed by more familiar terms, touched affectionately or otherwise, and described with stereotyped words – or excluded by sexist language ('founding fathers', 'masterful') and use of male exemplars.
- Men, and also women, talking about women in terms of their personal qualities, appearance and relationships rather than their professional skills and achievements.
- Identical behaviour being interpreted differently according to sex, with what women do being downgraded: women being seen as less dedicated, less promising, and their abilities disparaged.
- Faculty being less willing to work with women students – because men staff feel less comfortable with them or because women students are seen as having less potential.
- Women's success being attributed to their husbands, or to luck, and their not being given positive feedback.
- Work on areas of interest and relevance to women being seen as less valuable and less central to the field, as an optional extra; and those who raise women's issues in committees or take legal action to support women being disparaged. Similarly feminine pedagogic and leadership styles being less well regarded and seen as less effective.
- Women not being included to the same extent in informal or formal activities, and being given less powerful positions with lower budgets and resources.
- Frequent joking and sexualization of interactions, such that friendly collegial relations are read as 'being in a relationship' (hetero or homo), which result in some men feeling free to move in on women while others back off, especially when minority women are concerned.
- Men intentionally disrupting women's work.

(Sandler 1993: 177)

This is all fairly familiar, and certainly well evidenced by research in schools, colleges and workplaces in Britain, even if we don't have research evidence for higher education. However, because such behaviour is familiar does not mean we should underestimate how much it drags us down; and how particularly disheartening (and hypocritical) it seems when it occurs in universities with their ideals of merit and intellectualism and Equal Opportunities policies. My own experience suggests direct sexism in academe is increasing again, with the denigration of EO as 'political correctness' and cutbacks in pastoral support systems.

Overtly sexist behaviour also intersects with behaviour asserting other inequalities, and together they throw light on the commonality of *patterns* of discrimination and reconstruction of power relationships.

A central feature of some discussions with British ethnic minority research students was an attempt to characterize the nature of racism they perceived in British higher education and in other professional working environments. Also how it was muted and denied by supposedly liberal universities. The students felt they were constantly battling against being typecast by ethnicity and sex and resented having to jump over extra hurdles. They found white people have a sense of superiority and are unaware of how they stereotype other groups. This includes regarding ethnic minority groups as less intelligent or less able in various ways and judging them by standards they would not apply to other whites. For example, white students and staff expected ethnic minorities to be good only at certain (less demanding, less valued) subjects, and only to be interested in certain topics. The social scientists in the group related how it was commonplace for white people to assume that they were only interested in studying 'race', especially their own ethnic group, which was seen as natural and undemanding research.

People [ask] me what is your research topic and I say 'John Stuart Mill'... They say wow! You know, you are a little South Asian girl, you are not supposed to have a brain... People don't know what to do when you don't fit the stereotypes.

Even those white people who acknowledged the existence of racism tended to assume that the ethnic minorities should deal with it. But if an ethnic minority person took up this challenge they were then likely to be thought single-tracked.

What would happen if I meet two or three black students reasonably regularly, say twice a week, for lunch or coffee? I guarantee that you would see some eyebrows raised. People would be scared and nervous. And that is not because anything wrong was being done... It frightens people a lot. That is the reason why ethnic minority group behaviour does not come up [in culturally mixed groups]. It is undermined by the dominant culture. Because the dominant culture is so scared.

(Carter *et al.* 1999: 61–2 and 64, italics in original)

A colleague described the pleasures of attending an Indo-Caribbean group during Black History week as 'the privilege of being in the bosom of your own. Sharing the same food, the same films. It made me realize how every day I erase myself to make others feel comfortable. That way you are accepted. We have to do the work to make the mainstream feel comfortable.'

US studies have found Anglo and African Americans both want more contact on campus, but on different terms (Institute for the Study of Social Change 1991). Whites want interpersonal contact with Blacks, but seldom establish close friendships with them and resist formal learning about other cultures being included in the regular curriculum. African Americans, on the other hand, usually find same race friendships more comfortable and resonant with shared values and experiences, while for them antiracism means changing official organizational and institutional attitudes and behaviour.

Racism also consists in assuming that all women from 'the same group' (as defined by the dominant culture, the national census, or the university classification system) identify in the same way, and share the same historical experiences, language and cultural preferences. This would never be assumed of all Anglos, let alone all Europeans.

An exploratory study of ten Hispanic women doctoral students at a university in the USA, found that 'In general, ethnic identity was a concept of more interest to Latinas [those born and/or raised in the United States] than to Latin American women [born and raised in a central or South American country].' The Latin American women questioned whether the concept 'Hispanic' was appropriately applied to them.[2] Four out of the six, who came from middle and upper middle class backgrounds, found such analytical subgroup distinctions 'disagreeable and confusing'. They identified primarily as Caucasian and second-arily as Latin Americans. They also didn't identify as 'women of color' or as 'minority group members', except for one Mexican-born doctoral student who identified as Mexicana. She felt split in her ethnic identity. She enjoyed Latin American art, culture, and theatre as opposed to Chicano [Mexican-American] culture and said that in Mexico, the US Hispanic minority group is 'disdained, held in contempt and looked down upon because of class issues . . . [but] as I came to interact with Chicanos, I learned to appreciate the effects of their history of oppression and racism in this country. I now relate to both cultures.' The other Latin American doctoral student born in Puerto Rico identified as Puerto Rican. She explained, 'on official forms I have been marking off Hispanic because someone in my university told me that is what I am.' The authors comment that the experience of coming from a country where you are part of the racial majority, or where racial mixtures are the norm, to turn into a minority and experience overt racial discrimination, is a disorientating and alienating experience (Leal and Menjivar 1992: 98–9).

These and similar power dynamics are inevitably played out in the seminars and conferences which you need to attend as graduate student as part of your academic apprenticeship and where you must make your mark if you are to progress. All women, but especially non-white, working class women, find that they are given less attention, less possibility to contribute, and that they are less likely to be seen as 'rising stars' than (certain) men. But unlike similar situations in schools, few university teachers can credibly claim that they are forced to give more time to 'the boys' in order to maintain control in the classroom!

> [M]ale academics may listen to women but many do not hear or take up what women say. Men dominate speech interactions by monopolising turn-taking, by speaking longer and thereby maintaining the floor, and by turning up the vocal volume in order to assert dominance and mini-mise the potential for interruptions.
>
> (Purkiss 1994: 194)
>
> [In] a mixed seminar women will talk less than men, will have less im-pact on the course of the discussion, will be taken less seriously, will have their brilliant insights attributed to men, and will receive fewer detailed comments on their observations . . . [moreover] Reference to the scien-tific and literary canon of male authorship counts as cultural capital, not reference to feminist and/or post-colonial writers . . . The lecture and seminar discourse in the social and natural sciences and humanities, remains the terrain of patriarchal knowledge and modes of expression . . . Intellectual sparring and competitive one-up-'man' ship – the expres-sive mode of choice among men – is not women's discursive style and is not how most women go about the getting of knowledge.
>
> (Luke 1994: 213, 216 and 218)

Despite increased respect paid to women's intelligence and the increased numbers of women present in seminars, the style required in discussions, as in academic papers or consultancy (and in many other professions), is what Purkiss (1994: 194) calls a 'rhetoric of dogmatic certainty'. But if one is a scholar seeking after truth(s), can one not admit one has not read a par-ticular book? Or understood it? Or that there may be different answers to the same question? Or that other cultures might see things differently? Or that one may be wrong about something? Rhetorical certainty is a difficult style for everyone (men as well as women) who is diffident, and especially for those from other cultures who are insecure in their language and in their know-ledge of the 'relevant' background knowledge. This is revealed in, say, the different types of 'functional moves' such individuals make in meetings, and the total talking time they 'achieve' (Furneaux *et al.* 1991). This style, together with some directly antifeminist 'backlash', can provoke deep-seated reactions – which then only go to prove to the world that women *are* 'hysterical'.

> The sense of being a 'thicko' is something many women experience much of the time – as the gender positioned as irrational, feeling and therefore stupid – but it can be particularly stark at academic conferences. Tensions about visible ability intensify at the display of how much there is to

know, and how hard it is to 'get it right' – and how many things important Others know . . . Conference anxiety has many causes, for people of all backgrounds: re-activated early childhood fears of groups which can exclude and humiliate; a sense of desperate competitiveness caused by the employment practice of academic institutions; . . . [a sense of interacting with other participants who are not whole human beings but rather] intellectual aspects of the disembodied self . . .

For people multiply marginalized . . . the anxieties are cumulative and focus on social behaviour as well as the session content. Like the daily academy, this temporarily relocated academy is a site where illusions of social mobility are tested out intensively and repeatedly. For women of a working-class background with unhappy experiences of early formal education and of later alienation from middle-class circles, an academic conference of seemingly middle-class authority figures can trigger a range of overwhelmingly difficult reactions . . . [S]uch can be the force of these emotions – coupled with the learned habits of docile acceptance of the implicit values – that they immediately, but temporarily, cancel any abilities to cope . . . that we may have picked from assertiveness training, life, or good role models . . . When such early feelings re-emerge with all their force, some women may turn to angry retaliation . . . to disruption, [alcohol or] drugs, self-mutilation; others hide or go home. A daunting conference can require us to take a creative approach with great rapidity, if we are to enjoy it.

(J. Stanley 1995: 172–3)

Labs and field trips in archaeology, geography, botany and geology also produce specific problems for women – not so much direct discrimination, as variously threatening situations. The constant low level vigilance required are difficult to handle and debilitating; and women can also be assigned extra work.

Even Becher and colleagues (see pp. 61–2), who seldom mention gender, sometimes found it forced to their attention, for instance when six of the nine students they interviewed who definitely did not want an academic career after they finished their doctorate said it was because of their unhappy experiences as students, and five of the six were women.

It was noticeable that of the small number of women science students [interviewed], none mentioned the research group as a source of help and for [half] of them it provided a negative experience. The environment at two universities was described as chauvinist. Attitudes of male peers as well as the supervisor in a research group were oppressive and dismissive.

(Becher *et al.* 1994: 156 and 149)

A more recent study for the Royal Society of Chemistry of the factors that contribute to the discipline's inability to retain women, found that one issue was the culture of bravado towards hazardous substance in some university chemistry laboratories. This led to breaches of health and safety procedures which worried women particularly. Women researchers who had subsequently taken other jobs, said: 'They're stuck in the 1950s. You've always got this worry that what you are using could be very bad for you in the future.' Another: 'You had someone in my group working with cadmium who wasn't the tidiest of people, so we were on edge the entire time.'

(*THES* 10 March 2000)

In a lesbian and gay men discussion network, a geologist spoke of the culture of fitting in and not complaining, especially about conditions in the field. She had spent two weeks in a Scout tent on a Scottish island with two straight men students. 'That trip I had a terrible time being an out lesbian and got very little support, especially not from the staff, whose attitude when our cold water supply failed was "who needs water when there is whisky!" Tackling the whole culture and standing up for one's right to respect on a field trip can affect your career.' In addition, she said, women get put in charge of any mental health crises among other students precipitated by such trips. Another woman also spoke of the problems she had being 'out' at work and going on geography field trips. On one occasion there were not many women (and few rooms) and she found she had to choose without prior warning between sharing with a man member of staff and a woman student who was obviously very uncomfortable with the situation.

As a research student you will also have to take on jokes and malicious or stupid questions about your work. David Sternberg (1981) suggests trying for serious, in depth and good humoured replies (rationalizing to yourself that this is good practice in case you should get asked them by your examiners). I certainly have a list of stupid questions guaranteed to be asked after women/feminists give papers, and some good replies built up over time which will without doubt come in useful again in the future. The same could be said about practice in speaking out against one's 'terms and conditions' of work. But I think Sternberg's suggestion shows a lack of understanding of how carefully women have to tread a line, because when we respond cleverly, or if we protest, we get called a variety of names. Or worse, we can find ourselves being given the silent treatment – the collective cold shoulder: having cold water thrown on our successes and being invited to confess our faults and submit to mentoring from our peers (which was the technique used by the Chinese Red Guards in the Cultural Revolution).

> [E]ven when women have cracked the discursive codes of masculinist intellectual discourse and bureaucratic protocol, many . . . continue to downplay their discursive facility. The reason: verbally assertive women are quickly labelled with pejorative terms which mark these women as 'bitchy' and 'quarrelsome', 'ambitious' and 'aggressive' – the latter qualities valued in men but considered 'unseemly' in women.
>
> (Luke 1994: 216)
>
> He is confident. She is conceited.
> He is assertive. She is pushy.
> He follows through. She doesn't know when to quit.
> He gets angry because he cares about the job. She is emotional.
> He stands firm. She is hard.
> He isn't afraid to say what he thinks. She is mouthy.
>
> (Adapted from Sandler 1993: 181)

Paula Caplan (1994) suggests using body language to counter such behaviour and quietly but confidently taking up space when someone is putting you down. Continue talking while looking directly at a person and/or say 'I haven't finished' if interrupted. You can also try 'playing cracked record': repeating what you said over and over again. She also suggests refusing to take notes at, or to clear up after, mixed sex meetings, which can be as effective at upsetting patterns of domination as direct confrontation. But this does require considerable familiarity and confidence, so it is not surprising that in these sorts of situations, some women remain silent. Arguably this should be recognized as form of resistance: as a refusal to expose the self in what is recognized to be a power relationship (see p. 95). Women know what counts as authoritative discourse in public speech. But we also know that even if we were to reply in the approved terms, it would still be differently interpreted (and also in terms of our age, class, and ethnic background).

Having a critical mass of women students and several helpful members of staff is, however, undoubtedly better than having to tackle the chilly climate on an individual basis. Women's solidarity is the best way to 'normalize' women's interests and ways of working and to make it possible to mount collective (sometimes humorous) challenges. However, alongside this there needs also to be a much longer term project of getting universities, and graduate schools within them, to identify their own specific problems in this field (since there are local variations) and to set policies in place to overcome obstacle to their women research students' (and not just their women staff's) progress. This would require regular, systemic procedures to monitor, analyse and provide feedback information on the admissions process, the graduate curriculum, the supervising and mentoring of graduate students, and so on, with supportive backup available to supervisors and open lines of communication to the Dean through a student advisory group. It would mean departments taking more responsibility for the climate for graduate education and the experiences of their members; and for the power relations which exist in student societies and who it is that 'represents' a group being recognized, and student newsletters and WWW databases being regulated. It might involve giving certain groups extra help with job searches since having a job offer, or the prospect of one, can give encouragement at a crucial phase. This is all a long way from the minimalist, reactive, individualized state of most current EO practice (see pp. 33–5).

Harassment and violence

The routine put-downs of women can veer into major harassment and terrible violence – on campuses as in the rest of the world. Moreover, this is not a new problem.

> The object of the young gentlemen [in the 'Riot at Surgeon's Hall' at the University of Edinburgh on 18 November 1870] was to prevent the ladies from entering the building [to attend lectures in the medical faculty to qualify as doctors. The men] massed up in the street at the hour of the lecture, and when their five opponents appeared they began to sing and shout and jostle and throw mud, and finally they slammed the great doors of the courtyard in their faces . . . the janitor succeeded in opening a small door, and [the women] passed through and into their classroom . . . Inside . . . pandemonium reigned . . . it was long before the professor succeeded in turning out a band of intruders, who had forced their way in. He had hardly achieved this, and had begun to lecture . . . before the door opened again and a sheep was pushed hastily in . . . 'Let it stay,' said the angry professor, 'it has more sense than those who sent it here'.
>
> (Strachey 1978: 179)
>
> Fourteen women engineering students were separated from the men students and all shot dead at the University of Montreal's Ecole Polytechnique in December 1989 (Harris 1991).

What is relatively new is including 'sexual harassment' as a form of violence against women in higher education and the recognition that a high proportion of it is directed at minority women. The term was originally used to cover a demand for sexual contact from someone with power, backed by threats of reprisals (so-called quid pro quo harassment); but it was rapidly expanded to cover 'the creation of a generally discomforting work environments' (so-called environmental harassment). In the case of universities the latter also covers semi-social areas like student union bars, departmental parties, trips, conferences, and student halls of residence.

A young woman at Oxford was invited by a senior member of the college to a party in his rooms, which when she arrived she found consisted 'of a party of one'. She was embarrassed but quickly made excuses and left, despite his protestations about her misinterpreting him, about wasting food and wanting to talk about her work. She would have had no one to complain to even if she had considered it, since the person in question was also the person to whom she should complain – her 'moral tutor'.

Sexual harassment involves not only incursive, unwanted sexual attention and coerced sexual assault, but also 'accidental' touching, staring, comments, jokes, and insults to women, displaying pornographic material which makes women feel embarrassed, and general sexualization of interactions and locations. As such, it is too broad a term, since the appropriate response to each of these is different. But they have in common that they all ensure we never forget we are women, and emphasize our subordinate position. They give men a buzz by affirming *they* are not women, and they take up women's time and energy in coping with them. It is also recognized now that such harassment can come not only from senior men setting up 'casting couch' situations, but also from our peers and juniors (for instance women research students may get harassed by other research students, by porters or lab technicians, and by undergraduate students you are teaching). Occasionally women may harass men and women, though this is mainly the turnabout stuff that novels and plays are made of, for example David Mamet's travesty, *Oleanna*, where we are made to sympathize with the man and vilify the woman, and Hollywood male fantasies starring Demi Moore.

This is a much bigger topic in the USA than in Britain. When I was in the USA looking at graduate students I was amazed by the number of articles, special issues of journals and books on sexual harassment that have been produced since the mid-1970s. An early survey in 1976 found that 9 out of 10 American women in a sample of 9000 had had some experience of sexual harassment at work, and this led to a lot of media attention and academic analysis, notably by Lin Farley (1978) and Catherine MacKinnon (1979). At around the same time, sexual harassment was also found to constitute a form of sex discrimination by the courts and to be illegal under the terms of Title VII of the *Civil Rights Act 1964*. The same sort of protection was then held to extend to the educational sphere under Title IX of the same Act, which forbids sex discrimination in all institutions that receive federal money from grants, loans or contracts. Sexual harassment has maintained a high profile through other trials in this litigious culture, such as the Clarence Thomas/Anita Hill hearings, and allegations against Senator Robert Packwood and former President Bill Clinton.

In 1986 a case established that employers might be liable if an employee's harassing conduct created a 'hostile environment' for another employee (the subject of endless US lawyer-based soap operas like Ally McBeal) and also for rape on their premises. This allowed 'victims' to sue employers if the institution didn't have a policy clearly prohibiting sexual harassment and anti-rape strategies. This was also held to extend to educational institutions, which made their presidents sit up and take real notice. Most set about formulating policies and getting practices in place with immoderate haste; often taking their text pretty much straight from the Equal Employment Opportunity Commission's Sex Discrimination Guidelines. These are very broad and cover a range of behaviours from directly coercive (actual sexual assault or explicit or implicit threats of reprisal if the student doesn't engage in the desired conduct) through conduct which is invasive or threatening, though not explicitly coercive (repeated requests for dates or attempts to embrace, comments on a student's body, leers, and personal enquiries about the student's sex life or menstrual status) to conduct which is tasteless and offensive but not personally targeted (such as jokes in lectures and (unnecessary) use of sexually explicit material in seminars or leaving pornography on computer screens during tutorials).

If one wants to establish the incidence and prevalence of sexual harassment, the rate is obviously going to vary according to the definition and methodology one uses; and it must be said that some of the research in this field is wobbly. Sometimes the research instruments are unclear or leave decisions as to what to include up to the informant. But most women know such behaviour is not rare and the numbers affected are not small. Moreover, the issue is not so much behavioural and legal definitions and incidence, as the effects attempting to avoid sexual harassment has in constricting all women's geographical and social freedom, and the very distressing and seriously damaging effects experiencing it can have on individual women. The most common responses are pretending it is not happening or that it has no effect (denial), trying to ignore it and doing nothing or detaching psychologically (endurance), or blaming oneself for the behaviour of the harasser and attempting to avoid situations, or trying to put the harasser off without direct confrontation (appeasement). The *least* frequent response is to notify a supervisor or to bring a formal complaint. However if you experience sexual harassment you need to take some action because it often continues, and it does do you harm.

Sexual harassment is not monolithic – it can vary from a single incident to multiple exposure, from displaying soft porn to violent rape. Nor are its effects precisely predictable. How the recipient reacts depends on her relationship to the abuser; the kind of harassment and how long it continues; her pre-abuse psychological state; the way her disclosure and any investigation is handled; and the social support network available to her. But it may well affect her career progress and can have major psychological and physical effects, including serious depression and Post-Traumatic Stress Disorder (from O'Donohue 1997: 4).

The UK was slower to establish widespread concern about sexual harassment, both generally and specifically in relation to higher education. However there are now several published first hand accounts of sexual harassment in universities; several surveys of students and staff have been conducted since the mid-1990s; and a network of researchers in the field has been established. From the point of view of this book, there is an especially interesting account by Deborah Lee (1998) of interviews with fifty men and women, recruited through newspaper articles and radio broadcasts, which netted two women research students who independently responded to speak about their experiences while being supervised by the same man!

In British Law . . . sexual harassment is illegal in so far as it can be construed as an act of sex discrimination under the provisions of the 1975 Sex Discrimination Act (or when it results in unfair dismissal, under the Employment Protection Act). The first case in which it was successfully argued that sexual harassment was a form of sex discrimination (Porcelli *v.* Strathclyde Regional Council) reached the Employment Appeal Tribunal in 1986 when Jean Porcelli, a laboratory technician in a Scottish school, described how two male laboratory technicians had harassed her in a way they would not have harassed a man – by commenting on her physical appearance, brushing up against her, and making sexually suggestive remarks . . . [In addition] Following a commissioned Report in 1987, the European . . . Community issued a Recommendation and Code of Conduct on Sexual Harassment in 1991, which also covers the UK. This echoes the US legislation in identifying both 'quid pro quo' and 'environmental' harassment, and stresses the unacceptability of sexual harassment of any kind on the grounds that it is detrimental to 'the dignity of women and men at work'.

(Thomas and Kitzinger 1997: 5)[3]

As far as universities in the UK are concerned, however, reaction to sexual harassment of students has gone off in a rather odd direction because of an extraordinary case and the CVCP's response to it. Here, as often with sexual harassment cases, it is useful to distinguish what took place (the original events) from what happened as a result of the events (Eyre 2000).

In 1993, Austen Donnellan, a postgraduate student at King's College London, was acquitted at a rape trial amid intense media interest. He had accompanied a very drunk woman student to her room after a party, and sexual intercourse took place. The woman passed out and had little memory of the event, but the next day accused him of rape. She complained to the college authorities who 'informally' asked Donnellan to apologize, which he refused to do. He was asked to appear before a disciplinary tribunal, which could have suspended or expelled him. On the advice of his tutor (Lord Russell, the son of Bertrand Russell and a front bench spokesman for the Liberal Party in the House of Lords), he pre-empted this by contacting the police to insist he stand trial on the charge of rape. Inexplicably the Crown Prosecution Service went along with this. According to Sue Lees (1996: 84), it must be the only case of rape which has gone to a criminal court in order to clear a man's name.

At the trial the 'victim' became the bright, young, middle class male from a good home, championed by his famous tutor, with an anti-feminist press using this and other high profile 'date rape' cases at the time, to warn university administrators against acting on the complaints of 'sluttish' women students who live in a world with lots of sex, who get drunk and willingly engage in dangerous sexual behaviour which sometimes go wrong, and who are as much to blame as the young men.

British universities became desperate (or perhaps more desperate than ever) to steer clear of such issues, and the CVCP established a subcommittee post haste to consider how similar cases should be dealt with in future. The Zellick Report (1994), published a year after the Donnellan verdict, never mentions the case, though people from King's are the only named individuals consulted. Nor are rape and sexual assault prominently considered. But what it recommended is that universities should not do what King's had done. '[A]lleged misconduct, which also appears to constitute a criminal offence, should not be the subject of proceedings under the Code (of Student Discipline) unless there has already been a police investigation or prosecution' (Zellick 1994: 24). Whatever the evidence and whatever the distress, the university should stand on the sidelines.

(Account adapted from Hamilton 1997)

This continues a representation of the British university campus as a location where whatever crime there may be – be it theft, drug sales or assaults – is all perpetrated by outsiders. 'At all costs it seems the myth must be maintained that those who enter the university to study or teach are both intellectually and ethically superior to those unable to secure entrance' (Hamilton 1997: 110). Plus, Zellick (1994) says, universities should not get embroiled anyway. Provided that there are walls around the campus and closed-circuit TV in the entrance, there is no perceived need to publish information about the incidence of crimes and events on campus to warn students, nor any need for a system to support those members of the university community subjected to harassment and violence by other members. This means that if you are assaulted on university premises, you are likely to be given the impression that it is a one off incident, for which you are responsible, and you will be left to deal with it individually. If you are assaulted off the campus, even if it is clearly a university-related incident, the university will be unwilling to do anything damaging to another student or man colleague, or to undermine his autonomy, and/or will simply wash its hands.

> Colleges will close ranks to avoid scandal and publicity – in cases of theft, rowdiness and violence within the college, and certainly in cases of sexual offences. After all, to admit that the problem does exist is [often] to admit that a colleague is committing these offences.
> (Oxford University Student Union Women's Committee 1984)
>
> After a series of homophobic taunts in a student union, some lesbians were physically threatened and one fled. Jumping down a flight of concrete steps, she fell and severely injured her knee. The student union president and committee took the part of the aggressor, as he was a former miner, and the university absolved itself as the woman was 'only threatened', not actually physically attacked; and in any case the incident took place off its premises, in the student union. The police also considered the case but took no action. The man continued his course. The woman was hospitalized on and off for two years, with multiple operations and in pain – and dropped out of her course. She eventually took a civil case and got monetary criminal injuries compensation five years later.

The Commission on University Career Opportunity does, it is true, advise universities to have anti-harassment and EO policies, but *for staff*, and mainly in relation to racist harassment. It warns that not having such policies in place and not following the good practice of encouraging a culture that values personal dignity and welcomes diversity, in addition to dealing reactively with incidents, could result in legal actions against the institution at employment tribunals. But not in relation to students. This is in marked contradistinction to some US universities which fund rape crisis centres for students, staff and local women; which take far more responsibility for the impact of their students on local communities; and which may have well-established education and prevention programmes, including some targeted at 'sports Jocks' and other groups with reputations for violence and harassing behaviour. American HEIs are also legally obliged to publish statistics on campus crime. They will also, however, close ranks if and when they can.

One noteworthy aspect of sexual harassment (as against racist harassment) is how unwilling women are to *call* the everyday experiences of unwanted sexual attention 'sexual harassment'. Another is that since sexual harassment (or as Debbie Epstein (1996) argues, 'sexist harassment within a hetero-sexual matrix') is a response to threats to male supremacy, it is exercised *more* against higher status women. So although as a research student you will be used to dealing with sexist behaviour in general, and specifically within the university, even if it is hard to label it as such, you will probably find the level increases as you move from Masters to doctoral studies.

It is also really important to note the strength of the hostility encountered by – and danger to – anyone who tries to take this up as an issue, let alone to bring a legal case. Caroline Ramazanoglu (1987) suggests men's opposition is due to their freedoms being restricted and because it is no longer clear what they can and cannot do. But is certainly usually the woman's complaint that is seen as the problem. Even doing research on the issue can produce enormous aggravation for the researchers. In North America especially there have been a number of splenetic attacks on individuals and on reports and proposed codes of conduct designed to protect women from sexual harass-ment, including burning copies of a booklet on *Dealing with Harassment at MIT* and presenting the codes as 'puritanical' and 'Salem-like', inspired by 'feminazis' who are the enemies of free speech. Such campaigns have also been presented as attacks on academic freedom.

'I treasure academic freedom . . . but I have never known academic freedom to be used to protect women' (Dorothy Smith quoted in Eyre 2000: 303).

Feminism is fodder for the media and subject to increasing 'discourses of derision' for 'going too far' and irrelevance (since equity is presumed to have been achieved). Sexual harassment is a favourite topic for attack. Pro-viding 'balance' in print and air time apparently means giving space to right wing male journalists and such lecture circuit feminist/anti-feminist 'stars' as Camille Paglia and Daphne Patai, who present feminism as a juggernaut which positions women as victims and as punitive, fundamentalist and anti-sex. Katie Roiphe (1993) made her name arguing against Princeton's policy on sexual harassment, saying that women should simply cope with humdrum, minor instances of 'ordinary interaction between men and women' (that sexual harassment should be taken out of the public, political domain and put back into the personal arena). The media shape public knowledge of 'campus sex crimes' (as in the Donnellan case) by using men and women 'experts' who reproduce patriarchal points of view and by excluding or maligning those with a feminist position who are said to 'have an axe to grind'. The press particularly likes to focus on dissent (especially generational dissent) among feminists.

In 1995, Helen Garner, a well-known feminist author and member of the Melbourne literary set, wrote what would become a best seller within a week of its publication. *The First Stone* is about a sexual harassment case brought against Dr. Alan Gregory, the master of the prestigious Ormond College at the University of Melbourne. The book aroused more media interest than did the sexual harassment case. The legal case, which went to appeal, was ultimately dismissed because both sides were deemed to have equally defensible positions, hence creating 'reasonable doubt'. But by then, Gregory had resigned, and he [experienced] difficulty regaining an academic position.

The First Stone was a media event, not so much because the alleged harassment occurred at an elite university as because Garner, a well-known, middle-aged feminist author, sympathizes with the male defendant . . . [and] castigates young feminists for their intransigence, their 'priggishness', their lack of a sense of eros, their 'wimpishness', and their willingness to use institutional legal processes to gain redress for minor sexist (sexual?) encounters. [The Ormond case is unusual only in that it is the young who are cast as humourless man hater.] . . . Garner's position was well known even before the appearance of the book, as she wrote a sympathetic letter to the Master at the time the court case was made public. The media have [however] paid little attention to why such an incident was not appro-priately handled at the college level.

(Blackmore 1997: 75–6)

Matters can get even worse if the judiciary become involved, for then it is not a question of women's articulating their experience of a generally chilly climate (which most women empathize with); but rather of *proving* individual incidents and allegations, of charges and (what is taken to count as) evidence and what matters. Thus protecting gender asymmetry and making inequalities and the chilly climate invisible. When the going gets tough, feminists get little support from – indeed we may have to run the gauntlet of – equity agencies.

At the University of Victoria in Canada, women in the political science department were asked to write a report on why there were so few women students in their field. They discussed the chilly climate generally and included sexual harassment of women students at parties. They were then sued for defamation by senior men in the department. The women (consisting of a junior faculty member and research students) ended up being hauled before internal and external review committees and quasi-judicial equity agencies including the British Columbia Ombudsman, the Human Rights Commission, the Ministry of Women's Equality and the University of Victoria's own Equity Office (Brodribb 1996; Smith 1997).

How to handle sexual harassment

It is therefore difficult to know what to do if you experience sexual harassment. Just calling behaviour 'sexual harassment' is often treated as though it were a form of violence against men: an intrusion on their rights. They respond aggressively. You may even wonder if it has really occurred, since 'harassment' grades into general masculine behaviour (Figure 7.1). It is part of the pervasive sexism of the university and the surrounding culture, both majority and minority ethnic cultures, and all social class cultures. It depends on (generally) women's definition of the situation (or gay men's definition, in the case of some homophobic harassment), in opposition to the usual accepted authority: white, heterosexual men. It is especially hard to handle a combination of sexism and racism and national chauvinism – as in some national, cultural or religiously based student societies (see p. 164). It is especially dangerous for women who are not themselves heterosexual mothers; and especially difficult to deal with for those from outside the culture, since they may be accused of not 'reading' situations correctly, and because their 'exotic' female sexuality is stereotyped (for example African or Far Eastern women). Few women who fight academic discrimination encounter victory, and as Paula Caplan (1994) says, it is demoralizing to find that although the fight has a strong negative impact on the protesters, the institution itself changes little whether they win or lose.

There is of course a Catch-22. If we object, try to substantiate that harassment is occurring and demand action against it, we are accused of creating the problem by talking about it, or of lying, being hysterical, or selfish and vindictive in threatening good men's careers (with an added edge if we are Black or left-wing and the man in question is also Black and/or left-wing). But if we ignore such treatment, it 'proves' it is not there. Moreover if it is happening to you, you want the behaviour to stop, to get some sense of control of the situation, and to minimize the damage to yourself. So it is

Figure 7.1   © Jacky Fleming

important to take *some* action. But not the most common 'action' of thinking you can 'manage' it by avoidance – by giving up the class, course,
supervisor, or the whole university so as to avoid contact. Nor should you
lose confidence because you think the person in question, who had initially
expressed interest in your work and encouraged you, must have been doing
this only because of his sexual interest – so you are really *not* intellectually
competent after all. You are. Equally, do not be too optimistic. Recognize
that you are as, or more, likely to be affected and damaged by grievance
procedures than the person(s) you are complaining about. Take action early
on, but don't rush into things.

The best option seems to be the one recommended by occupational psychologists and trade unions. Record what has happened as dispassionately as possible, and having talked it through with other women and sought confidential support, directly confront the individual in writing with what you do not like and what has to stop. This seems to work in about 50 per cent of cases, and being assertive in itself builds confidence.

A research student who had just finished her thesis was offered a half-time research job by a man in a department where she had done occasional interviewing and data processing the previous year. He met her on the way to the binders with her thesis and insisted on taking her out for lunch to celebrate. Hard to refuse! She was however wary of him from a previous occasion when he had encouraged (and paid for) her to go to a conference. She felt then that he might have ulterior motives – he was also attending – but as it was a key conference in her field she very much wanted to go. On that occasion she had sought 'protection' against being left alone with him from her supervisor, who was also attending.

She tried to get out of the lunch by saying she didn't have time, but he summoned a taxi. During the meal he was 'all over' her and her big day was ruined. 'I felt like just running away and hiding.' However she was also frightened that her first real job offer would be withdrawn. She was in tears, feeling degraded and that she should have handled it better. Despite being a feminist activist, she was totally unaware of the institution's formal harassment procedures when she needed them.

She talked with her supervisor about what to do, and the supervisor stressed that the man was not socially inept (as the student suggested in excuse/to protect him!), that he did know what his actions meant, that he had persevered despite her evident discomfort, and that he was abusing his position of power. The two of them then went to the head of her home department and the student described in confidence what had happened, so it was formally noted. The head of department was very sympathetic and mentioned several other women who had also had problems with the same man. The student then wrote a letter which was explicit about the behaviour she found offensive:

Dear Y

I would like to thank you for your support and encouragement over the past year. I am pleased we may be able to continue working together. However, during our discussion over lunch on Friday, you advised me to develop my 'professional image'. I appreciated this and, having thought about it, I feel it is important in terms of my own sense of being a 'professional' to let you know that some of your behaviour made me feel uncomfortable. I am sorry

> *to inform you of this by letter, but I find it difficult to say face-to-face (as you are, after all, my boss). I know we all have different ways of relating to colleagues, but I feel very awkward when you initiate physical contact, as you did last week and have done a few times in the past – hand holding, touching my knee, hugging, and sitting very close. I hope you will appreciate that in order to be confident about myself and my work I need to feel at ease with the manner in which we relate to each other as colleagues. I am sure you will understand and respect my wishes in this regard.*
> *Thanks again for all of your help.*
> *Best wishes*

The guy realized, of course, that another important reason for her writing rather than talking was to put the matter on record: that this was a 'first formal warning'. He made no reference to it for many weeks, but the behaviour ceased. The woman worked out the contract, even though she never felt entirely easy with him, and she moved on to another job.

If such a letter doesn't work, then you will need to use the formal grievance procedures. But start low and work up slowly and steadily; keep records; use someone who has more power and who knows the politics of the institution better than you do as an advocate, such as a departmental head or your professor; talk to your trade union representative and their women's officer (and if appropriate race and other units); and keep your biggest guns of legal action till last. Avoid journalists.

If you do find yourself in such a situation, try also not to beat yourself up over it. It is not the way you dressed or how you responded, nor could you have 'handled it better'. How one reacts is not rational and the same harassing behaviour can produce different responses in different students, or from the same student at different times and in different circumstances. You should respect yourself however you reacted. But be prepared for the man concerned seeing (or at least presenting) the situation very differently. He may well contest the accusation and even complain that he himself is being harassed: that *he* is suffering emotional stress from the accusation, or being victimized because he is a foreigner, and so on. He may recruit some women to his side. Be prepared mentally to resist attributions of malign intent, or of outright lying, or of your having misinterpreted his naturally affectionate approach to lots of people; or that you are a deprived child desperate for attention; or even counter-suits for defamation. (The last has occurred even when there have been multiple complainants against a particular individual.) Feel angry not guilty.

Taking a more general perspective, we need to press universities to support women students more by taking the uncomfortable and difficult issue of their students' and staff's behaviour more seriously, and being publicly very clear that they are concerned for their members' safety (beyond the level of putting adequate lighting on paths, cutting back hedges, putting peepholes in students' doors, and supplying personal alarms). They need not only to have sexual harassment grievance procedures in place, but also, and more importantly in the long term, to tackle their own (dominant group) members' behaviour, and to make clear that it is unacceptable to harass and invade the personal space of women, Black and gay students. Such behaviour serves either to drive us out of the organization or at least to stress our lack of fit. To do this, institutions need to have active (not paper or moribund) support structures, with responsible individuals who are skilled at nipping such behaviour in the bud (and not themselves some of the prime culprits!). More generally, they need to work to change the institutional climate by increasing the institutional power held by pro-equity groups. In the short term there should be a rethinking of if and when universities should themselves take action, changing the spirit of the Zellick Report (1994) and reviewing what student activities they actually support.

> [F]raternity norms and practices influence members to view the sexual coercion of women, which is a felony crime, as sport, a contest, or a game . . . This sport is played not between men and women but between men and men . . . The use of women in this way encourages fraternity men to see women as objects . . . In a fraternity context, getting sex without giving emotionally is 'cool' masculinity . . . it poses no threat to the bonding and loyalty of the . . . brotherhood . . . Drinking large quantities of alcohol before having sex suggests that 'scoring' rather than intrinsic sexual pleasure is a primary concern.
>
> (Martin and Hummer 1993: 128)

Dangers of research and teaching

Issues of safety when doing research are barely mentioned in textbooks, though when you start to look there are various instances of danger to women recorded. The experience of those who do research on sexual harassment is itself an interesting case in point. Recklessness in the lab was mentioned above (p. 207); and empirical work in the social sciences obviously often puts women into situations we would otherwise generally avoid while asking questions about sensitive topics. In anthropology the extreme danger of women getting into sexual relationships while in the field, which has resulted in deaths, is passed down by word of mouth.

Neither of us [Lorna McKee and Margaret O'Brien] experienced physical abuse throughout our research with men, although in two cases [out of 59] in the lone fathers project the interviewer began to feel worried about possible attack and in another two cases was pestered some days after the interview for further contact. In these interviews, the researcher employed a variety of strategies to offset any risk of sexual confrontation: taking conscious decisions about make-up and clothes; and maintaining a 'professional' manner when ambiguities arose. The *props* were . . . the tape-recorder, the clip-board and interview schedule . . . [and a prior decision not to include direct questions on sex, but] the boundaries between women as 'scientific observer', confidant, and sexual being are sometimes finely negotiated and often conflated . . .

Mr Last was a draftsman who had looked after his two children for the last ten months. At home, where his parents looked after the children during the interview, he appeared reasonably even-tempered but exploded when driving the interviewer to the railway station afterwards. He claimed that his ex-wife and her new lover were teaching his son to masturbate and that he could not entrust his children to their care. He became more angry and bitter, eventually driving *past* the station. When he drove past the next station, the interviewer became very worried, tried to calm him down and neutralise the topic of conversation. At the *third* station she insisted that he stop and let her out there. This was an anxious moment because during the interview he had described his karate skills and drawn attention to his general physical prowess and strength. Although he did not initiate any physical contact, his unpredictable behaviour in the car left the interviewer very relieved to have 'escaped' and at that point very glad that the study was not longitudinal in nature!

(McKee and O'Brien 1983: 157–8)

My own experience of doing surveys has found me wandering around empty housing estates after dark, knocking on doors and trying to get interviews with families. This has included going voluntarily into a 'strange' man's house, which would certainly have been seen judicially as a form of contributory negligence should there have been problems. I would now definitely advocate two people working together in such situations, and having mobile phones and personal alarms. Women doing anthropological fieldwork are obviously in even more exposed situations – useful though one's gender may be in giving one access to places where men could never go, and to information they would never get.

Some clever researchers have turned this around and researched threatening experiences as a form of self-defence: a way of dealing with the experience. For example Sue Wise and Liz Stanley dealt with the obscene phone calls they received while working on a lesbian support telephone line by recording and analysing them, and writing one of the first British books on sexual harassment (Stanley and Wise 1979; Wise and Stanley 1987).

We should also not underestimate the emotional stress and psychological effects of researching certain topics, such as rape or domestic violence, and of asking questions in volatile situations, across sectarian divides or of criminals or people with a history of psychological disturbance. Sara Scott describes the 'nasty dent in your ontological security' and associated physical symptoms she experienced when 'researching the unbelievable, hearing the unthinkable' of ritual abuse (Scott 1998: para 5.14).

Whilst I try to rationally assess the merits of my research, this is often futile. It is agonizing to think clearly when I am distressed by insomnia. I find it strenuous to write because I often suffer acute panic attacks and computer blues. The motivation to study disappears as I worry about my vomiting and difficulty with eating. I really believe that doing research can seriously damage your health. I'm not sure whether this is a widespread tendency or one that is restricted to anti-establishment/ pro-Black/women's studies. All that I know is that my bouts of fear, nervousness and anxiety seem to be linked to my 'status' on the margins of intellectual life. I persevere despite misgivings about my potential to complete my thesis.

(Marshall 1994: 121)

Teaching also exposes one to threats, including on fortunately rare occasions to stalking. Anecdotally it appears that universities are much more prepared to support men in such circumstances, for example in getting injunctions against women, than vice versa.

One [ethnic minority research] student described how she had to teach a class which included an Enoch Powell supporter. She felt that her institution had been extremely supportive, but nevertheless his presence was a test for her and she was conscious that she was being watched by the whole class to see how she dealt with him. It had been a frightening experience, which did not stop with the end of the class: 'It was awful. I was always nervous every time when I had to go to that class. And leaving the class, every night I was checking whether anybody is behind me. I was so scared.'

(Carter *et al.* 1999: 62)

Intimate relationships between staff and students

Many would want to separate out harassment, and certainly violence, which is clearly unwanted, from 'consensual sexual relations' between supervisors or other faculty members and students. It is however difficult to draw the line, given the assumptions of male dominance and female resistance embedded in heterosexuality and the eroticization of power in western culture. In any event, relationships with staff (of either sex) are seductive for research students partly because authority figures are sexy and also because they see themselves as getting support from someone who shares the excitement of intellectual endeavour, who understands their goals and ambitions, who has access to helpful inside information and contacts, and who will increase their chances of success. The supervisory relationship is also framed to proceed through 'intimate interaction and structural dependencies', giving it a charge of strong feelings (of gratitude, resentment, frustration, love) and memories of past 'significant [parental] others'. But just as the medical profession and therapists warn against this type of intimacy as being both unethical and detrimental to the treatment process, so there are arguments against amorous relationships between teachers and students.

Such relationships are surprisingly common. One study at a prestigious US university found 37 per cent of the faculty had attempted to date, and more than 25 per cent reported actually having dated, at least one of their students (Fitzgerald *et al.* 1988); while a survey of 500 postgraduate and trainee psychologists – most of them women – found that nearly half had had intimate relationships with their supervisors which they subsequently regretted (Glaser and Thorpe 1986). To warn against getting involved in this way is not to be a kill joy who cannot recognize that knowledge is sexy. Nor is it to infantilize students and make women into victims by denying them the opportunity or suggesting they are incapable of making decisions about how they live their lives. On the contrary, it is to recognize, as Diane Purkiss (1994) argues, that pedagogy and seduction have been semiotically intertwined since Plato (at least); and that such relationships can possibly be more of a problem where there is not a huge age difference. While 18-year-old students may be less vulnerable because they are part of a peer group which can provide a strong defence against dirty old men, older woman may set more store by a new relationship, and research students are particularly dependent on specific individuals and hope for an intertwining of romantic and academic input.

The cause for concern is, first, that some members of staff (almost always men) can only be described as predatory. They (attempt to) run through each new woman graduate and staff member, and many of the undergraduates, who come on to campus, leaving the women feeling stupid and distraught when their seduction becomes public knowledge. These men are vituperative if they hear that warnings about them are being given to students by their colleagues.

It is the serial nature of the relationships on the part of staff that is their most damning indictment. If we were to see them as the happy flowering of true love we would not expect lecturers to have several of these liaisons in one year.

They do not occur because academics are unusually sexy or attractive. 'As a student officer contemptuously put it "no-one would give them a second glance in the street". Rather it is their position with all its cultural and social signs and symbols, which gives them a special kind of power and allure vis-à-vis students.' But allure with a cost.

As one student who had a brief relationship with her tutor that he abruptly ended prior to commencing a relationship with another [student] found: 'my worst fears at the onset of what might happen could not have been worse than what did happen.' . . . other students turned against her . . . stories of her relationship reached her [social work] placement causing such acute embarrassment she eventually asked to be pulled out. It was even reported to her that she had been branded a liar and a cheat by a colleague of the lecturer. This is not an atypical example, one student counsellor informed us that in every case she had dealt with the student who complained about exploitation had 'been victimised to some extent or another'.

(Carter and Jeffs 1995: 16, 20, 23)

Second, such affairs have long-term consequences. Were you thinking of having such a relationship, you should know for just how long any success you may have will be (at least partly) attributed to it. Ten, twenty, thirty years on, people in the discipline will still be saying: 'She only got through her viva because she was sleeping with Y' – whether it is true or not. Moreover, lovers can make you unemployable in their university; and even if the relationship should end in marriage, this is not necessarily a 'positive supportive consequence' for the woman involved, but may be the entry into a different form of exploitative relationship.

Finally, contrary to expectations, a supervisor who loves you can do you more damage than an indifferent one. He may not read with critical care. He may encourage you to be romantically disorganized in the early stages of a happy love affair. Then, when you or he becomes disenchanted, angry or jealous, he can act to ensure your dissertation is doomed, especially if he is supposedly the only person qualified to supervise you.

It is overwhelmingly men academics who abuse their power and/or kid themselves about romance in relationships with students since most supervisors are men, most such relationships are heterosexual, and heterosexual relationships are typically initiated by men. But similar comments can apply to same-sex relationships and to women staff members' involvement with men students – though the way sexual dynamics are constructed in our society affects the power balances in these less common cases.

Jane Gallop (1997) has mounted a sophisticated defence of her own sexual relationships with both men and women students (after two women graduate students charged her with sexual harassment). Drawing on Queer Theory, she argues teachers should use every means at their disposal – including the sexualization of pedagogic interactions and the thrill of transgressive behaviour – to intellectually excite students. She claims to make a spectacle of herself, to perform, to seduce, in order to turn her audience on, literally and figuratively: to shock, entertain – and to make people think. 'It is no more possible to really teach without at times eliciting powerful and troubling sensations than it is to write powerfully without producing the same sort of sensation.' She argues that sexual and other role reversals involve a student taking power over or with a teacher, to play with and explore power and conventional limitations. This makes women sexually active and powerful, the desire fills them with energy and drive and they become more engaged, productive and confident – also as scholars (Gallop 1997: 100–1).

But is sex as deliberate and controllable and malleable as Gallop says? So equally good for both parties? Do you have to have sex with your tutor to to be powerful (sexy, smart, successful) alongside him or her? Does Gallop perhaps not over-stress agency as much as she presents others as underplaying it? Whatever the possibilities of playful Queer transgression or the more mundane specifics of conventional adulterous relationships, the fact that sexual relations between (men) staff and (women) students (are allowed to) occur, means that women students and staff have constantly to be circumspect in their dealings with men staff. Moreover, it means that if and when women are sponsored and included in the informal learning situations which are so important in the process of entry into the discipline, this may be (and there is always the underlying possibility that it is, or that it will be read as being) on different terms and conditions from men (even from homosexual men).

Phillips and Pugh (2000) comment that 'When a male student goes for a drink with his (male) supervisor he is perceived as an ambitious and sociable person; but when a female student is in the same situation she is in danger of being perceived as flirtatious or even as already being "involved" with her supervisor.' They then go on to say that a 'Innocent and perfectly acceptable social contact between staff and students becomes tainted with gossip and innuendo' (Phillips and Pugh 2000: 137–8). But it is rather that an always problematic and unequal relationship (between tutor and student and between men and women) is used to reconstitute women as women, and to keep them in their place, both within the individual relationship and within the wider public domains of academic work and social life.

Consensual sexual relationships between staff and students are detrimental both to the learning of the student involved *and* to all others (especially to all women) in the same department. They involve much wider issues about the part played by heterosexuality in gender relations (and vice versa) and about what constitutes 'consent' in unequal relationships.

They also raise the issue of whether there are not more general problems in *all* close friendships between staff and students. Some have argued these constitute favouritism because such students are given extra time and advice and other goodies. The professoriate has diffuse power and controls access to future advancement in a host of ways – by providing research and teaching opportunities for students and recommendations and references. Such 'friendships' are indeed a way in which men students are routinely given preference by the largely male faculty (see mentoring pp. 166–9) and why a vicious circle exists for minority groups because of the serious shortage of non-white, non-English-speaking background and 'out' lesbian and gay sponsors.

While I don't believe staff–student relationships should be universally banned and generally subject to disciplinary procedures (nor should they be included in sexual harassment policies), I do think they should be regarded as problematic and a breach of professional conduct. Indeed policies produced by university staff trade unions in Britain, Canada and Australia have all recommended it should be regarded as unethical and reprehensible for an academic to have a sexual, or indeed a family or financial relationship, with any student under his or her supervision or whose work they will be marking.

But more than this, the masculine code of silence and support for such behaviour needs to be broken. Such relationships should be talked about, and the general issue debated within the wider context of how far teachers and students, and especially supervisors and research students, should get involved in each others lives. Should we talk about our personal relationships (how openly and fully)? Be physically affectionate? Meet socially for a drink or a meal in twos or in groups? Or go travelling together? The issue is not to deny students the right to sexual consent, but to problematize what that means. Can there be a consensual relationship between staff and students: how free are students to choose? How is choice constructed? It is also to recognize the complexity of each encounter. Meanwhile, the university should support, not attack, those of its members who do occasionally 'blow the whistle' on their colleagues.

Pressure on and from personal relationships and jobs

> Are you able to say no to favors, fun times, fund-raising chair positions, family reunions, and frolicking in the park on Sunday afternoons? Because if you are ever going to gain control over your days and nights, and manage your time efficiently, the first lesson is to learn to say no. Say it regretfully, say it remorsefully, say it with clenched teeth, or say it with joy – but say it loud and clear. The world is full of Time Zappers who will steal your time if you allow them, so put all your good deeds on hold and use the word no freely. You'll be glad you did.
>
> (Fitzpatrick *et al.* 1998: 97)

The thesis demands can cause, or be attributed responsibility for, a deterioration in relationships with your 'significant' others. You may lose friends because you can't be spontaneous and because of reducing across the board social time; you may have to travel for sources, facilities and fieldwork; or you may find you now have little in common. Partners and children have to learn to live with a problem person – one struggling to write a difficult and lonely dissertation. They too may need a support group comparable to Al-Anon (for the partners of alcoholics).

> Every time I look at my daughter – she's 5 now – I think 'I should have called her Thesis'!

Either sex may feel 'the thesis is coming between me and my partner' because of its demands for time and one's head always being in it, or because men and women feel they have outgrown a past way of life. (Of course some may seek a thesis as an intellectual or material way out of an unsatisfying domestic or employment situation.) But men's demands, and especially demands from children and elderly or sick relatives, are harder for women to manage (see pp. 118–22).

> Ernest Rudd (1985) suggests that 'In general what interferes with postgraduate study is not marriage but a family. It is here and only here, that there is a sharp divide between the experience of men and the women I interviewed. Many of the special difficulties the women meet are clear and obvious'. He

then goes on to give examples of women interviewees being called away to pick up a sick child from school, suffering from nausea and medical problems in pregnancy, becoming absorbed in a new baby, and of the demands of caring for pre-school infants. He stresses that mothers have no frequent long stretches of free time and less time overall to study or for the life of the university. He also remarks on women students' husbands moving job and their having to cope with the removal and a new university. At the end, however, he suggests that things can also work the other way round, and that children may be used as a way of getting out of doing a thesis which is not going well – just as child-free women, and men generally, may use getting a job as their excuse (Rudd 1985: 51–5).

However when Rudd talks of marriage he talks of 'spouses' and does not differentiate wives and husbands, even though he found at least twice as many of his respondents got divorced as might be expected, and that the disparity was highest among women. He spends some time considering why there is this correlation, and whether it is causal, commenting that it could be because of the strains doctoral work puts on marriage – he cites low income and women not doing the chores – even though he says many 'spouses' are supportive. On the other hand he suggests it could be that the same skills are needed to maintain marriage as to complete a PhD and so those who fail one, fail the other.

Other work on divorce has as a commonplace that women who divorce are more likely to be in paid employment, but whether it is the employment and its demands (or the confidence it gives) which leads to divorce, or whether it is that women who are at a particular points in their lives when marriages are liable to split, or who are thinking of divorce, who get jobs, is less clear. It is undoubtedly an interactive process; similarly with doctorates.

I have deliberately said relatively little about women's domestic responsibilities in this book, partly because it feels a bit obvious: like telling readers how to suck eggs, and partly because this gets over-stressed in mainstream work on higher education like Rudd's. When women do get a mention it is to explain our dropout and slow completion in terms of motherhood, disregarding gender discrimination *within* the university and the fact that many women do not have small children. Amazingly too, such studies never seem to have found any homosexual students.

However, while it is important to stress that women's return to studying is no more likely to produce a more equal division of labour at home than does their entry or return to the labour market, not all women are in heterosexual couples nor do most have dependent children, and single heterosexual or lesbian women with no children, or grown up children, *also* have demands on their time (again see pp. 118–22).

A colleague said that when donors make general funding cutbacks and reduce allowances for spouse and children,

> a woman who does take a scholarship, particularly if she is a mature age
> student, may encounter what I call the 'mother hen syndrome'. It was
> quite common for lonely single or unaccompanied students (both male
> and female) to gravitate to a mature age female student for various
> forms of support. This is not necessarily a bad thing ... but it can often
> lead to ... extra curricular distractions ... This could manifest in not
> finishing studies on time and we tried to take this into account when
> dealing with requests for extensions.

Finally, to repeat, getting a new job is not a smart move if you are trying
to finish a doctorate, although it is forced on many after their third year on
a grant. If you do get a job, get one which is not demanding; and if you get
one in academia, try to get a research assistantship rather than a teaching
post. If possible work part-time.

Pressures from your self

A theme throughout this book has been many women's chronic low self-
esteem and lack of confidence. Many of us go on questioning whether we
can manage a doctorate and whether it is worth its personal and professional
costs throughout the time we are working on it (and beyond) – despite the
good academic results we have achieved and/or the professional expertise
we displayed in our jobs before undertaking doctoral studies. However, we
also feel we have to be circumspect in revealing these uncertainties and
distress because otherwise people 'may find out that we got in by mistake'.

This chapter has stressed that this comes not just from within women's
heads, as a result of childhood socialization and 'lack of role models', but
also from the contexts we continue to find ourselves in. Present day social
interactions in academia make us feel uncomfortable and doubt our abilities
– so we become less productive and able, hence we may fall behind and
leave. Universities are said to prize rationality and objectivity and to be
meritocratic. But it is not merit alone, but also a lot of other things –
including sponsorship and male bonding – that determines who is successful.
Academia also supposedly involves a cooperative search for knowledge,
with rewards for honesty and collaboration, but it is in fact often duplicitous,
competitive and exploitative. It does not often reward, indeed it sometimes
does not even allow, collaboration, as is evident in the PhD itself. (This
is less true of professional doctorates, thanks to pressures from outside.)
Moreover, as is well attested experimentally, women's work is routinely
less well evaluated – because of what it is about, how it is done, and straight-

forwardly because it has a woman's name on it. While male success is attributed to solid abilities, women's achievements are said to be due to luck or hard work. Women who are scholarly and ambitious are 'hard faced'; women who are not 'should not be keeping a deserving man out of a job'. To counter this women need extra support – to start, to continue and to finish.

For all students, getting to the end of a thesis is likely to feel like being on an emotional rollercoaster. Doubt, desperation and depression alternate with confidence, elation and satisfaction in waves – over the length of the research and from day to day. Troughs which can feel like nervous breakdowns are caused by hearing someone else is working in your field, by fieldwork crises, data not panning out, being overwhelmed by what is left to be done, and trouble with your supervisor. Highs come from . . . (you fill it in). But, especially for women, they rarely come from positive feedback. ('Your paper was brilliant. Reading that made my day!')

Some common talking down of oneself can be relatively easily countered.

I picked the wrong topic!

There is no 'wrong' topic – rethink your angle on it.

What have I got myself into!? I'm stupid: I always make the wrong decisions!

Remember why you decided to do a PhD, and go back to your notes on why you made what were good decisions at the time, and your careful planning. Don't generalize to your whole being.

The data's come out all wrong!

Some data always do come out other than expected. Restructure your attitude towards 'scientific procedure' and emphasize serendipity and radical methods.

Nothing comes when I sit down to write!

Periods of blockage are inevitable. Everyone has them. The only way through is to put in some time every day. Take it slow and steady. The worst thing is just stopping for weeks.

I'm overwhelmed by what there is left to do!

You have your plan. Revise it, and work on slowly and steadily. Remember no dissertation is ever perfect. If you revise it ten times more, and pursue all possible angles or new books to read, it will be a different dissertation not a better one.

I've left out something which the examiners will jump on!

There will always (there has to be) something left out. If they ask you, you can defend its omission and the other 350 pages will get you through.

(Adapted from Sternberg 1981)

If you need to do this exercise time and again and you seem stuck in repetitively punishing patterns or with ambivalences and contradictions which are not amenable to rational explanation, you might consider finding more therapeutic support that the departmental seminar and your study group. There *are* constraints, not only in the climate around us, but also 'in our heads': embedded, gendered, blockages to our being successful. These are fluid, contradictory and irrational – not at all what socialization or role theory presents as 'gender'. Chryssi Inglessi (1998) explored them in her work counselling university students in Greece, especially women who were not completing their theses. In the end she wrote her own thesis on this topic.

[T]he very content of my thesis was a reflection of my personal experience as well as that of the women I met as a psychologist in my [clinical] practice: it was about the impasses, the confusions, and the inhibitions which run through our life stories, marring our successes, blunting our initiatives. My subjects were twenty-five feminist women with a university education. Their biographies, narrated to me, served as material for the analysis. Different as each story was, when juxtaposed to the others, they tended to reveal certain constant patterns which belied the romantic ideal of an uninterrupted progression of life-plans, as expected of this talented, politically-aware population. The women had all been brilliant in their school-years; as young students their future looked promising, and their aspirations were high. Educationally, as well as professionally, however, the women did not advance in a straight line. A closer reading of the biographies showed that strange coincidences seemed to put an abrupt end to plans which were heavily invested in effort; it seemed that every time a new decision was taken it was because a different kind of priority had replaced the older one: an 'irresistible' love affair, a 'sudden' decision to marry, an 'unwanted' pregnancy, a change of orientation. Every time, it was as if the women had been caught unaware. At the time of our meeting, when the women told me their stories, years had passed after the actual events, but a strong sense of frustration still coloured their words of thwarted ambitions.

My reading brought into relief how the fabric of our individual lives is woven from the imperatives and prohibitions that determine our very fem-ininity in the Greek patriarchal society. It is a double bind which inhibits our entering the territories of sexuality openly and with ease, and attenuates our commitment to higher education and a career, traditionally defined as male. Despite the process of modernization, at a symbolic level these areas still remain forbidden to women. Our inner conflicts arise from a 'false permissiveness', the same as that which de-

> termines our strategies of survival. The unaccounted for retreats and confusions that fill the pages of the women's stories are in fact psychological manoeuvres aimed at appeasing the fear of punishment for transgression. Caught between the permitted and the forbidden, women have recourse to trade-off strategies in order to counterbalance their advance into forbidden territory. They may be seen as pledges of allegiance to the female destiny. The stories should be told the other way round: we do not stop our studies because we fall in love, because we get married or have a baby: we do it in order to stifle a symbolically forbidden desire, a desire which is too threatening.
>
> (Inglessi 1998: 70)

Working with groups of women, Inglessi originally thought there would be a 'before' (when they were inchoate and conflicted), then their consciousness would be raised and a 'click' would occur when they suddenly made connections, and they would start to fly. But this didn't happen. Feminists tread on men's turf and do enter the public sphere, including the university, but we do it with a lot of self-recrimination and self-blame. We get exhausted by the process. 'We carry weights on our feet.' Although looking at things from a feminist perspective is painful, because it makes us see what is done to us, it is much better than what went before (see Bartky quote on p. 5). But seeing this does not mean we escape our situation or our selves. There is a repetitive confusion: something not closed or resolved in the psyche of academic women, interconnecting sexuality, competition, higher education, career and feminism. Feminism is a transgression. Inglessi's informants advanced on certain fronts, but when success was in sight, they turned away, or made trade offs. 'If you want career success, you give up sex (i.e. have a period of aestheticism); and then go on to have a child.'

Her account has things in common with earlier work on women's 'motive to avoid success' (or 'fear of success'), and on the mixed messages given to daughters by their parents, especially their fathers. But it is more fluid and more tied in with 'compulsory' (hetero)sexuality and desire. Individual or group feminist therapy may help women ventilate emotions and untangle the specific ways in which we (seek to?) shoot ourselves in the foot. It may also help untangle needy, unrealistic expectations of our supervisors (for perfect mothering: boundless and powerful care, guidance and nurturance), our sometime over-eagerness to please combined with resentment, and/or our thwarted desires (envy and competition) in relationships with our peers. The lines between past and present relationships and selves and positions can intersect, interfere and confuse each other, damming-up our creative energies.

Further reading

Encountering and countering chilly climates

Various of the books recommended in earlier chapters describe the dimensions of the 'chilly climate' and engagements with it.

Caplan, P. (1994) *Lifting a Ton of Feathers: A Woman's Guide to Surviving in the Academic World*. Toronto: University of Toronto Press. On North America.

Morley, L. (1999) *Organising Feminisms: The Micropolitics of the Academy*. London: Macmillan. On the matrix of power relations of the academy in Britain and parts of Europe.

Toth, E. (1997) *Ms. Mentor's Impeccable Advice for Women in Academia*. Philadelphia, PA: University of Pennsylvania Press.

Particular dimensions further explored

Clark, V., Garner, S. N., Higonnet, M. and Katrak, K. H. (eds) (1996) *Antifeminism in the Academy*. New York: Routledge. On the 'intellectual harassment' backlash: the vilification, distortion, racism, and even violence from some men and women intended to ridicule feminist activism and to overturn the achievements made since the 1970s.

Mahony, P. and Zmroczek, C. (eds) (1997) *Class Matters: 'Working-class' Women's Perspectives on Social Class*. London: Taylor and Francis. The majority of contributors have come from working class backgrounds and been through higher education. Valerie Hey, Janet Parr and Bogusia Temple (among others) discuss the influence this has had on the research they have done and their position as researchers.

Mintz, B. and Rothblum, E. D. (eds) (1997) *Lesbians in Academia: Degrees of Freedom*. New York: Routledge. Very readable autobiographical accounts by American lesbians who comprised the 'first women in the faculty', during the women's movement, and the most recent 'generations' of lesbians in universities. They discuss being closeted or 'out' in elite and community colleges and in southern, mid-west and urban locations.

Responses

Most professional associations and publishers can provide guidelines on non-sexist and antiracist language in your field.

EOC (no date) *Sexual Harassment – What You can Do About it!* Pamphlet available free from the Equal Opportunities Commission.

Maher, F. A. and Tetreault, M. K. T. (2001) *The Feminist Classroom*, 2nd edn. New York: Basic Books. Based on observation of classrooms and interviews with feminist professors and students in six colleges and universities in the USA, it provides detailed accounts of alternative, women-friendly pedagogies.

Harassment and violence against women

Bacchi, C. (1999) *Women, Policy and Politics: The Construction of Policy Problems*. London: Sage. The chapter on sexual harassment rephrases the question to 'what kind of problem is sexual harassment represented to be?': that is, what behaviours are included and in what ways are these seen as problems? She stresses requiring institutions to set in place not specific procedures to 'deal' with sexual harassment so much as broad changes to the whole organization to challenge 'women-hating harassment' aimed at stressing women's 'lack of fit'.

Craig, G., Corden, A. and Thorton, P. (2000) 'Safety in Social Research', *Social Research Update*, Issue 29, Department of Sociology, University of Surrey. A useful four-page pamphlet.

Kelly, L. (1988) *Surviving Sexual Violence*. Cambridge: Polity. An important text that explores feminist theory and attempts to account for the link between men's interests and the abuse of women and suggests looking at various forms of sexual violence (rape, sexual abuse, domestic violence) as on a continuum.

Thomas, A. M. and Kitzinger, C. (eds) (1997) *Sexual Harassment: Contemporary Feminist Perspectives*. Buckingham: Open University Press. The editors provide an excellent historical introduction and include chapters looking at the press 'coverage' of sexual harassment.

Trioli, V. (1996) *Generation F: Sex, Power and the Young Feminist*. Kew, Vic.: Minerva. Following on from the Ormond debate in Australia, a young Australian journalist responds to the 'paranoid' account of feminism as priggish and overbearing with an account of how it is alive and well and kicking, but not Stalinist, in the next generation.

Consensual relations

Barale, M. A. (1994) The romance of class and queers: academic erotic zones, in L. Garber (ed.) *Tilting the Tower: Lesbians Teaching Queer Subjects*. New York: Routledge. A counter to Jane Gallop's arguments.

Cahn, S. M. (ed.) (1990) *Morality, Responsibility, and the University: Studies in Academic Ethics*. Philadelphia, PA: Temple University Press. Includes discussion of the fundamental obligations of university teachers to all their students and why miscreants (in this or any other professions) should not be treated lightly.

Carter, P. and Jeffs, T. (1995) *A Very Private Affair: Sexual Exploitation in Higher Education*. Ticknell: Education Now Books. An exploratory qualitative study of 'consensual' relations which their evidence suggests consists mainly of planned, serial abuse by men academics.

Wolf, S. and Dolan, J. (1997) Consenting to relations: the personal pleasures of 'power disparity' in lesbian–teacher partnerships, in B. Mintz and E. D. Rothblum (eds) *Lesbians in Academia: Degrees of Freedom*. New York: Routledge. They defend their relationship. Other articles in both these last two collections engage with this debate from various sides.

Pressure from personal relationships

Delphy, C. and Leonard, D. (1992) *Familiar Exploitation: A New Analysis of Marriage in Contemporary Western Societies*. Cambridge: Polity. Discusses marriage as a labour relationship and how and why women have different rights to leisure, time and 'family' money from men in family households.

Shaw, J. (1995) *Education, Gender and Anxiety*. London: Taylor and Francis. An account from a psychoanalytic frame of reference of how education can give rise to all kinds of unconscious anxieties.

Notes

1 At least eleven Freemasons lodges are attached to British universities (*THES* 13 March 1998).
2 'Hispanic' in the USA includes those with Mexican, Puerto Rican, Cuban, as well as Central and South American orgins, and covers those coming directly from another country and second generation US citizens.
3 An Employment Tribunal ruling in 2000 in a case against Wigan and Leigh College established that universities and colleges could be held liable for sexist and racist behaviour of their students *to staff*. (Three 16-year-old students had harassed a Black woman lecturer.)

8 | COMPLETION, THE VIVA AND LIFE AFTER THE DOCTORATE

> The PhD is not meant to be flawless and definitive. It is a research training. It is a 'master piece' in the old guild sense of the carefully-done job which shows that an apprentice is now qualified to practice this trade. PhD theses always have limited scope, are never definitive, and always have errors and misjudgements. If examiners did not recognise this, no thesis would ever be passed. The point is not to produce perfect research, but to produce research that is adequate, in quality and amount, to justify the award of a doctorate.
>
> (Connell 1985: 38)

The form of doctoral assessment

The doctoral degree as introduced to UK universities at the end of the First World War used forms of assessment familiar in medieval universities but no longer common in undergraduate or Masters degrees: a relatively lengthy thesis or dissertation which is 'defended' to the satisfaction of examiners in a viva voce examination. Both these elements have been subject to some discussion, though not as much as one might expect given the attention to other aspects of the PhD and to assessment in higher education generally since 1985. They are coming under reconsideration again with professional doctorates.

Assessment specialists say that a good test should measure what you want a candidate actually to be able to do, in circumstances close to the actual situation in which the skills will be deployed in future, and in conditions which allow the candidate to work in optimal fashion. The criteria should be explicit, the process clear and widely known, and the procedure for review prompt and credible. So how do doctorates measure up?

None of the research projects on the UK doctorate noted elsewhere has looked at the actual assessment process. Standard texts on assessment in higher education are focused on undergraduates and also have little to say about vivas, which get subsumed under 'orals'. The latter are used, for instance, to assess consultation skills in medicine and law, presentations in architecture and design engineering, oral proficiency in foreign languages, and to help with decisions in marginal cases (when students might be awarded first class degrees or might fail). Such discussion as there is of doctoral assessment tends to come in occasional reports from student associations and accounts of individual experiences, which tend to focus on difficult cases and can be alarmist. Becher and colleagues emerged sanguine from their systematic study of research students, however, and say that 'Assessment at the PhD level may not (any more than it is in other contexts) be a rigorously scientific process, but it is not a lottery either' (1994: 137). Although quality may be more easily recognized than defined, especially across disciplines, they claim most students get a 'fair but not over generous hearing' (p. 138). Others are less sure and my own experience suggests the choice of examiners can sometimes be haphazard. Since one bad report on a thesis can have very serious repercussions, it is a topic which needs revisiting.

Why have a thesis?

Most disciplines and most universities continue to require a 50,000–100,000 word thesis for a PhD (with variation in the length by discipline). In the sciences it is said to be the research rather than the thesis which is assessed, but a social scientist is expected to produce a mature continuous exposition which is judged as a book. For professional doctorates, a portfolio of coursework and/or professional publications, a work-based project and a short thesis may all be assessed. There is also a lobby which argues that a portfolio of published articles with a literature review might be a better alternative to a thesis for PhD candidates too (and this is now allowed in a few UK universities and some disciplines, notably economics).

> Not only does writing a traditional dissertation become a heavy burden on students, the very length of the presentation may act against the usefulness of the research. Far from being a significant contribution to knowledge, the frequently excellent work presented in dissertations all

> too often lies collecting dust in university libraries. There are enough analyses of citation indexes, orders placed for copies of theses listed in Dissertation Abstracts International, etc., to convince us that the dissertation has never established itself as a useful tool for the communication of knowledge. Few academics can remain unaware of the increased difficulty of having monographs published as traditional publishers of academic work become more and more cost-conscious and less interested in work with a limited audience . . . indications are that knowledge might be better advanced by less extended presentations of postgraduate research.
>
> (Nightingale 1984: 143)

There are also concerns that the taught methodology courses which are now mandatory in social science and science PhDs are not included in the assessment procedure (and this will also apply in similar fashion to any other courses on 'transferable skill elements' which may be introduced in future). If the British PhD is now about *general* research training, as well as about breadth of background knowledge and an original contribution to a particular sub-field (cf pp. 22–5), how are generic research skills to be judged (compare the coursework for professional doctorates)? Also how 'original' and how 'substantial' does the contribution to the field have to be? Or even, how much more substantial and how much more original than a Masters dissertation? Must it *also* be satisfactorily presented *and* contain material suitable for publication *and* be well defended? If it fails on any one of these, does it fail overall?

> It is almost impossible to get any clear information on what a thesis is or should be. Marvellously ambiguous phrases, like 'a contribution to knowledge', are bandied around by the authorities. But, what students who are embarking on their first really major pieces of solo work need are some clear guidelines. And these they do not get. At [the University of New South Wales in Australia], the conditions for the award of degrees in the Graduate Study section of the Calendar give more precise information on the size of the paper to be used and the margins to be left on each side of the sheet than on the university's understanding of what a thesis is.
>
> (Nightingale 1984: 145)

There have been attempts to define the 'how much' a thesis should contribute to knowledge by suggesting it should be the amount of work that can be done in three years by 'a competent and reasonably diligent candidate' which is 'satisfactory for the level of this degree'. Getting consensus on the latter – what is 'satisfactory for this level of degree'/the quality of the thesis – is however tricky because, as various reports have noted, 'The purpose (or purposes) of the PhD have not been set down in such a way as would attract unequivocal and widespread agreement' (ABRC 1993: 3) and different stakeholders have different views on what constitutes 'quality' in postgraduate education and different disciplines mean different things by 'knowledge'. Consensus is also tricky because the imperative for originality of material and of presentation and the need for highly specialist examiners mean that judgements of worth are difficult (impossible?) to standardize. They certainly cannot fit into a set framework of measurement and outcomes-based approaches.

The PhD is obviously a criterion-referenced assessment. One candidate is not marked against a set of others, with their scores expected to give a normal (bell-shaped) distribution, but against certain criteria which have to be met. It is judged on a simple pass/fail basis, not a series of gradations. Standards are ensured through having peer examiners who are assumed to know the thresholds for the awards, even if the criteria are not (and cannot be) very explicit. Each university has general criteria but these may also vary somewhat between disciplines, much is implicit especially in the pre-1992 universities, and there is considerable room for interpretation. Moreover, in disciplines where there are not agreed dominant paradigms, the evaluation of a particular text can vary from one examiner to another (as Australian studies make clear, see p. 241). The doctorate is also unusual in that it is the gateway for students to move into full membership of the discipline (to become a supervisor and future examiner), and so in doing a doctorate they can be expected also to be able to generate the criteria for assessing their own performance and to evaluate what counts as evidence of excellence.

You should discuss with your tutor and others in the department both the specific criteria for the award of a doctorate in your field in your university (according to the guidelines issued to examiners by your university) and what counts as evidence of fulfilment of them generally in the discipline, and support this by looking at a number of recent, successful, 'good' theses in your university's library. You can also get guidance on how your work is being received within the discipline by some prior exposure of your ideas on your website or through email lists and by giving presentations to research groups and at conferences (see pp. 244–5). If you have a formal upgrade (from an MPhil to PhD) this can also be really helpful. It is also ideal to get some papers published en route to your viva. The aim is for you yourself to recognize when your work fulfils (current, disciplinary) criteria of academic good taste or excellence (see Estelle Phillips' work on 'originality' and 'excellence', pp. 64–6). 'You must know it when you see it'. But the 'it' is not an absolute property or quality, but rather something interactively produced and evaluated by context-dependent social relations.

Why have a viva?

The advantages claimed for oral examinations generally are that it is difficult to cheat in them and that they allow follow-up questions and probing in
a way denied to other forms of assessment. For example, if the work presented in a thesis has been done by the candidate as a member of a team, the
viva allows an assessment of how much responsibility the candidate has had
for the product. Vivas can make apparent a candidate's problem-solving
abilities or their excessive reliance on other people; vivas allow examiners to
take account of flaws in design if these are the result of problems in a larger
project or if they suspect a poor thesis is the result of negligent supervision;
and vivas allow a final assessment to be made on the spot. Even though in
general good examinations should make candidates relaxed and establish
rapport so that they can present and defend their work to the best advantage, it is appropriate that the qualification for entry to an academic career
should include a requirement to be clear and articulate and to defend one's
ideas when challenged, and even under stress (a simulation of teaching and
conference presentations to come!).

On the other hand, vivas are time consuming and costly. It is also well
established that the gender and race of a candidate affect evaluation, selection
and classification in other sorts of face-to-face interviews and examinations
(hence the warnings given in formal EO practice about the need for training
and guidelines when interviewing to improve consistency and fairness, and
the use of anonymous marking of exam scripts). So PhD outcomes ought to
be monitored for biases – but this isn't done. In fact HESA doesn't even
collect statistics on the incidence of passes and fails, let alone cross-correlating
these by discipline and characteristics of candidates.

Some countries with broadly comparable education systems to Britain, such
as Australia and South Africa, seldom have vivas, using instead two or three
carefully chosen (?) anonymous examiners to report on the thesis. Candidates
do not know who their examiners are, and not all of the examiners' comments get passed on to the student. Regulations allow for a viva but they are
relatively rare. When the examiners' reports disagree – and they often do, to
a considerable extent (one study of this was published as an article entitled
'Which thesis did you read?': Kamler and Threadgold 1997) – they are re-
viewed by the university's postgraduate committee and the issues 'resolved',
sometimes by involving another external examiner. This system has caused
some concern because too many students get referred and required to resubmit
their theses. Some staff have proposed having vivas so that minor differences
of opinion between examiners, and misunderstandings of students' work, can
be clarified. (Alternatively, it is suggested, a subcommittee might try to get
minor things sorted out before the main postgraduate committee meeting.)

In the USA 'the examination' usually refers to the 'comprehensive examination' (three exams in three areas) taken before work on the dissertation is actually begun (see pp. 74–5). The thesis itself is examined by the members of the dissertation committee who have worked with the student for some years, together with other members of the faculty and a few professors from other departments in the same university (who may know little about the particular field). Half the time during the examination is devoted to the candidate giving a presentation of the work. That is to say, there may be between four and eight people at the oral, most of whom are well known to the candidate. This can be a problem: past history and personal likes and dislikes can get played out during the defence. But there is no one voice, certainly no 'external', previously unknown, very powerful voice suddenly intervening.

In various continental European countries, on the other hand, the viva is a major, staged public performance. For instance,

In Finland the thesis can consist of a normal monograph with conventional chapters or it may consist of about five papers that have been published or accepted for publication, with an introductory and concluding chapter . . . The thesis is initially examined by two external examiners. If they deem it satisfactory it is then bound and published as a book. Following this there is a public defense with one or two leading professors playing the role of 'devil's advocate'. This defense normally lasts two hours but it can go on for as long as four hours before the degree is formally awarded. Following this the candidate is expected to host a doctoral dinner.

(Hartley 1999: 40)

What does this say for comparability of qualifications and reciprocal recognition in the increasingly international world of higher education employment? It will certainly become a practical issue as higher education becomes central to cultural globalization and in terms of the cost-effectiveness of different modes of study and assessment as universities compete for students. It is already causing concern within the EU as it seeks greater 'degree harmonization'.

The process of completion

If you are doing a PhD, many universities register you initially for a generic degree or an MPhil and have a more or less formal upgrading event somewhere along the way. There is a wide variety of ways in which this gets handled, from almost a formality after a year or so, to a very formal procedure with mandatory chapters in draft and a panel interview based around these. Where it is very minimal, students can go all the way through to the end without anyone other than their supervisor engaging in depth with their work; where it is very formal, students can get anxious and even blocked, especially if what is required is not made clear. It helps if your graduate school can establish reasonably uniform practice and standards because then you can benefit from upgrading as a useful quality check along the way: giving you an idea of the standard set by the department, picking up problems and suggesting developments. It is a useful dry run for your actual viva. In professional doctorates the other 'hurdles' along your way serve similarly to give to a sense of the level you are expected to reach.

Let's hope, if your supervisor was well chosen and your research project interesting and realistically set up, things will run relatively smoothly. You will have people to talk to about your problems even when you are not too clear what it is that is causing you trouble. Never lose touch with your supervisor(s); do not let problems drift on; and take periodic advice from your mentor once you have located someone who will help you in this sort of capacity (see pp. 166–9). The data processing, analysis and writing up phases are often a let down after data gathering and it can be really hard to stick at them. Moreover, it often takes much longer than you expect to give a clear account of a complex project and its results. A lot is monotonous, it is easy to get bogged down in details, and all too common to try to put in too much. Better to write a short, crisp thesis and another separate book or series of articles rather than one very long and complex thesis. (The latter could change several times in the writing *because* it takes so long.)

Use your supervisor to help with the overall plan, to accept rough drafts so as to pace you with a series of deadlines which keep the overall process moving, and to reassure you that the whole thing is not a waste of time, not badly designed, not about a trivial problem, and not hopelessly ambitious. Your supervisor should also tell you if there are additional sections needed and supplement your own checking of whether there are new books and articles to be included. You must put limits on the job – referring back to your original plans. As you go on you will develop the feel for this: it is an important element in acquiring academic skills – though often easier to do for someone else than with your own work. So also use your peers to help you and learn by helping them in turn.

If you have serious problems with your supervisor, it is probably better to change the individual person even at a late stage, or to supplement with a second supervisor, rather than getting into complex interpersonal engagement – in pseudo-therapy (for yourself or for your supervisor) – when you should be working on your dissertation. Difficulties can of course be a projection of your own problems on to your supervisor, but even if it is an issue of your 'father complex' or other emotional blocks (see pp. 230–3) or whatever, dissertation supervision is not meant to be therapy. Go look for the latter elsewhere. Note, too, that you can submit your thesis against your supervisor's advice: it is *your* thesis.

> It is better to settle for 85 per cent of what you wanted and to deliver it at a determinate time, than to try to deliver 100 per cent at some time in the future (which is quite possibly never).

Giving presentations

It helps enormously to clarify your argument to give papers in the later phases. (It is also useful as a way of demonstrating you have another skill employers are looking for.) If you are not used to giving a presentation, do a short course. Make sure you give your first paper (and also probably subsequent ones) to a sympathetic 'home' audience (perhaps to other research students in your department) before you go public. Maybe your university will have departmental seminars and an annual research student conference where you can first watch others in action and then try out your own work.

> I strongly recommend not *reading* a paper, however nervous you feel, because you cannot then maintain eye contact and vary your delivery to talk to your audience. Your listeners will therefore cut off quite rapidly. Also do make the structure of your talk super clear, and be fairly brief. Break up the monotone with jokes, overhead transparencies, video clips and getting other people to read sections, and so on.
>
> Work from a few overhead transparencies (OHTs) and a set of cards.
>
> - First have a device (a cartoon or an anecdote) to grab people's attention and make a point about what is to come. Then explain the structure of the paper and its main argument. Get that across while people are still fully listening.
> - Then have about three cards, each with one point on it and some supporting evidence. Talk around what is on each card for about five minutes, using interesting examples.
> - Go on to a final card which reminds people of what you have said, and draw your conclusions.
>
> A presentation should be a performance and you will always and necessarily leave things out. These can come up in the discussion. If you want to make fine points and develop theoretical ideas, have these in a paper which you hand

out at the end (or collect in people's addresses and email it to them later). But having to pare things down and still get your ideas across explicates your thinking markedly. Most academics give a paper two or three times, revising it in between times, before submitting it for publication.

I'm greatly in favour of students getting one or two articles published before they complete (especially given many people's reluctance in practice to look at their thesis again after the viva). In the sciences this means being one of the senior authors in the list of the team, and in the social sciences and humanities you are sole author (or joint with your supervisor). Publishing gives you confidence and it is harder for examiners to refuse to pass a thesis if a peer-reviewed journal has seen fit to publish sections of it. Thinking about publication also requires you to think how clean you want to come about the difficulties you encountered during the research; and about ethical issues of confidentiality and disguising sources if you have human subjects. You may feel a thesis is hidden away, but it is officially 'published' and accessible in your university's library. It is also available on inter-library loan – unless you specify to the contrary (and it is anti-academic to do this: see Table in p. 155). So be careful. Do not think your informants and/or the press won't find it; and you would also be well advised not to do too much of an intellectual 'striptease' too early in your career.

Thesis writing

Academic writing has its own generic features, but a thesis is obviously different from even other forms of academic writing, such as postgraduate essays.

Mark Torrance and Glyn Thomas stress that

> Research writing is not simply a description of the researcher's activities, but a constructive process that uses research findings as raw materials to build one of several possible accounts of a programme of research. In the course of writing the researcher makes decisions about what audience to aim his or her account at, what results to report, the theoretical framework in which to set the account, what conclusions to draw and so forth. Each of these decisions constrains not only the rhetoric but also the meaning of the text that is produced. Research writing is, therefore, not simply a communication of knowledge but a negotiation of knowledge claims.
>
> (Torrance and Thomas 1994: 109)

During their project on doctoral students' writing skills, which was part of an ESRC Research Training Programme, they distinguished two approaches.

- The first, traditional approach typically involves a think-then-write strategy in which content is decided largely in advance of composing the text. This is the one most often taught in British schools and recommended in guides to under-graduate study. Torrance and Thomas call this approach 'knowledge telling'.
- More experienced writers have usually become aware of the power of writing to develop their thinking and adopt a different, 'knowledge transforming' approach. This involves setting out ideas in full sentences but postponing final decisions over the content and structure of the text until late in the writing process. Such writing they describe as 'a recursive process in which planning, drafting and revising are interleaved' (Torrance and Thomas 1994: 110).

Torrance and Thomas found students who were working successfully with both approaches and they suggest that a knowledge telling approach works well for writing up routine research within a well-established theoretical framework in any discipline. It also can be more productive in terms of words per hour worked. But developing theoretical ideas and exploring competing conceptualisations benefits from a revising strategy. Students who mix up the two strategies, however, have the most worries and difficulties.

Not only are there generic features of academic writing, but there are also subject specific genres and conventions. Art and design, history, cultural studies, engineering, psychology, and physics are each characterized by different discourses and discourse practices, that is by different ways of constructing knowledge in talk and in writing. They also vary in how much your personal voice can be heard, issues of impartiality (how you present views with which you disagree), and what constitutes 'quotable bookwork'. Moreover, there are also political differences *within* many disciplines, and feminist approaches in particular in many fields have encouraged the 'writing in' of the researcher and her voice (see pp. 189–92). Given this variance, it may well be helpful to go to specialist academic literacy sessions and get expert advice on developing your own particular 'voice', especially if your supervisor is not particularly good at explicating style criteria. This can happen even if they write a lot, successfully. Or they may be set in a mode they have developed which works for them, but not for you. There are a number of books which may also help, though choose ones which are relevant to your discipline since disciplinary differences and politics extend even to, say, the form of the review of the literature.

Some feminists have been in the vanguard of extending the limits of what can count as 'a thesis'. Jannette Rhedding-Jones, for instance, wrote a prize-winning postmodern thesis which deliberately set together different methodologies and ways of writing, and both used and deconstructed each of them. She suggests the researching and writing of 'signs, representations and multiple meanings in events and sites' is 'more women's prerogative', and that this can open doors to different ways of writing a thesis and of going about theorizing. In a subsequent article she sets out the techniques she used:

> I hope that readers who are doctoral students, supervisors or examiners can see what may be done. Showing the insides of a garment, by turning it inside out, is not necessarily postmodern. My grandmother worked as a dressmaker, which meant paying attention to bodies, fashions, pragmatics and arts. In much the same way, as a PhD student who was at the same time a university lecturer who taught throughout her candidacy, I attempted to do the same.
>
> (Rhedding-Jones 1997: 194–5)

Such complex patching and sewing of a thesis is possible thanks partly to word processing, which has made writing and editing an easier and continuous process. It is also more common in the humanities and social sciences. Although 'knowledge transformation' also occurs in science, 'writing up' here generally starts later and theses are shorter. But in all disciplines things have to be said in the 'right' order so as to be read from an outsider's perspective, making the path travelled by the reader fully comprehensible; and there has to be a rigorous argument constructed in a form which is recognizably a doctoral thesis – however much you may want to push at its boundaries. You have to define the problem and its importance, explain the research design, display the evidence, state the implications fully (especially the contribution to the discipline and field) and enthuse the reader about the topic. You need to say what you have discovered, rolling the drums whenever you are about to do something clever. To see just how much a weak argument can be strengthened and a good piece further improved by moving material around and tightening up the threads of the argument, get a good editor to work on parts of your own text; and try editing and proof-reading other people's work. (Another useful 'transferable skill' for your CV.) In general go for quality not quantity. Try to leave time to set the penultimate version aside for a while so you can revisit it afresh and improve it. Finally, proof-read the typescript carefully, check the referencing and bibliography, and be sure you meet the formal requirements of your particular university. Check the length, size of margins and font, colour of binding, number of copies, and length of the abstract allowed. Anticipate delays when printing out. Machines can tell when users are in a hurry and choose that moment not to cooperate!

Examiners

It is helpful to know who your examiners are going to be before you finish the thesis. It helps to write any text or talk for a known audience and you should have read and referenced their work and familiarized yourself with their interests and investments. They are representatives of the academic peer group and gatekeepers of your access to it, but they are also located within it.

The usual practice (at least outside the most dominant paradigm sciences) is for your supervisor to be responsible for suggesting a short list of examiners, one from your university (internal) and one from elsewhere (external), which they will usually talk over with you, or at least put their names to you to check there are no personal animosities. They should certainly not be someone with whom you have had either a close or an antagonistic present or past relationship, nor someone whose work you deeply disagree with. They could well be people to whom you already make frequent reference. The various possibilities will also be discussed with other staff in the department and probably go to a formal departmental board.

The choice of examiners is strategic, not only in terms of empathy but also because your thesis will be evaluated by where you did it and who the examiners were (at least until you publish). You need professional and respected people. (If I hear X and Y were used, I think 'Uh oh . . . strategic choice . . . weak candidate'.) Also certain people in each discipline are mavericks: they have their own excellent research records but they are devils when examining. Obviously you don't want someone totally hostile to your methods or perspectives. On the other hand, you do want someone with good contacts in the field. The demography of people who act as supervisors and examiners has changed recently with the 'massification' of numbers of research students and with the 'new' universities awarding their own doctorates. There has been little time for the (small) old guard to transmit their expertise by co-examining with novices (there is no formal required training) and the Council for National Academic Awards which used to guide and regulate the former polytechnics has been disbanded. The latter's legacy, however, continues in the 'comprehensive and detailed specifications' of the independence, academic credentials and experience required of examiners in the post-1992 institutions (Tinkler and Jackson 2000). The Regulations for some of the old universities are surprisingly sparse.

Potential examiners agree to serve largely out of the goodness of their hearts. It is very low paid work. According to an AUT (1999) survey, the fee is an average of £98 for about three working days and attending the viva. (It should be more like £415 if the union's recommended minimum was adhered to.) The higher status universities and the sciences pay the least. It is much less pro rata than doing undergraduate and Masters degree examining – though much more interesting.

Once the thesis is presented (that is once you have delivered it to your Registry, bound or unbounded as local requirements specify), it is sent out to the examiners by the university with details of its regulations. Your supervisor is usually the one who fixes a date for the viva. This is generally several weeks, even months, ahead so as to find space in people's diaries, to give the examiners several weeks to read your tome, and for the university's bureaucratic procedures. This can be a problem for those waiting to return to their home countries, so if this applies to you, try to give your supervisor due notice of your intentions so arrangements can be made ahead of time as far as possible.

The viva

In most universities in the UK the two examiners now write separate reports beforehand and meet an hour before the viva to discuss their recommendations and how to handle the event. You and the examiners then meet, in private, usually in someone's office. Your supervisor may usually be present but not speak. The external examiner usually takes the lead and chairs the meeting. They ask you to come in, they grill you for as long as they wish, generally from one to three hours, they may then ask you to wait outside while they deliberate, and then they tell you whether you have passed or not.

It is a pretty daunting experience but also often stimulating, interesting and, in retrospect, enjoyable. (Yes, really.) It should have a structure and purpose. Having read each other's reports, the examiners should have agreed where they stand and the order and nature of the questions to be asked. These should cover the ideas and assumptions in the research, the empirical work, the results and interpretations, and what might be published.

Unfortunately some students are very unclear about what to expect and what to provide in the viva. Surprisingly, tutors and the taught courses provided by the doctoral school often don't discuss it and students don't ask. Some supervisors (in the sciences) don't even tell the candidate who the examiners are going to be prior to the viva. University regulations can be skimpy and you have anyway to seek them out; and textbooks stop at *preparation* for the viva and don't talk much about the event itself. Nobody has done systematic research about what goes on in vivas and how people feel about them. So we are left with personal stories, including some horror stories.

Sara Delamont and Jim Egglestone (1983) analysed responses to a questionnaire to research students in education on how they prepared for their viva examinations, using a threefold categorization of 'playing the system' (derived from an earlier study of undergraduate law students:

- **Cue-seekers** who believe in technique and 'deliberately interact with the system'. They seek contact with lecturers and set out to impress them with their ability and level of interest. They ask staff about the form and content of their examinations, who the examiners are going to be, and what they specialize in.
- The **cue-conscious** who are alert to hints about assessment but take no active steps to acquire such organizational knowledge. They believe in luck.
- So called **'cue-deaf'** students who believe that hard work and virtue are rewarded. They see lecturers as distant authority figures and do not believe that impressing staff is relevant to the examination process. They don't hear cues even when they are given.

Cue-seeking research students could give Delamont and Egglestone long replies when questioned about what features of their thesis would be judged and what criteria used to assess it. They actively planned their presentation, found out what was important and made sure they complied with the formal and informal rules. (Even they were vague, however, about the importance of getting an appropriate external examiner.) The **'cue-deaf'** did not know or were very uncertain about what criteria might be used by examiners; or they thought the issue of whether a thesis is worth a PhD or not was a question of the time spent and the number of words written; or that there are no objective criteria and it depends upon the external examiner (but they had no idea how examiners were chosen). In the survey, 21/84 respondents were in this last category, which as Delamont and Egglestone say is '21 too many'. Some students in this category did none the less get their PhDs.

Do seek out information, read your university's regulations, and practise your viva either by proxy (by giving some seminar and conference papers during the course of your research) or more directly at the time of upgrading from MPhil to PhD. It is also worth organizing a mock viva with your peers or your tutor. Delamont and colleagues (1997) describe how their university (Cardiff) holds mock vivas where two staff members grill a third one about an article the latter has recently written, in the mode of a viva, and students can observe. In any event, keep a record of the questions asked when you give papers and think of good answers; get your supervisor to ask difficult questions; and/or ask your dissertation group to role play the viva with you.

Your examiners will probably ask questions in uninterrupted blocks, first one examiner and then the other, followed by a period of crossfire. They may well start by asking you to give an account of your most interesting findings, or 'the substance of your thesis', and/or what you would have done differently if you knew at the start what you know now. Towards the end they will probably ask you where you think you might publish it and how you think you will change it for publication. So be prepared for these questions. If there are areas where you know the thesis is weak, have a response ready. ('I would like to have done it differently, but . . .')

Otherwise, prepare by visiting the room beforehand, if you are not familiar with it; dress to impress – smart and business-like to show you appreciate the importance of the occasion, while comfortable in your clothes; and use body language of composed listening and reflecting! You will be totally in command of the substance of the dissertation and neither examiner knows half of what you do. But do *remember to take a copy with you* so you can check points with the examiners.

If they say 'I am worried about x', it does not mean you will fail because of it. Say 'Yes, me too, but . . .' This is a thesis *defence* – so defend your ideas, but don't be defensive. Do not get emotional or personal. If you are unclear what a question means, ask for clarification; or say 'do you mean, why did I . . .' (with a question you can answer!). Concede some points (but not too many). Don't give too long answers (examiners like to talk too). Don't make comments of a self-deprecating, task-irrelevant kind; and respond to questions rather than initiating topics. Assertiveness may be difficult for you, if you don't like arguing with your seniors, or criticism, or challenging people. But in my experience most candidates get a huge boost from engaging with people who have paid their work extended close attention; and no student has gone down in the examiner's estimation during any viva I have attended. On the contrary, several have picked themselves up and covered sections the examiners were unhappy about, and passed because of a good demonstration of professional competence.

Your examiners will probably know each other, though possibly more by reputation than by close personal acquaintance. They are therefore relatively unlikely to be playing complex interpersonal games (compare the US literature). But they may display to each other; and the whole procedure is set up to encourage them to criticize – so don't be surprised if they do just that.

Let's hope your supervisor will avoid the following examiners, but if not, take them in your stride. They won't stop you getting the degree.

- The proof-reader, who spends the viva going through the thesis making detailed corrections of spelling, punctuation and grammar.
- The committee man, who takes up points page by page, in the order they occur in the thesis, rather than synthesizing them into key questions.
- The hobby horse rider, who applies highly personal preferences and prejudices ('I see you haven't quoted my friend/enemy Lovejoy?') rather than whether the candidate is aware of the main relevant work.
- The kite flyer, who targets questions to items tenuously related to the study as defined by the candidate.

- The reminiscer, who uses the viva for their own memories or indulgences ('I see you're from Liverpool, did you know Professor Smith in the Psychology department?')

(Brown and Atkins 1988)

You don't have to reply brilliantly, or even adequately, to every question; and if you do get rattled, admit you are nervous and take your time, referring back to the thesis itself which is sitting in front of everyone. If it should all go *very* pear-shaped, excuse yourself and go to the toilet and breathe slowly before returning (and hope your supervisor turns the conversation to positive things in your absence). Stop the momentum of the other team. If your supervisor is there (and they don't have to be) the examiners may ask if they have any comments to add at the end, and they can say: 'I don't think X did herself justice with the answer to such and such a particular question. Could you ask it again?' Or if the examiners ask you if there is anything you want to add, you could do something similar.

If your examiners ask you something you think you have already covered fully in the thesis, it could be because they haven't read it properly. All vivas are put together with difficulty and shoe-horned into examiners' schedules, so it is possible one or other may not have read it word for word, reprehensible though that is. But it is more likely they are checking that it *is* your own work and/or that you can repeat the argument, or in order to gauge your understanding of the ideas and the limits of your evidence. So say politely that you think you covered that in the section on . . . (and you can take the time to look through your thesis and find the relevant passages). Or just say it again, and use the occasion to spotlight again your original contributions (methodological, theoretical and empirical).

Possible outcomes

There are various possible outcomes to a viva, so prepare yourself not to get an unconditional acceptance. The options open to the examiners are to recommend to your university that you be awarded:

- an outright pass
- a pass subject to minor changes
  (often correcting typos and/or omissions from the bibliography)
- a pass subject to major revisions
  (which must be submitted to one examiner for approval within a set period, for example you must develop the implications of the study further in a new final chapter within a few months)

- referral for a major revision and resubmission,
    to be re-examined by both examiners, and possibly (though rarely) involving another viva
- an MPhil[1]
- or they may indicate that you have failed.

Neither HESA nor the funding councils keep statistics of how many people get a clear pass, a pass with minor revisions, and so on. The most that is recorded is the time to submission, not even the time to examination. However, indicative figures for 100 psychology graduates who had vivas in 1997–9 show that

16 were accepted outright
69 required minor amendments
11 required major amendments
3 had to be resubmitted with a further viva, and
1 was rejected (Hartley and Jory 2000).

This study found few differences by sex or between full- and part-time students; and 44 per cent of the respondents said they had a positive experience, 16 per cent said it was okay or an anti-climax or exhausting; but 39 per cent found it awful, devastating or scary. The great majority (82 per cent) of those who were asked to make some changes thought these were fair. The figures are perhaps optimistic because the sample was derived by asking heads of departments for names, and there was then only a 75 per cent response rate, both of which mean that respondents who did not do well would be likely to be lost.

If you get through to presenting your thesis, your chances of being successful are high. But be self-protective and realistic. While a pass subject to minor or even major revisions is not as existentially satisfying as an outright pass, it does nonetheless constitute a pass if you go the extra mile. This also seems to be becoming increasingly common because, with the pressure to submit 'on time', the examination has become almost 'formative'. 'Unfinished' theses are being submitted within four years to fulfil research council requirements and to see what the examiners will require for a minimal pass. Referral, or at least the expectation of writing some extra sections after the viva, may be becoming almost the norm.

One very good candidate I knew had deliberately chosen high status examiners. Unfortunately, one of them liked things done the way *she* would have done them if she had written the thesis. So she insisted on some rewriting and an extra appendix. This was disappointing and in the supervisor's opinion unnecessary. But they took only two extra weeks.

Even the fourth option shouldn't lead you to go into a down spin. A requirement to do substantial specified rewriting is still essentially an acceptance, and if you do what is required within the time set, you get your degree. So get straight on with the work. This means leaving the exam knowing exactly what you have to do. Get a 'strict' (narrow) written interpretation of what is wanted. Make sure you know exactly what each examiner is asking for (and don't volunteer anything else you remember they critiqued!) and make sure your supervisor photocopies any relevant comments. But take the longest length of time you are offered. You can resubmit as soon as you are ready.

> One student whose thesis caused the examiners considerable concern managed to convince them her work was worthy of a PhD during the viva. But they required her to write an additional new chapter and to get the whole thing thoroughly sub-edited and proof-read. The regulations said she could be offered one or six months within which to do this; but she insisted she needed only one month, and this was what was recorded. This was not very smart because it looked as if she thought their objections were minor and she wasn't taking them seriously. It was also a practical mistake because this ran her into the Christmas period and she had to renegotiate a couple of extra weeks (by arguing it was 'one working month'). Even so, she still did not get the new chapter done in time to get it properly proofed – which annoyed one examiner so much he did not want to act as a referee subsequently.

The moral of which is that it is best not to schedule a celebration party for the night of the viva, but rather to phone round after the viva for an event a few days or even weeks later.

Appeals

The element of 'taste' in evaluations, and the uncertain way in which examiners are selected, does mean that PhD examining in the UK can sometimes be precarious. Some go so far as to say say that the potential for abuse is 'awesome' (quoted in Noble 1994: 69). Since explicit criteria are not possible for assessing originality, there should at least be explicit processes and transparent appeals procedures – especially since face-to-face assessments have known and worrying fallibilities. However, there is neither research on, nor any individual institutional monitoring of submission and success rates by discipline, age, race or sex. Nor is there any practice of moderating and 'second examining' a sample of PhDs to see the reliability of the existing system. There is therefore no knowing if there *is* cause for concern.

A senior supervisor recommended two well-known individuals in his field as examiners for one of his students, who was already a lecturer in another university. This suggestion did not go through a departmental research committee, which was a tactical mistake because one of the examiners was notorious (to staff other than the supervisor) for his intolerance. This maverick managed to persuade the other examiner to go along with his negative assessment of the thesis, and they required the candidate to make major revisions and to resubmit and be re-examined. The supervisor was furious because he was certain the thesis was good. The candidate was devastated. Fortunately the intolerant guy was also incompetent and failed to produce the required paperwork within three months of the viva. The department did not remind him and it was therefore able, on a technicality, to appoint new examiners and hold a new viva, at which the candidate passed.

Occasionally appeals around doctoral examinations do become known along the grapevine, through tales in professional newsletters and by reports in the *THES*. These include descriptions of what appear to be 'an appalling mix of highly selective reading arising out of prejudice on the part of the external examiner'; theses which get referred but the candidate is not given access to the examiners' report nor any written guidance as to what revisions are expected; or where it takes six months to hear about a thesis which had be re-presented and where the candidate is then offered an MPhil with no possibility of a second viva and no apology or explanation (Anon 1993).

The QAAHE published a new *Code of Practice for Postgraduate Research Programmes* in 1999, but this does not deal with the ticklish issues of *who* is selected to be the examiners for a doctorate, nor how the viva itself should be conducted. It merely states that 'research assessment processes should be clear and operated rigorously, fairly, reliably and consistently' (QAAHE 1996b: 12), thus throwing back onto institutions themselves a requirement to 'consider' the mechanisms and procedures to achieve this. Such an informed consideration of 'mechanisms and procedures' is difficult in the current absence of systematic, research-based information on the formal *and informal* viva procedures actually in place across the sector.

Student union advisers or the National Postgraduate Committee may perhaps be able to give you some support if you do have problems with the assessment of your doctorate, especially if the issue is 'inadequate assessment' or 'prejudice'. However the chances of overturning the decision on a failed thesis (in any country) are slim unless your supervisor is strongly behind you and you have evidence your examiners behaved badly. But some internal university appeals *are* successful even though the actual processes involved at present are varied and complex.

The Dearing Report (1997) called for the QAA to produce 'fair and robust' procedures for student complaints and appeals, including an 'independent external element' (generally taken to be a student Ombudsman) by summer 2000. But the CVCP supported universities in guarding their institutional autonomy and in their worries concerning freedom of information issues and the need for discretion over the release of data to complainant students. If you are lucky, you will find your university has an independent appeals body, but a survey by the NPC in 1998 revealed that one-third of institutions didn't have even any internal complaints procedure, and that most of those that did exist 'did not bear scrutiny nor satisfy even the most basic recommendations of Dearing' (*THES* 25 September 1998: letter from Don Stanford). Many use an ancient 'Visitor' system involving members of the Royal family as arbiters. You could be consigning yourself to years of hell with little chance of ultimate vindication, let alone victory. Law suits are unlikely to succeed because there will be a precedent and assumption of competence and sound academic judgement on the part of faculty, which will act against you as appellant. It might be better to get supportive counselling and move on.

Publication

Those of you in science and engineering will probably have published a few articles as part of a team by the time you complete your doctorate, and those in the social sciences and humanities should have given some papers and be on the way at least to having an article or one or two chapters published by the time of your viva (or you may even submit a portfolio of several articles as your 'thesis'). But do try to get some of your doctoral research published (and used) after the event, despite an understandable desire to relax or collapse after completion. You need to *keep* padding onwards, at perhaps a less obsessive pace, into postdoctoral research and to a renewed recognition that you were not writing to be read by three people.

If you chose your topic and methodology with a larger audience in mind, and if you had human subjects whom you told that you would write a book, you must start work on publication and other ways of disseminating your ideas and feeding back to relevant parts of the outside world. Minimally put a report on to the university website. There is also a considerable literature you might find useful, including free pamphlets from the research councils (see p. 261), on other ways of getting your ideas across, including patenting or issuing press releases to get media interest. You also need to publish to establish intellectual property rights and in the social sciences your thesis is a major source of intellectual capital. You can call on help from your supervisor, your examiners and your mentor(s) on how best to use it. If your examiners don't raise the issue of publication towards the end of the viva, you (or your supervisor) should ask them which journals they think might be interested in parts of the work and maybe which publishers would be interested in it as a book.

To make any thesis into a publication requires considerable 'translation' and cutting back; but if you are thinking in terms of a book, you need to recognize how hard it is now to get a social science or humanities monograph (as opposed to a textbook) published, and that it needs to be 'sold'.

> There is a basic contradiction in modern publishing which . . . creates many problems: it is the discrepancy between the image that publishers still have of themselves to an extent as . . . people with liberal views . . . interested in books and Culture, and the change in the market, whereby small publishing houses have been taken over by larger groups, which are themselves often owned by media empires like Granada or Rupert Murdoch, which makes it impossible to be any such thing . . . 'cultural' responsibility comes a poor second to making a profit.
>
> (Adapted from Cadman *et al.* 1981: 19)

In the 1970s a number of women's presses (and printers and periodicals and radical distributors) were established precisely to counter the gatekeeping which made it difficult for women to get published. But most of those in the UK (see p. 196) suffered badly from a series of takeovers and then the recession of the 1980s. Today, although 'women' have been a profitable 'product' for some years and many mainstream academic presses (Falmer, Polity, Sage, Open University, Routledge, Zed) have lists of what they variously call Feminist Theory, Women's Studies and Gender Studies; it is still (or rather, once again) difficult to get radical work accepted, but now for commercial rather than political reasons. Some professional associations are starting their own new publishing companies to get 'minority' books made available.

Publishers tend to hype just a few books which have a lot invested in them: to concentrate limited resources on a few products and for a short space of time (i.e. they no longer keep books in print for very long). Bookshops also favour books with big advertising budgets; and many American books are published in Britain because all the editing and printing costs have been covered for the larger market and it is just a case of a slightly larger print run. If British books get published, the cost and hence the price is high, so they don't sell in large numbers and the prophecy is self-fulfilling.

The RAE has established a slightly different hierarchy of publications (see pp. 17–18). Access to the most prestigious 'outlets' – the university presses and international refereed journals – requires going through peer review, which even the Royal Societies comment is 'self-evidently not neutral'. You may receive damaging (hostile) anonymous reviewers' reports which knock your confidence. But sometimes, although there seem to be two lines of praise and two pages of criticism, in fact what is being said is that if you make some amendments, the piece will be accepted. So read carefully before throwing it in the bin!

On the other hand, there are now many more academic journals than there used to be and many in fields where women are strongly represented. Mentors will probably advise against 'limiting' yourself to publishing in only overtly feminist fields and feminist journals, even if you work in the field of gender, because these count less: they may be seen as lower quality because they are not 'objective' or because they addressing 'minority' concerns. But if you want to get political ideas across, there is the worldwide web which avoids all the need for duplication, distribution and sales of pamphlets which we used to have to go through in the 1970s (even if it doesn't count as publishing for RAE purposes). And you can get feedback from your readers.

Returning to your previous life

Perhaps one of the biggest surprises about doing a PhD is that many people feel anything but straightforwardly elated afterwards. You may feel detached, as if it hasn't really happened, or a lack of purpose, as if this is the end not the beginning of research, and of life generally. Experience suggests (I know of no research) that postpartum exhaustion and paralysis can lead to years of unproductive drifting, so be compassionate and self-healing. Get someone else to organize your celebration, take a brief holiday, and then publish the material in your dissertation and push on to a new project.

Some of the depression is due to a loss of a sense of achieving something each day. It may also be partly due to a continuing belief in dissertation myths (see p. 231). You still believe either that you don't deserve it or that it wasn't really good enough, leading to loss of confidence – despite the fact that to the world you have precisely demonstrated your worth and ability. Some of the flatness may be due to disrupted or broken friendships and relationships. If you have a partner or children who have been waiting for 'it' to be over, they will not welcome you getting involved in a new project – and yet you need to. If you are, or become, an academic it will never be over: you will continue to need swathes of time in your office on your own. Again (as stressed on pp. 118–22), men are more likely to get the support of wives in a continuing intellectual drive and long-term projects. Most heterosexual women have to be expressive and instrumental, including taking (back) primary responsibility for domestic concerns.

The need to demonstrate that you are now available again and not much changed personally after you have your doctorate, may be exacerbated if you have been self or family funded and incurred financial and emotional debts. This may be especially marked if you have travelled to study and face the issue of reintegration into your home society. The separation and often very large adaptations you needed to make to live in another country – in time-keeping, diet, self-sufficiency, dress, and tolerance for different minority views – have to be worked through again on return. Once again the gender relations of the two cultures you are moving between are very important. Men may be under greater economic pressures than women to succeed so as to meet their future obligations within the family, but women often have to handle greater demands to conform to conventional (non-western) (sexual) mores to show they have not 'rejected' their home culture. You may also have to help your children, who have either been separated from you or spent time abroad with you, to adjust to their new situation. Perhaps your university in the UK will run not only induction courses but also sessions for students returning home, which encourage you to think about the dimensions of this process before you leave. Something similar might also be welcomed by 'home' students.

> In the approach to a book you often come across acknowledgements. The author greets you like a host with his visitors' book and gives you a ceremonial run-down of the people without whom . . . etc., etc., though they are not of course responsible for any errors that may have slipped through. Dedications were originally intended by the publisher to prove that the author was not a hack, that he had respectable friends . . . Most important, this kind of prefatory note is a formal recognition that authorship is a social process, that the book did not spring fully formed like Athene from the brain of Zeus but was shaped in a context of relationships and put together by many different kinds of work – from the spark of ideas to the sweat of proof-reading . . .
>
> I share the crude curiosity that plagues writers who give autographs or visit schools and colleges in their official capacity: 'How much do you earn?' 'How hard do you work?' 'How long does it take?' . . . It may be useful to confront literary achievement with the challenge that the worker in Brecht's poem brought to the Great Names of History: 'Someone wins on every page. Who cooked the winner's banquet?' Yes indeed: 'Did you do it all by yourself?' How many hot dinners, how many changes of shirt, how many delegated chores make a book? This is not a

trivial or reductive question. If you believe, as Karl Marx and Jean-Paul Sartre and I do, that 'the mode of production of material life generally dominates the development of social, political and intellectual life', then the maintenance of the writer's workplace and the divisions of labour within it are far from irrelevant. They have a decided bearing on what [gets written].

(Glastonbury 1978: 27–9)

Further reading

Writing a thesis

Becker, H. S. (1986) *Writing for Social Scientists: How to Start and Finish your Thesis, Book, or Article.* Chicago: University of Chicago Press. A classic guide which is especially good at exemplifying the power of editing in the 'knowledge transforming' mode of writing. Lots of jokes and 'worked examples'.

Evans, D. (1995) *How to Write a Better Thesis or Report.* Carlton, Vic.: Melbourne University Press. Very straightforward and direct, focused on the structure rather than the style of a (fairly conventional) thesis. Also useful on proof-reading and presentation.

Lea, M. R. and Stierer, B. (eds) (2000) *Student Writing in Higher Education.* Buckingham: SRHE and Open University Press. Aimed at practitioners but should give you a sense of what 'academic literacy' has to contribute, not only if you are working within a traditional disciplinary genre, but also to work in non-traditional settings (such as practice-based research) and through non-traditional writing practices within traditional disciplines. It sees writing not as a homogeneous and transferable skill you acquire once and for all, but a contextualized social practice. Particular writing constitutes and perpetuates privilege within disciplines, but practices are mediated to students somewhat individualistically by different courses within the same field and by individual staff. There is considerable fluidity despite the fact that most people persist in advising that there is *a* model essay or thesis form. It looks at nursing, teacher training, environmental sciences, philosophy, social anthropology and dance; and the tensions (for professional doctorates) between 'real-world' and 'academic' learning and writing.

The viva examination

Burnham, P. (1997) Surviving the viva, in P. Burnham (ed.) *Surviving the Research Process in Politics.* London: Cassell.

Delamont, S., Atkinson, P. and Parry, O. (1997) *Supervising the PhD: A Guide to Success.* Buckingham: SRHE and Open University Press. Provides ideas about running demonstration and practice vivas. It is well worth reading to see the viva from the supervisor's or examiner's point of view.

Evans, G. R. (1999) *Calling Academia to Account: Rights and Responsibilities*. Buckingham: SRHE and Open University Press. Should you find yourself in dispute, this has chapters on forming academic judgements, ensuring sound procedures and resolving disputes, and on what 'openness' should mean for universities following the *Report of the Nolan Committee on Standards in Public Life* (1996), the Dearing Report (1996) and the *Public Interest Disclosure Act* (1998).

Getting published

Black, D., Brown, S., Day, A. and Race, P. (1998) *500 Tips for Getting Published: A Guide for Educators, Researchers and Professionals*. London: Kogan Page

Blaxter, L., Hughes, C. and Tight, M. (1998) *The Academic Career Handbook*. Buckingham. Open University Press. Has a good chapter on the importance and ways of writing, on co-authorship, getting work accepted by journals, and producing a book proposal; with a long annotated bibliography.

ESRC (1993) *Pressing Home Your Findings: Media Guidelines for ESRC Researchers* and (1995) *Writing for Business: How to Write Reports that Capture the Attention of Businesses*. Swindon: Economic and Social Research Council. Available free.

Roberts, H. (1984) Putting the show on the road: the dissemination of research findings, in C. Bell and H. Roberts (eds) *Social Researching: Politics, Problems, Practice*. London: Routledge and Kegan Paul. Useful warnings about the problems of publishing for a wider readership or audience. The author uses three pieces of research on which she worked to discuss the politics of popularization and the (sometimes unexpected) media interpretations of projects, and strategies to get through to areas where our research may have some effect (not always the corridors of power).

Walford, G. (1998) Compulsive writing behaviour: getting it published, in G. Walford (ed.) *Doing Research about Education*. London: Falmer. Substantially autobiographical and funny account of how Geoffrey keeps on running . . .

Returning to one's past life

Unterhalter, E. and Hayton, A. (1993) *Homeward Bound: A Pack for Tutors Organising Courses for Students Returning to their Home Countries after Studying in the UK*. London: UKCOSA.

Future careers

Basalla, S. and Debelius, M. (2001) *So What Are You Going To Do With That? A Guide to Career-Changing For M.A.'s and Ph.D.'s*. New York: Farrar, Straus and Giroux. To broaden your thinking; for faculty as well as students. US based but with a useful appendix of Web addresses.

Collins, L. H., Chrisler, J. C. and Quina, K. (1998) *Career Strategies for Women in Academe: Arming Athena*. Thousand Oaks, CA: Sage. Useful if you are thinking of working in North America, but also generally helpful especially in relation to negotiating one's (starting) salary.

Warrior, J. (1997) *Cracking It: Helping Women to Succeed in Science, Engineering and Technology.* Watford: Training Publications. Readable and enthusiastic. Discusses planning a career, how to increase your chances of getting a particular job or research contract, and networking. It includes profiles of successful women. All the chapters have further reading and resource lists, with suggestions for some alternative possible careers with a science base (specialist publishing, the law, public life and so on).

Note

1 It is argued that giving an MPhil essentially as compensation for a failed PhD downgrades all MPhils. The QAAHE's new higher education qualifications framework proposals (1999b) propose to abolish this option.

REFERENCES

Aaron, J. and Walby, S. (eds) (1991) *Out of the Margins: Women's Studies in the Nineties*. London: Falmer.

ABRC (Advisory Board for the Research Councils) (1982) *Report of the Working Party on Postgraduate Education* (Swinnerton-Dyer Report), Cm 8537. London: HMSO.

ABRC (1993) *The Nature of the PhD – A Discussion Document*. London: HMSO.

Acker, S. and Feuerverger, G. (1996) Doing good and feeling bad: the work of women university teachers, *Cambridge Journal of Education*, 26(3): 401–22.

Acker, S., Black, E. and Hill, T. (1994a) Research students and their supervisors, in R. Burgess (ed.) *Postgraduate Education and Training in the Social Sciences*. London: Jessica Kingsley.

Acker, S., Hill, T. and Black, E. (1994b) Thesis supervision in the social sciences: managed or negotiated?, *Higher Education Review*, 28(4): 483–98.

ACU (annual) *British Universities' Guide to Graduate Study*. London: Association of Commonwealth Universities.

Adkins, L. (1995) *Gendered Work*. Buckingham: Open University Press.

Aisenberg, N. and Harrington, M. (1988) *Women of Academe: Outsiders in the Sacred Grove*. Amherst, MA: Massachusetts University Press.

Ali, S., Coate, K. and wa Goro, W. (eds) (2000) *Global Feminist Politics: Identities in a Changing World*. London: Routledge.

Allan, G. and Skinner, C. (eds) (1991) *Handbook for Research Students in the Social Sciences*. London: Falmer.

Allen, F. (1994) Academic women in Australia: progress real or imagined?, in S. Stiver Lie, L. Malik and D. Harris (eds) *The Gender Gap in Higher Education*. London: Kogan Page.

Allen, J. A. (1997) Strengthening women's studies in hard times: feminism and challenges of institutional adaptation, *Women's Studies Quarterly*, 1 and 2: 358–87.

Allen, S. and Leonard, D. (1996) From sexual divisions to sexualities: changing sociological agendas, in J. Weeks and J. Holland (eds) *Sexual Cultures: Communities, Values and Intimacy*. London: Macmillan.

Ang-Lygate, M., Corrin, C. and Henry, M. (eds) (1997) *Desperately Seeking Sisterhood: Still Challenging and Building*. London: Taylor & Francis.

Anon (1993) A conspiracy of silence, *Network: The Newsletter of the British Sociological Association* 56: 7.

Arregui, B. (1991) Personal views, in G. Allan and C. Skinner (eds) *Handbook for Research Students in the Social Sciences*. London: Falmer.

Ashenden, D. and Milligan, S. (annual) *Postgraduate and Career Upgrade Courses and Campuses*. Melbourne: Mandarin.

Astin, H. S. and Malik, L. (1994) Academic women in the United States: problems and prospects, in S. Stiver Lie, L. Malik and D. Harris (eds) *The Gender Gap in Higher Education*. London: Kogan Page.

AUT (1994) *Long Hours, Little Thanks: A Survey of the Use of Time of Full-time Academic and Related Staff in the Traditional University*. London: Association of University Teachers.

AUT (1999) *Cheating the Examiners*. London: Association of University Teachers.

AUT, NUS and NPC (1996) *Survey of Postgraduate Teachers 1995*. London: Association of University Teachers.

Bacchi, C. (1999) *Women, Policy and Politics: The Construction of Policy Problems*. London: Sage.

Bagilhole, B. (2000) Too little too late? An assessment of national initiatives for women academics in the British university system, *Higher Education in Europe*, XXV(2): 139–45.

Barale, M. A. (1994) The romance of class and queers: academic erotic zones, in L. Garber (ed.) *Tilting the Tower: Lesbians Teaching Queer Subjects*. New York: Routledge.

Barry, A-M. (1993) 'Women-centred' politics: a concept for exploring women's political perceptions, in J. de Groot and M. Maynard (eds) *Women's Studies in the 1990s: Doing Things Differently?* London: Macmillan.

Bartky, S. L. (1990) *Femininity and Domination: Studies in the Phenomenology of Oppression*. New York: Routledge.

Basalla, S. and Debelius, M. (2001) *So What Are You Going to Do With That? A Guide to Career-Changing For M.A.'s and Ph.D.'s*. New York: Farrar, Straus and Giroux.

Becher, T. (1989) *Academic Tribes and Territories: Intellectual Enquiry and the Cultures of Disciplines*. Milton Keynes: SRHE and Open University Press.

Becher, T. (1993) Graduate education in Britain: the view from the ground, in B. Clark (ed.) *The Research Foundations of Graduate Education: Germany, Britain, France, United States, Japan*. Berkeley, CA: University of California Press.

Becher, T., Henkel, M. and Kogan, M. (1994) *Graduate Education in Britain*. London: Jessica Kingsley.

Becker, H. S. (1986) *Writing for Social Scientists: How to Start and Finish your Thesis, Book, or Article*. Chicago: University of Chicago Press.

Bell, C. and Roberts, H. (1984) *Social Researching*. London: Routledge and Kegan Paul.

Black, D., Brown, S., Day, A. and Race, P. (1998) *500 Tips for Getting Published: A Guide for Educators, Researchers and Professionals*. London: Kogan Page.

Blackmore, J. (1997) Disciplining feminism: a look at gender-equity struggles in Australian higher education, in L. G. Roman and L. Eyre (eds) *Dangerous Territories: Struggles for Difference and Equality in Education*. New York: Routledge.

Blake, M. and La Valle, I. (2001) *Who Applies for Research Funding? Key Factors Shaping Application Behaviour Among Women and Men in British Higher Education Institutions*. London: Wellcome Trust.

Blaxter, L., Hughes, C. and Tight, M. (1996) *How to Research*. Buckingham: Open University Press.

Blaxter, L., Hughes, C. and Tight, M. (1998) *The Academic Career Handbook*. Buckingham: Open University Press.

Blundell, R., Dearden, L., Goodman, A. and Reed, H. (1997) *Higher Education, Employment and Earnings in Britain*. London: Institute for Fiscal Studies.

Bogdanor, V. (1997) Review of Michael Power's *The Audit Society: Rituals of Verification*, *THES* 21 November: 22.

Booth, A. (1999) Study for the Royal Economic Society's Committee on Women in Economics, reported *THES* 20 August: 2.

Bott, G. (ed.) (1958) *Selected Writings of George Orwell*. London: Heinemann.

Bourdieu, P. (1988) *Homo Academicus*. Cambridge: Polity.

Bourgeois, E., Duke, C., Guyot, J-L. and Merrill, B. (1999) *The Adult University*. Buckingham: SRHE and Open University Press.

Braidotti, R. and Vonk, E. (eds) (2000) *The Making of European Women's Studies: A Work in Progress Report on Curriculum Development and Related Issues*. Utrecht: ATHENA Universiteit Utrecht.

Brodribb, S., Bardon, S., Newhouse, T. and Spencer, J. (1996) The equity franchise, *Women's Education*, 12(1): 12–20.

Broughton, T. (1993) Cross purposes: literature, (in)discipline and women's studies, in J. de Groot and M. Maynard (eds) *Women's Studies in the 1990s: Doing Things Differently?* New York: St Martin's Press.

Brown, G. and Atkins, M. (1988) *Effective Teaching in Higher Education*. London: Methuen.

Brown, S., McDowell, L. and Race, P. (1995) *500 Tips for Research Students*. London: Kogan Page.

Bulbeck, C. (1999) *Re-orientating Western Feminism: Women's Diversity in a Postcolonial World*. Cambridge: Cambridge University Press.

Burgess, R. G. (ed.) (1994) *Postgraduate Education and Training in the Social Sciences: Processes and Products*. London: Jessica Kingsley.

Burgess, R. G. (ed.) (1997) *Beyond the First Degree: Graduate Education, Lifelong Learning and Careers*. Buckingham: SRHE and Open University Press.

Burnham, P. (ed.) (1997a) *Surviving the Research Process in Politics*. London: Pinter.

Burnham, P. (1997b) Surviving the viva, in P. Burnham (ed.) *Surviving the Research Process in Politics*. London: Pinter.

Butler, A. (1998) Creating space: the development of the feminist research group, in D. Malina and S. Maslin-Prothero (eds) *Surviving the Academy: Feminist Perspectives*. London: Falmer.

Cadman, E., Chester, G. and Pivot, A. (1981) *Rolling our Own: Women as Printers, Publishers and Distributors*. London: Minority Press Group.

Cahn, S. M. (ed.) (1990) *Morality, Responsibility, and the University: Studies in Academic Ethics*. Philadelphia, PA: Temple University Press.

Caplan, P. J. (1994) *Lifting a Ton of Feathers: A Woman's Guide to Surviving in the Academic World*. Toronto: University of Toronto Press.

Carter, J., Fenton, S. and Modood, T. (1999) *Ethnicity and Employment in Higher Education*. London: Policy Studies Institute.

Carter, P. and Jeffs, T. (1995) *A Very Private Affair: Sexual Exploitation in Higher Education*. Ticknell: Education Now Books.

Channell, J. (1990) The student–tutor relationship, in M. Kinnell (ed.) *The Learning Experience of Overseas Students*. Buckingham: SRHE and Open University Press.

Charities Aid Foundation (biennial) *Directory of Grant Making Trusts, Charities and Foundations*. Tonbridge: Charities Aid Foundation.

Chodorow, N. (1978) *The Reproduction of Mothering: Psychoanalysis and the Sociology of Gender*. Berkeley, CA: University of California Press.

Clark, B. (ed.) (1993) *The Research Foundations of Graduate Education: Germany, Britain, France, United States, Japan*. Berkeley, CA: University of California Press.

Clark, S. M. and Corcoran, M. (1993) Perspectives on the professional socialization of women faculty: a case of accumulative disadvantage?, in J. S. Glazer, E. S. Bensimon and B. K. Townsend (eds) *Women in Higher Education: A Feminist Perspective*. Needham Heights, MA: Ginn Press.

Clark, V., Garner, S. N., Higonnet, M. and Katrak, K. H. (1996) *Antifeminism in the Academy*. New York: Routledge.

Clarke, J. and Newman, J. (1997) *The Managerial State*. London: Sage.

Cockburn, C. (1991) *In the Way of Women: Men's Resistance to Sex Equality in Organizations*. London: Macmillan.

Coffield, F. and Vignoles, A. (1997) *Widening Participation in Higher Education by Ethnic Minorities, Women and Alternative Students*, National Committee of Inquiry into HE, Report 5. London: HMSO.

Cohen, D., Lee, A., Newman, J. *et al.* (eds) (1999) *Winds of Change: Women and the Culture of Universities. Conference Proceedings*, 2 vols. Sydney: Equality and Diversity Unity, University of Technology, Sydney.

Cole, J. R. (1979) *Fair Science: Women in the Scientific Community*. New York: Free Press.

Collins, L. H., Chrisler, J. C. and Quina, K. (1998) *Career Strategies for Women in Academe: Arming Athena*. Thousand Oaks, CA: Sage.

Connell, R. W. (1985) How to supervise a PhD, *Vestes*, 2: 38–41.

Connell, R. W. (1995) *Masculinities*. Cambridge: Polity.

Connor, H. (1994) Doctoral social scientists and the labour market, in R. Burgess (ed.) *Postgraduate Education and Training in the Social Sciences: Processes and Products*. London: Jessica Kingsley.

Connor, H., Court, G., Seccombe, I. and Jaggar, N. (1994) *Science PhDs and the Labour Market*. Brighton: Institute for Employment Studies.

Cooper, C. (1990) Coping strategies for managing transitions, in S. Fisher and C. Cooper (eds) *On the Move: The Psychology of Change and Transitions*. New York: John Wiley.

Cordis focus (2000) Women scientists use science to press for gender equality, 24 April. Available on Cordis website.

Cowen, R. (1996) Last past the post: comparative education, modernity and perhaps post-modernity, *Comparative Education*, 32(2): 151–70.

Cowen, R. (1997) Comparative perspectives on the British PhD, in N. Graves and V. Verma (eds) *Working for a Doctorate: A Guide for the Humanities and Social Sciences*. London: Routledge.

CRAC (annual) *Postgraduate: The Students' Guide to the Development of Graduate Studies*. London: Hobsons.

Craig, G., Corden, A. and Thornton, P. (2000) Safety in social research, *Social Research Update*, 29, Department of Sociology, University of Surrey.

Cryer, P. (1996) *The Research Student's Guide to Success*. Buckingham: Open University Press.

Cryer, P. (1997a) *Handling Common Dilemmas in Supervision*. London: SRHE and *THES*.

Cryer, P. (1997b) How to get ahead with a PhD, *THES Research Opportunities Section*, 16 May, I.

David, M. and Woodward, D. (eds) (1997) *Negotiating the Glass Ceiling: Careers of Senior Women in the Academic World*. London: Routledge Falmer.

Davies, C. (1996) The sociology of professions and the profession of gender, *Sociology*, 30(4): 661–78.

Davies, S., Lubelska, C. and Quinn, J. (eds) (1994) *Changing the Subject: Women in Higher Education*. London: Taylor & Francis.

Dearing Report (1997) *The National Committee of Inquiry into Higher Education*. London: HMSO.

de Groot, J. and Maynard, M. (1993) Doing things differently? A context for women's studies in the next decade, in J. de Groot and M. Maynard (eds) *Women's Studies in the 1990s: Doing Things Differently?* New York: St Martin's Press.

Delamont, S. (1989) Gender and British postgraduate funding policy: a critique of the Winfield Report, *Gender and Education*, 1(1): 51–7.

Delamont, S. and Egglestone, J. (1983) A necessary isolation? A report on students' attitude to their higher degree research, in J. Egglestone and S. Delamont (eds) *Supervision of Students for Research Degrees with Special Reference to Education Studies*. Crewe: British Education Research Association.

Delamont, S., Atkinson, P. and Parry, O. (1997) *Supervising the PhD: A Guide to Success*. Buckingham: SRHE and Open University Press.

Delamont, S., Atkinson, P. and Parry, O. (2000) *The Doctoral Experience: Success and Failure in Graduate School*. London: Falmer.

Delphy, C. and Leonard, D. (1992) *Familiar Exploitation: A New Analysis of Marriage in Contemporary Western Societies*. Cambridge: Polity.

Denicolo, P. (2000) *Supervising Students from Public Sector Organisations*. London: SRHE and *THES*.

Department of Trade and Industry (2000) *Excellence and Opportunity: A Science and Innovation Policy for the 21st Century*. London: Stationery Office.

Devine, F. and Heath, S. (1999) *Sociological Research Methods in Context*. London: Macmillan.

DfEE (1999) *The European Choice: A Guide to Opportunities in Higher Education in Europe*. Nottingham: DfEE.

Dunne, G. A. (1998) 'Pioneers behind our own front doors': new models for the organization of work in partnerships, *Work, Employment and Society*, 12(2).

Dunne, G. A. (1999) A passion for 'sameness'? Sexuality and gender accountability, in E. Silva and C. Smart (eds) *The 'New' Family?* London: Sage.

EOC (no date) *Sexual Harassment – What You can Do about It!* Equal Opportunities Commission. Manchester.

Epstein, D. (1996) Keeping them in their place: hetero/sexist harassment, gender and the enforcement of heterosexuality, in J. Holland and L. Adkins (eds) *Sex, Sensibility and the Gendered Body*. London: Macmillan.

ESRC (1993) *Pressing Home your Findings: Media Guidelines for ESRC Researchers*. Swindon: Economic and Social Research Council.

ESRC (1995) *Writing for Business: How to Write Reports that Capture the Attention of Businesses*. Swindon: Economic and Social Research Council.

Evans, D. (1995) *How to Write a Better Thesis or Report*. Carlton, Vic.: Melbourne University Press.

Evans, G. R. (1999) *Calling Academia to Account: Rights and Responsibilities*. Buckingham: SRHE and Open University Press.

Eyre, L. (2000) The discursive framing of sexual harassment in a university community, *Gender and Education*, 12(3): 293–307.

Fallon, H. (1998) *WOW Women on the Web: A Guide to Gender-related Resources on the Internet*, 2nd edn. Dublin: Women's Education Research and Resource Centre, University College, Dublin.

Farish, M., McPake, J., Powney, J. and Weiner, G. (1995) *Equal Opportunities in Colleges and Universities: Towards Better Practices*. Buckingham: SRHE and Open University Press.

Farley, L. (1978) *Sexual Shakedown: The Sexual Harassment of Women on the Job*. New York: Warner.

Feminist Studies (1998) Special issue on 'Disciplining feminism? The future of women's studies', 24(2).

Fitzgerald, L. F., Weitzman, L., Gold, Y. and Ormerod, M. (1988) Academic harassment: sex and denial in scholarly garb, *Psychology of Women Quarterly*, 12: 329–40.

Fitzpatrick, J., Secrist, J. and Wright, D. J. (1998) *Secrets for a Successful Dissertation*. Thousand Oaks, CA: Sage.

Fleet, A., Holland, S. and Leigh, B. (1999) Women as researchers: room at the top, in D. Cohen *et al.* (eds) *Winds of Change: Women and the Culture of Universities. Conference Proceedings*. Sydney: Equity and Diversity Unit, University of Technology, Sydney.

Fox Keller, E. and Longino, H. E. (eds) (1996) *Feminism and Science*. Oxford: Oxford University Press.

Francis, H. (1997) The research process, in N. Graves and V. Verma (eds) *Working for a Doctorate: A Guide for the Humanities and Social Sciences*. London: Routledge.

Furneaux, C., Locke, C., Robinson, P. and Tonkyn, A. (1991) Talking heads and shifting bottoms: the ethnography of academic seminars, in P. Adams, B. Heaton and P. Howarth (eds) *Socio-Cultural Issues in English for Academic Purposes*. London: Macmillan.

Gallop, J. (1997) *Feminist Accused of Sexual Harassment*. Durham, NC and London: Duke University Press.

Garner, H. (1995) *The First Stone*. New York: Free Press.

Gibbons, M., Limoges, C., Nowotny, H. *et al.* (1994) *The New Production of Knowledge: The Dynamics of Science and Research in Contemporary Societies*. London: Sage.

Gillon, E. (1999) Report on the doctorate for the AUT, NATFHE, NUS and NPC. See A. Goddard, The workhorses of the system, *THES*, 4 June: 8–9.

Glaser, R. D. and Thorpe, J. S. (1986) Unethical intimacy: a survey of sexual contact and advances between psychology educators and female graduate students, *American Psychologist*, 41(1): 43–51.

Glastonbury, M. (1978) Holding the pens, in S. Elbert and M. Glastonbury (eds) *Inspiration and Drudgery*. London: Women's Research and Resources Centre.

Glazer, J. S., Bensimon, E. M. and Townsend, B. K. (eds) (1993) *Women in Higher Education: A Feminist Perspective*. Needham Heights, MA: Ginn Press.

Goldsmith, J. and Shawcross, V. (1985) *It Ain't Half Sexist, Mum: Women as Overseas Students in the United Kingdom*. London: World University Service.

Gorry, J. (1997) Investigating methodologies: a comparison of MA and PhD process, in P. Burnham (ed.) *Surviving the Research Process*. London: Pinter.

Graves, N. and Verma, V. (eds) (1997) *Working for a Doctorate: A Guide for the Humanities and Social Sciences*. London: Routledge.

GRIF (1989) *Women's Studies: Concept and Reality*. Brussels: Les cahiers du Grif.

Griffin, G. and Andermahr, S. (eds) (1997) *Straight Studies Modified: Lesbian Intervention in the Academy*. London: Cassell.

Griffin, G., Hester, M., Rai, S. and Roseneil, S. (eds) (1994) *Stirring It: Challenges for Feminism*. London: Taylor & Francis.

Gross, R. (1994) Accommodation of research students, *Journal of Graduate Education*, 1: 21–4.

Gundara, J. (1997) Intercultural issues and doctoral studies, in N. Graves and V. Verma (eds) *Working for a Doctorate*. London: Routledge.

Habu, T. (2000) The irony of globalization: the experience of Japanese women in British higher education, *Higher Education*, 39: 43–66.

Hacking, I. (1992) The self-vindication of the laboratory sciences, in A. Pickering (ed.) *Science as Practice and Culture*. Chicago: University of Chicago Press.

Hall, R. M. and Sandler, B. R. (1982) *The Classroom Climate: A Chilly One for Women?* Washington, DC: Association of American Colleges.

Hall, R. M. and Sandler, B. R. (1984) *Out of the Classroom: A Chilly Campus Climate for Women?* Washington, DC: Association of American Colleges.

Halladay, F. (1998) *THES*, 22 May: 12

Halsey, A. H. (1992) *Decline of Donnish Dominion: The British Academic Professions in the Twentieth Century.* Oxford: Clarendon.

Hamilton, R. (1997) Researching sexual violence in higher education, in V. Merchant (ed.) *Harassment and Bullying in Higher and Further Education.* Preston: University of Central Lancashire.

Hanmer, J., Baradotti, R. and Ní Chárthaigh, D. (1995) *Women's Studies and European Integration.* Brussels: Commission of the European Communities.

Haraway, D. J. (1989) *Private Visions: Gender, Race, and Nature in the World of Modern Science.* New York: Routledge.

Harris, D. W. (1991) Keeping women in our place: violence at Canadian universities, *Canadian Women Studies*, 11(4): 37–41.

Harris Report (1996) *Review of Postgraduate Education.* Bristol: HEFCE, CVCP and SCOP.

Hartley, J. (1999) Lifting the veil on the viva: the experiences of psychology PhD candidates in the UK, mimeo, Department of Psychology, University of Keele.

Hartley, J. and Jory, S. (2000) Lifting the veil on the viva: the voice of experience, mimeo paper to BERA seminar, Faculty of Education and Community Studies, University of Reading, June.

Hatt, S., Kent, J. and Britton, C. (eds) (1999) *Women, Research and Careers.* London: Macmillan.

Hernández, A. (1997) *Pedagogy, Democracy and Feminism: Rethinking the Public Sphere.* Albany, NY: SUNY Press.

Higher Education Statistics Agency (HESA) (2000b) *Students in Higher Education Institutions 1998/99.* Cheltenham: Higher Education Statistics Agency.

Hey, V. (1997) *The Company She Keeps: An Ethnography of Girls' Friendship.* Buckingham: Open University Press.

Hill Collins, P. (1990) *Black Feminist Thought.* London: Unwin Hyman.

Hinds, H., Phoenix, A. and Stacey, J. (eds) (1992) *Working Out: New Directions for Women's Studies.* London: Falmer.

Hockey, J. (1994) New territory: problems of adjusting to the first year of a social science PhD, *Studies in Higher Education*, 19: 177–90.

Hockey, J. (1995) Change and the social science PhD: supervisors' responses. *Oxford Review of Education*, 21: 195–206.

Hockey, J. (1997) A complex craft: UK PhD supervision in the social sciences, *Research in Post-Compulsory Education*, 2: 45–66.

Hogan, J. (1994) *Graduate Schools: The Organisation of Graduate Education.* Warwick: CEDAR, University of Warwick.

Holden, P. (1988) *Constraints to Increasing the Proportion of Women Benefitting from O.D.A. Funded Training Awards.* Unpublished report to the Overseas Development Agency, London.

Howe, F. (1997) 'Promises to keep': trends in women's studies worldwide, *Women's Studies Quarterly*, 25(1 and 2): 404–20.

Hudson, L. (1960) Degree class and attainment in scientific research, *British Journal of Psychology*, 51(1): 67–73.

Hudson, L. (1977) Picking winners: a case study in the recruitment of research students, *New Universities Quarterly*, 32(1): 88–107.

Iantaffi, A. (1996) Women and disability in higher education: a literature search, in

L. Morley and V. Walsh (eds) *Breaking Boundaries: Women in Higher Education*. London: Taylor and Francis.

Inglessi, C. (1998) A malady of leisure and travel: the autobiography of a scholar, in M. David and D. Woodward (eds) *Negotiating the Glass Ceiling*. London: Falmer.

Institute for the Study of Social Change (1991) *The Diversity Project: Final Report*. Berkeley, CA: Institute for the Study of Social Change, University of California.

Jackson, S. and Jones, J. (eds) (1998) *Contemporary Feminist Theories*. Edinburgh: Edinburgh University Press.

Jary, D. and Parker, M. (eds) (1998) *The New Higher Education: Issues and Directions for the Post-Dearing University*. Stoke-on-Trent: Staffordshire University Press.

Johnson, L., Lee, A. and Green, B. (2000) The PhD and the autonomous self: gender, rationality and postgraduate pedagogy, *Studies in Higher Education*, 25(2): 135–47.

Kamler, B. and Threadgold, T. (1997) Which thesis did you read? in Z. Golebiowski (ed.) *Policy and Practice of Tertiary Literacy. Selected Proceedings of the First National Conference on Tertiary Literacy: Research and Practice*. Melbourne: Victoria University of Technology.

Keeling, C. and Cole, E. (2001) *Setting Up Peer-Mentoring with Postgraduate Research Students*. London: SRHE and THES.

Kelly, L. (1988) *Surviving Sexual Violence*. Cambridge: Polity.

Kennedy, M., Lubelska, C. and Walsh, V. (eds) (1993) *Making Connections: Women's Studies, Women's Movements, Women's Lives*. London: Taylor & Francis.

Kerlin, S. P. (1995) Surviving the doctoral years: critical perspectives, *Education Policy Analysis Archives* (electronic journal) 3(17), November.

Knorr-Cetina, K. D. (1999) *Epistemic Cultures*. Cambridge, MA: Harvard University Press.

Knorr-Cetina, K. D. and Mulkay, M. (1983) *Science Observed: Perspectives on the Social Study of Science*. Beverly Hills, CA: Sage.

Kramarae, C. and Spender, D. (eds) (1993) *The Knowledge Explosion: Generations of Feminist Scholarship*. London: Harvester Wheatsheaf.

Kunkel, C. A. (1994) Women's needs on campus: how universities meet them, *Initiatives*, 56(2): 15–28.

Langmead, D. (1999) International women postgraduates in Australian university marketing materials: identity, representation and location. BLitt thesis, Deakin University, Geelong, Vic.

Lawton, D. (1997) Problems of supervision, in N. Graves and V. Verma (eds) *Working for a Doctorate: A Guide for the Humanities and Social Sciences*. London: Routledge.

Lea, M. R. and Stierer, B. (eds) (2000) *Student Writing in Higher Education*. Buckingham: SRHE and Open University Press.

Leal, A. and Menjivar, C. (1992) Xenophobia or Xenophilia? Hispanic women in higher education, in L. B. Welch (ed.) *Perspectives on Minority Women in Higher Education*. New York: Praeger.

Lee, D. (1998) Sexual harrassment in PhD supervision, *Gender and Education*, 10(3): 299–312.

Lees, S. (1996) *Carnal Knowledge: Rape on Trial*. London: Hamish Hamilton.

Leonard, D. (1980) *Sex and Generation: A Study of Courtship and Weddings*. London: Tavistock.

Leonard, D. (1998) Gender and international graduate studies, *Journal of International Education*, 9(2): 26–34.

Leonard, D. (2000) Transforming doctoral studies: competencies and artistry, *Higher Education in Europe*, 25(2): 181–92.

Leonard Barker, D. and Allen, S. (eds) (1976a) *Dependence and Exploitation in Work and Marriage*. London: Longman.

Leonard Barker, D. and Allen, S. (eds) (1976b) *Sexual Divisions and Society: Process and Change*. London: Tavistock.

Leonard, D. and Allen, S. (eds) (1991) *Sexual Divisions Revisited*. London: Macmillan in association with the British Sociological Association.

Lewins, H. (1990) Living needs, in M. Kinnell (ed.) *The Learning Experiences of Overseas Students*. Buckingham and Bristol: SRHE and Open University Press.

Lipman-Blumen, J. (1984) *Gender Roles and Power*. Englewood Cliffs, NJ: Prentice Hall.

Locke, L., Spirduso, W. and Silverman, S. (1993) *Proposals that Work: A Guide for Planning Dissertations and Grant Proposals*. Newbury Park, CA: Sage.

Luke, C. (1994) Women in the academy: the politics of speech and silence, *British Journal of Sociology of Education*, 15(2): 211–30.

McKee, L. and O'Brien, M. (1983) Interviewing men: 'taking gender seriously', in E. Gamarnikow, D. Morgan, J. Purvis and D. Taylorson (eds) *The Public and the Private*. London: Heinemann.

MacKinnon, C. A. (1979) *Sexual Harassment of Working Women*. New Haven, CT: Yale University Press.

McNamara, D. and Harris, R. (eds) (1997) *Overseas Students in Higher Education: Issues in Teaching and Learning*. London: Routledge.

McNicoll, I., McCluskey, K. and Kelly, U. (1997) *The Impact of UK Universities and Colleges on the UK Economy*. London: CVCP.

Maher, F. A. and Tetreault, M. K. T. (2001) *The Feminist Classroom*, 2nd edn. New York: Basic Books.

Mahony, P. and Zmroczek, C. (eds) (1997) *Class Matters: 'Working-class' Women's Perspectives on Social Class*. London: Taylor & Francis.

Malina, D. and Maslin-Prothero, S. (eds) (1998) *Surviving the Academy: Feminist Perspectives*. London: Falmer.

Marginson, S. (1997) *Markets in Education*. St Leonards, NSW: Allen and Unwin.

Marginson, S. (1998) Keynote address at the 1998 'Quality in Postgraduate Research Conference' in Adelaide, *Postgraduate Review: A Publication of the University of Melbourne Postgraduate Association Inc.*, 4(3): 17–23.

Marshall, A. (1994) Sensuous Sapphires: a study of the social construction of Black female sexuality, in M. Maynard and J. Purvis (eds) *Researching Women's Lives from a Feminist Perspective*. London: Taylor & Francis.

Martin, P. Y. and Hummer, R. A. (1993) Fraternities and rape on campus, in P. B. Bart and E. G. Moran (eds) *Violence Against Women: The Bloody Footprints*. Thousand Oaks, CA: Sage.

Maxwell, T. W. and Shanahan, P. J. (1997) Towards a reconceptualisation of the doctorate: issues relating to the EdD degree in Australia, *Studies in Higher Education*, 22(2): 133–50.

Maynard, M. and Purvis, J. (eds) (1995) *(Hetero)sexual Politics*. London: Taylor & Francis.

Maynard, M. and Purvis, J. (eds) (1996) *New Frontiers in Women's Studies: Knowledge, Identity and Nationalism*. London. Taylor & Francis.

Merrill, B. (1999) *Gender, Change and Identity: Mature Women Students in Universities*. Aldershot: Ashgate.

Merton, R. K. (1957) *Social Theory and Social Structure*. Glencoe, NY: Free Press.

Miller, G. W. (1970) *Success, Failure and Wastage in Higher Education*. London: Harrap and London Institute of Education.

Millett, K. (1971) *Sexual Politics*. London: Abacus.

Mintz, B. and Rothblum, E. (eds) (1997) *Lesbians in Academia: Degrees of Freedom*. New York: Routledge.

Mirza, H. S. (1995) Black women in higher education: defining a space/finding a place, in L. Morley and V. Walsh (eds) *Feminist Academics: Creative Agents for Change*. London: Taylor & Francis.

Mirza, H. S. (ed.) (1997) *Black British Feminism: A Reader*. London: Routledge.

Morley, L. (1999) *Organising Feminisms: The Micropolitics of the Academy*. London: Macmillan.

Morley, L. and Walsh, V. (eds) (1995) *Feminist Academics: Creative Agents for Change*. London: Taylor and Francis.

Morley, L. and Walsh, V. (eds) (1996) *Breaking Boundaries: Women in Higher Education*. London: Taylor & Francis.

Moses, C. G. (1998) Made in America: 'French feminism' in academia, *Feminist Studies*, 22(2): 241–74.

Moses, I. (1990) *Barriers to Women's Participation as Postgraduate Students*. Canberra: Australian Government Publishing Service.

Moses, I. (1992) Issues in women's participation, in D. J. Cullen (ed.) *Quality in PhD Education*. Canberra: CEDAM and the Graduate School, ANU.

Moses, I. (1994) Planning for quality in graduate studies, in O. Zuber-Skerritt and Y. Ryan (eds) *Quality in Postgraduate Education*. London: Kogan Page.

Moses, I. (1996) Women and research, paper presented to CHESS Workshop: *Women and Management in Higher Education*, Port Moresby, Papua New Guinea, May 1995.

Muijlwijk, M. van (1999) *Funding and Private Resources for Women and Gender Studies*. Utrecht: Women's International Studies Europe (WISE).

Munt, S. R. (1997) 'I teach therefore I am': lesbian studies in the liberal academy, *Feminist Review*, 56: 85–99.

Murrell, G., Huang, C. and Ellis, H. (1990) *Research in Medicine: A Guide to Writing a Thesis in the Medical Sciences*. Cambridge: Cambridge University Press.

Neal, S. (1998) *The Making of Equal Opportunities Policies in Universities*. Buckingham: SRHE and Open University Press.

Nelson, C. and Watt, S. (1999) *Academic Keywords: A Devil's Dictionary for Higher Education*. New York: Routledge.

Nerad, M. (1992) Using time, money and human resources efficiently and effectively in the case of women graduate students, paper prepared for the conference proceedings of Science and Engineering Programs: On Target for Women?, mimeo.

Nerad, M. and Cerny, J. (1991) From facts to action: expanding the educational role of the graduate division, *Communicator*, special edition (May).

Nerad, M. and Miller, D. S. (1996) Increasing student retention in graduate and professional programs, in J. G. Haworth (ed.) *Assessing Graduate and Professional Education: Current Realities and Future Prospects*. San Francisco: Jossey-Bass.

Nerad, M. and Stewart, C. L. (1991) Assessing doctoral student experience: gender and departmental culture. Paper presented to the 31st annual conference of the Association for Institutional Research, San Francisco, May 26–9.

Nightingale, P. (1984) Examination of research theses, *Higher Education Research and Development*, 3(2): 137–50.

Nishio, A. (2001) The experience of Japanese postgraduate students at the University of London, with special reference to gender. PhD thesis, University of London.

Nkomo, M. (1989) Foreign policy and scholarship programmes for Black South Africans: a preliminary critical assessment, *Perspectives in Education*, 11(1): 1–18.

Noble, K. A. (1994) *Changing Doctoral Degrees: An International Perspective*. Buckingham: SRHE and Open University Press

Nolan Report (1996) *Second Report of the Committee on Standards in Public Life*, 2 vols, Cm 3270–1 and 3270–11. London: HMSO.

NPC (1992) *Guidelines on Codes of Practice for Postgraduate Research*. Troon: National Postgraduate Committee.

NPC (1993) *Guidelines for the Employment of Postgraduate Students as Teachers*. Troon: National Postgraduate Committee.

NPC (1995a) *Guidelines on Accommodation and Facilities for Postgraduate Research*. Troon: National Postgraduate Committee

NPC (1995b) *The Postgraduate Book*. Troon: National Postgraduate Committee.

NPC (1998) *Guidelines for the Conduct of Research Degree Appeals*. Troon: National Postgraduate Committee.

NWSA (annual) *Guide to Graduate Work in Women's Studies*. College Park, MA: University of Maryland.

Oakley, A. (1972) *Sex, Gender and Society*. London: Temple Smith.

Oakley, A. (1974) *Housewife*. London: Allen Lane.

O'Donohue, W. (ed.) (1997) *Sexual Harassment: Theory, Research, and Treatment*. Boston, MA: Allyn and Bacon.

Oerton, S. (2000) *Feminisms on the Edge: Politics, Discourses and National Identities*. Cardiff: Cardiff University Press.

Office of Science and Technology (1993) *Realising our Potential: A Strategy for Science, Engineering and Technology*, Cm 2250. London: HMSO.

Okorocha, E. (1997) *Supervising International Research Students*. London: SRHE and *THES*.

Open University (2000) *Support for Part-time Teachers of Sociology*. Milton Keynes: Centre for Higher Education Practice, The Open University.

Orlans, K. P. M. (ed.) (1994) *Gender and the Academic Experience*. Lincoln, NB and London: University of Nebraska Press.

Oxford University Student Union Women's Committee (1984) *'The Ones who just Patronise Seem Genial by Comparison . . .' An Enquiry into Sexual Harassment of Women in Oxford University*. Oxford: Oxford University Student Union Women's Committee.

Ozga, J. (1998) The enerepreneurial researcher: re-formations of identity in the research marketplace, *International Studies in Sociology of Education*, 8(2): 143–53.

Pearson, R., Seccombe, I., Pike, G., Holly, S. and Connor, H. (1991) *Doctoral Social Scientists and the Labour Market*. Brighton: Institute for Employment Studies.

Peters, R. L. (1997) *Getting What You Came for: The Smart Student's Guide to Earning a Master's or Ph.D.*, revised edn. New York: Noonday Press, a division of Farrar, Straus and Giroux.

Phillips, E. (1983) The PhD as a learning process. PhD thesis, University of London.

Phillips, E. M. (1994) Quality in the PhD: points at which quality may be assessed, in R. Burgess (ed.) *Postgraduate Education and Training in the Social Sciences*. London: Jessica Kingsley.

Phillips, E. M. and Pugh, D. (2000) *How to Get a PhD: A Handbook for Students and their Supervisors*, 3rd edn. Buckingham: Open University Press.

Plimpton, G. (ed.) (1977) *Writers at Work: The Paris Interviews*. New York. Penguin.

Pole, C. J., Sprokkereef, A., Burgess, R. G. and Lakin, E. (1997) Supervision of doctoral students in the natural sciences: expectations and experiences, *Assessment and Evaluation in Higher Education*, 22(1): 49–63.

Power, M. (1997) *The Audit Society: Rituals of Verification*. Oxford: Oxford University Press.

Purkiss, D. (1994) The lecherous professor revisited: Plato, pedagogy and the scene of harassment, in C. Brant and Y. Lee Too (eds) *Rethinking Sexual Harassment*. London: Pluto.

QAAHE (1999) *Code of Practice for the Assurance of Academic Quality and Standards in Higher Education: Postgraduate Research Programmes*. Gloucester: Quality Assurance Agency for Higher Education.

Ramazanoglu, C. (1987) Sex and violence in academic life or you can keep a good woman down, in J. Hanmer and M. Maynard (eds) *Women, Violence and Social Control*. London: Macmillan.

Reay, D. (2000) 'Dim dross': marginalised women both inside and outside the academy, *Women's Studies International Forum*, 23(1): 13–21.

Rhedding-Jones, J. (1997) Doing a feminist poststructural doctorate, *Gender and Education*, 9(2): 193–206.

Roberts, H. (1984) Putting the show on the road: the dissemination of research findings, in C. Bell and H. Roberts (eds) *Social Researching: Politics, Problems, Practice*. London: Routledge and Kegan Paul.

Robinson, D. and Richardson, V. (eds) (1997) *Introducing Women's Studies: Feminist Theory and Practice*, 2nd edn. London: Macmillan.

Roiphe, K. (1993) *The Morning After: Sex, Fear and Feminism*. London: Hamish Hamilton.

Rose, H. (1994) *Love, Power and Knowledge: Towards a Feminist Transformation of the Sciences*. Cambridge: Polity.

Rose, S. M. (1985) Professional networks of junior faculty in Psychology, *Psychology of Women Quarterly*, 9: 533–47.

Rudd, E. (1985) *A New Look at Postgraduate Failure*. Guildford: SRHE and NFER-Nelson.

Rudd, E. and Hatch, S. (1968) *Graduate Study and After*. London: Weidenfeld and Nicolson.

Rudd, E. in association with Simpson, R. (1975) *The Highest Education: A Study of Graduate Education in Britain*. London: Routledge and Kegan Paul.

Russell, C. L., Plotkin, R. and Bell, A. C. (1998) Merge/emerge: collaboration in graduate school, in E. Peck and J. S. Mink (eds) *Common Ground: Feminist Collaboration in the Academy*. Albany, NY: SUNY Press.

Ryan, Y. and Zuber-Skerritt, O. (eds) (1999) *Supervising Postgraduates from Non-English Speaking Backgrounds*. Buckingham: SRHE and Open University Press.

Salmon, P. (1992) *Achieving a PhD – Ten Students' Experiences*. Stoke-on-Trent: Trentham.

Sandler, B. (1993) The campus climate revisited: chilly for women faculty, administrators, and graduate students, in J. S. Glazer, E. M. Bensimon and B. K. Townsend (eds) *Women in Higher Education: A Feminist Perspective*, Needham Heights, MA: Ginn Press.

Sandler, B. and Hall, R. M. (1986) *The Campus Climate Revisited: A Chilly One for Women Faculty, Administrators, and Graduate Students*. Washington, DC: Association of American Colleges.

Schön, D. (1987) *Educating the Reflective Practitioner*. San Francisco: Jossey-Bass.

Scott, P. (ed.) (1998) *The Globalization of Higher Education*. Buckingham: SRHE and Open University Press.

Scott, S. (1998) Here be dragons: researching the unbelievable, hearing the unthinkable, *Sociological Research Online*, 3(3), http://www.socresonline.org.uk/socresonline/3/3/1.html.

Scott, M. (1997) Students writing arguments: a metaphoric process. Unpublished paper to a conference on Argument, Middlesex University, September, mimeo.

Segerman-Peck, L. (1991) *Networking and Mentoring: A Woman's Guide*. London: Piatkus.

Shaw, J. (1995) *Education, Gender and Anxiety*. London: Taylor and Francis.

Sims, A. (1997) Financing a doctorate, in N. Graves and V. Varma (eds) *Working for a Doctorate*. London: Routledge and Kegan Paul.

Smith, A. and Gilby, J. (2000) *Supervising Students on Industrial-based Projects*. London: SRHE and THES.

Smith, D. (1978) A peculiar eclipsing: women's exclusion from man's culture, *Women's Studies International Quarterly*, 1(4): 281–95.

Smith, D. (1997) Report and repression: textual hazards for feminists in the academy, in L. G. Roman and L. Eyre (eds) *Dangerous Territories: Struggles for Difference and Equality in Education*. New York: Routledge.

Spender, D. (1982) *Women of Ideas and What Men have Done to Them: From Aphra Behn to Adrienne Rich*. London: Routledge and Kegan Paul.

Stacy, H. (1999) The law, policies and ethics: supervising postgraduate NESB students in an era of internationalization, in Y. Ryan and O. Zuber-Skerritt (eds) *Supervising Postgraduates from Non-English-Speaking Backgrounds*. Buckingham: SRHE and Open University Press.

Stanley, J. (1995) Pain(t) for healing: the academic conference and the class/embodied self, in L. Morley and V. Walsh (eds) *Feminist Academics: Creative Agents for Change*. London: Taylor & Francis.

Stanley, L. (ed.) (1990) *Feminist Praxis*. London: Routledge.

Stanley, L. and Wise, S. (1979) Feminist research, feminist consciousness and experiences of sexism, *Women's Studies International Quarterly*, 2: 359–74.

Steiner, J. M. (1990) *How to Survive as a Working Mother*. London: Kogan Page.

Sternberg, D. (1981) *How to Complete and Survive a Doctoral Dissertation*. New York: St Martin's Press.

Strachey, R. (1978, first published 1928) *The Cause: A Short History of the Women's Movement in Great Britain*. London: Virago.

Taylorson, D. (1984) The professional socialization, integration and identity of women PhD candidates, in S. Acker and D. Warren Piper (eds) *Is Higher Education Fair to Women?* Guildford: SRHE and NFER-Nelson.

Teichler, U. and Maiworm, F. (1997) *The ERASMUS Experience: Findings of the ERASMUS Evaluation Research Project*. Luxembourg: Office for Official Publications of the European Communities.

The Times Good University Guide (annual). London: Times Books/HarperCollins.

Thomas, A. M. and Kitzinger, C. (eds) (1997) *Sexual Harassment: Contemporary Feminist Perspectives*. Buckingham: Open University Press.

Thomas, K. (1990) *Gender and Subject in Higher Education*. Buckingham: Open University Press.

Threfall, M. and Langley, G. (1992) *Constraints on the Participation of Women in Technical Cooperation Training due to Lack of English Language Skills*. London: Overseas Development Administration.

Tinkler, P. and Jackson, C. (2000) Examining the doctorate: institutional policy and the PhD examination process in Britain, *Studies in Higher Education*, 25(2): 167–80.

Torrance, M. S. and Thomas, G. V. (1994) The development of writing skills in doctoral research students, in R. W. Burgess (ed.) *Postgraduate Education and Training in the Social Sciences: Processes and Products*. London: Jessica Kingsley.

Toth, E. (1997) *Ms. Mentor's Impeccable Advice for Women in Academia*. Philadelphia, PA: University of Pennsylvania Press.

Trioli, V. (1996) *Generation F: Sex, Power and the Young Feminist*. Kew, Vic.: Minerva.

Trow, M. (1994) Managerialism and the academic profession: the case of England, *Higher Education Policy*, 7(2): 11–18.

UKCOSA (1998) New approaches to orientation, UKCOSA Training Day, London, 7 May.

UNESCO (1998/1999) *Study Abroad*. Paris: UNESCO.

Unterhalter, E. and Green, D. (1997) *Making the Adjustment: Orientation Programmes for International Students*. London: UKCOSA.

Unterhalter, E. and Hayton, A. (1993) *Homeward Bound: A Pack for Tutors Organising Courses for Students Returning to their Home Countries after Studying in the UK*. London: UKCOSA.

Unterhalter, E. and Maxey, K. (1995) *Educating South Africans in Britain and Ireland: A Review of Thirty Years of Sponsorship by the Africa Educational Trust*. London: RESA, Institute of Education, University of London.

Vartuli, S. (ed.) (1982) *The PhD Experience: A Woman's Point of View*. New York: Praeger.

Wajcman, J. (1991) *Feminism Confronts Technology*. Cambridge: Polity.

Walby, S. (1986) *Patriarchy at Work: Patriarchal and Capitalist Relations in Employment*. Cambridge: Polity.

Walford, G. (1998) Compulsive writing behaviour: getting it published, in G. Walford (ed.) *Doing Research about Education*. London: Falmer.

Warrior, J. (1997) *Cracking It! Helping Women to Succeed in Science, Engineering and Technology*. Watford: Training Publications.

Weneras, C. and Wold, A. (1997) Nepotism and sexism in peer review, *Nature*, 387: 341–3; reprinted in *New Scientist*, 24 May 1997.

Whelehan, I. (1995) *Modern Feminist Thought: From the Second Wave to 'Postfeminism'*. Edinburgh: Edinburgh University Press.

Wilson, T. (1991) The proletarianisation of academic labour, *Industrial Relations Journal*, 22(4): 250–62.

Wise, S. and Stanley, L. (1987) *Georgie Porgie: Sexual Harassment in Everyday Life*. London: Pandora.

Wisker, G. (1996) *Empowering Women in Higher Education*. London: Kogan Page.

Wolf, S. and Dolan, J. (1997) Consenting to relations: the personal pleasures of 'power disparity' in lesbian–teacher partnerships, in B. Mintz and E. D. Rothblum (eds) *Lesbians in Academia: Degrees of Freedom*. New York: Routledge.

Women's Studies Quarterly (1992) special issue on 'Women's Studies in Europe', 20(3 and 4).

Woodward, D. and Ross, K. (2000) *Managing Equal Opportunities in Higher Education*. Buckingham: SRHE and Open University Press.

Wright, C. (1997) Gender matters: access, welfare, teaching and learning, in D. McNamara and R. Harris (eds) *Overseas Students in Higher Education: Issues in Teaching and Learning*. London: Routledge.

Wright, T. and Cochrane, R. (2000) Factors influencing successful submission of PhD theses, *Studies in Higher Education*, 25(2): 181–95.

Wright Mills, C. (1970, first published 1959) *The Sociological Imagination*. New York: Oxford University Press.

Yeatman, A. (1994) Contractualism and graduate pedagogy, *Connect: Newsletter of TASA Women's Section*, 2(2): 2–5.

Yeatman, A. (1998) Making research relationships accountable: graduate student logs, in A. Lee and B. Green (eds) *Postgraduate Studies, Postgraduate Pedagogies*. Sydney: Centre for Language and Literacy, University of Technology, Sydney.

Zellick Report (1994) *Student Disciplinary Procedures: Notes of Guidance*. London: CVCP.

Ziman, J. (1991) Talk at a Research Supervision Workshop organised by CHES, Institute of Education, 16 May.

Ziman, J. (2000) *Real Science: What it is and What it Means*. Cambridge: Cambridge University Press.

Zmroczek, C. and Duchen, C. (1989) Women's studies and feminist research in the U.K., *Women's Studies International Forum*, 12(6): 603–10.

Zmroczek, C. and Duchen, C. (1991) Women's studies and feminist research in the European community, in J. Aaron and S. Walby (eds) *Out of the Margins: Women's Studies in the Nineties*. London: Falmer.

AUTHOR INDEX

SUBJECT INDEX

ability, *see* confidence
ABRC (Advisory Board for the
    Research Councils), 61, 64,
    239
academic life
    as gendered, 7, 43–5, 50, 56–7, 181
    homosocial culture, 4, 201–2, 226–7,
        230
        see also chilly climate for women
    as raced and classed, 57, 148, 234
    as sexualized, 95, 202, 210, 215,
        225–7
    as symbolic community, 50, 232–3
academic literacy, 80, 151, 244–6, 260
academic staff
    additional requirements on women,
        167, 207, 248
    administrators and support staff, 82,
        141–2, 164–5, 173
        see also welfare and welfare offices
    age profile, 12
    part time university teaching and
        contract research, 4, 40, 55–6,
        132, 137–42, 148, 192
    terms and conditions of employment,
        9–10, 18, 40, 50, 57, 71, 88–9,
        148–9, 183, 192, 248
    trade unions, *see* AUT; NATFHE

accommodation needs of research
    students
    residential, 24, 39, 107–8, 110,
        119–20, 126–9
    work and office, 63, 106–8, 125–6,
        140, 144, 148, 173
activist research, 154–5, 191–2
age, differences among students, 34, 57,
    66, 76–7, 183, 201, 224, 229–30,
    234
agriculture and related fields, 68, 103,
    142
AHRB (Arts and Humanities Research
    Board), 19, 25, 41, 198
AIOFE (Feminist Education and
    Research in Europe), 185
anthropology, 70, 80, 87, 111, 152, 177,
    195, 221–2, 260
anti-feminism, 35, 183, 188–9, 201, 210,
    215–17, 234
    in media, 213, 215–16, 234
        see also harassment, sexual
    in seminars and conferences, 204–8
    and religious fundamentalism, 109
    resistance to it by women, 208,
        212
anti-racism, *see* race, racism and
    ethnicity